Travelers in Ancient Lands

TRAVELERS IN ANCIENT LANDS

A Portrait of the Middle East, 1839–1919

LOUIS VACZEK

GAIL BUCKLAND

Boston · New York Graphic Society

First Edition

Designed by Katy Homans
Typeset in Monotype Bell by Michael & Winifred Bixler

New York Graphic Society books are published by Little, Brown and Company.

Published simultaneously in Canada by Little, Brown and Company
(Canada) Limited.

Preceding the title page:

George Eastman took this picture of "Ruth" in Thebes, in 1890, with his Kodak No. 1 camera.

A dahabiyah is prepared for departure from Kosheh on the Nile. Horst Schliephack, Breasted expedition, 1906–1907.

The ruins of San, ancient Tanis (biblical Zoan), are being excavated by archeologists from the Louvre. Workmen are carrying away sand on their heads. Henri de Banville, 1863–1864.

Because even commoners could afford to be mummified, mummies choked the sands of Egypt. One of the preservatives, a cure-all bituminous substance called mummiyah *in Arabic, made pulverized mummy a sought-after medicine in Asia and Europe. Countless unknown mummies were peddled whole or in parts throughout the nineteenth century.* Bonfils, after 1867.

Barber shop in Cairo. Anonymous, before 1877.

Athletes in trousers of embroidered leather performed ritual exercises to the chanting of verses from the Shah-nameh, Persia's national epic. Sevruguin, after 1880.

These wealthy Turkish ladies are posing in a studio. Anonymous, before 1877.

Constantinople's Galata Bridge, across the Golden Horn, connects the city (now Istanbul) with its suburb Galata-Pera (now Beyoglu). Abdullah Frères, ca. 1890.

Chicago baseball players atop the Sphinx. Anonymous, ca. 1880.

Library of Congress Cataloging in Publication data will be found on the last page.

PRINTED IN THE UNITED STATES OF AMERICA

To Peace in the Middle East

Acknowledgments

The Arnold H. Crane Collection, one of the finest, if not the finest, private assemblages of photographs in the world, is particularly rich in images of the Middle East. Arnold Crane allowed the authors liberal access to his collection for research and for choosing pictures. We acknowledge his help and that of the former curator of the collection, Mary E. Fanette.

The team at the Harvard Semitic Museum — Dr. Carney Gavin, Ingeborg O'Reilly, and Elizabeth Carella — have been doing the premier research on Middle Eastern photographers for a number of years. They were consulted on the biographies of many of the lesser-known cameramen and supplied all the material on Bonfils. Donna Stein, an art historian who is one of the leading authorities on early Persian photography, directed the authors to the Freer Gallery of Art, which houses the Sevruguin archives, and graciously discussed her as yet unpublished research. François Lepage, assistant to Gérard Lévy, identified Comte A. de Moustier, W. Hammerschmidt, and other photographers whose work is in Gérard Lévy's fine collection of Middle Eastern views.

We are grateful to all the individuals who allowed us to reproduce their photographs. The picture credits at the end of the book identify them. We particularly would like to thank Daniel Wolf, whose two magnificent anonymous albums, compiled before 1877, provided some of the most beautiful pictures in our book; Gilbert

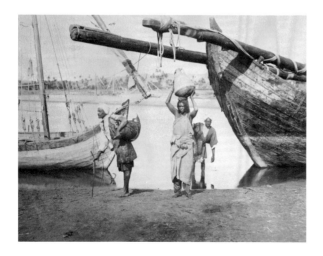

Gimon, whose rare daguerreotypes appear for the first time in a book; and the following: Harold Allen, Chicago; Deborah Bull, New York; Frances Dimond, Curator, Photographic Collection, Royal Archives, Windsor Castle; Paula Fleming, National Anthropological Archives, Smithsonian Institution; Gillian Grant, Archivist, Middle East Centre, St. Anthony's College, Oxford University; Diane Guzman, Librarian of the Wilbour Library, The Brooklyn Museum; Julia Van Haaften, formerly of the Art and Architecture Division, New York Public Library; George S. Hobart, Curator, Documentary Photography, Prints and Photographic Division, Library of Congress; Isaac Lagnado, New York; John A. Larson, Ronnie L. Burbank, and David Nasgowitz, the Oriental Institute, University of Chicago; Donald Lorimer, New York; Sarah Newmeyer and Holly Edwards, Freer Gallery of Art; Nissan Perez, Curator of Photography, Israel Museum, Jerusalem; and Professor Joel Snyder, University of Chicago.

Eyal Onne's book *Photographic Heritage of the Holy Land 1839–1914*, Julia Van Haaften's *Egypt and the Holy Land in Historic Photographs: 77 Views by Francis Firth*, and Ritchie Thomas's articles have been particularly useful and should be noted by those interested in the field; see the Bibliography.

This book could not have been written without the help of innumerable friends who for five years (1936–1941) taught Louis Vaczek how to live in villages and cities and in the desert: farmers, bedouin, servants, craftsmen, poets, police chiefs, diplomats, political agents, explorers, pashas, sheikhs, ship captains, generals, bankers, laborers, camel drivers, patriots, renegades, cabaret girls, teachers, Islamic scholars, smugglers, empire builders, mullahs, nuns and monks, tourists, archeologists, a king, people of the street and people of the oases — from Istanbul to Aden and Alexandria to Tehran.

We are also deeply grateful to our editor, Robin Bledsoe, who with great taste, tact, and persistence helped us pull together everything and guided the making of this book.

CONTENTS

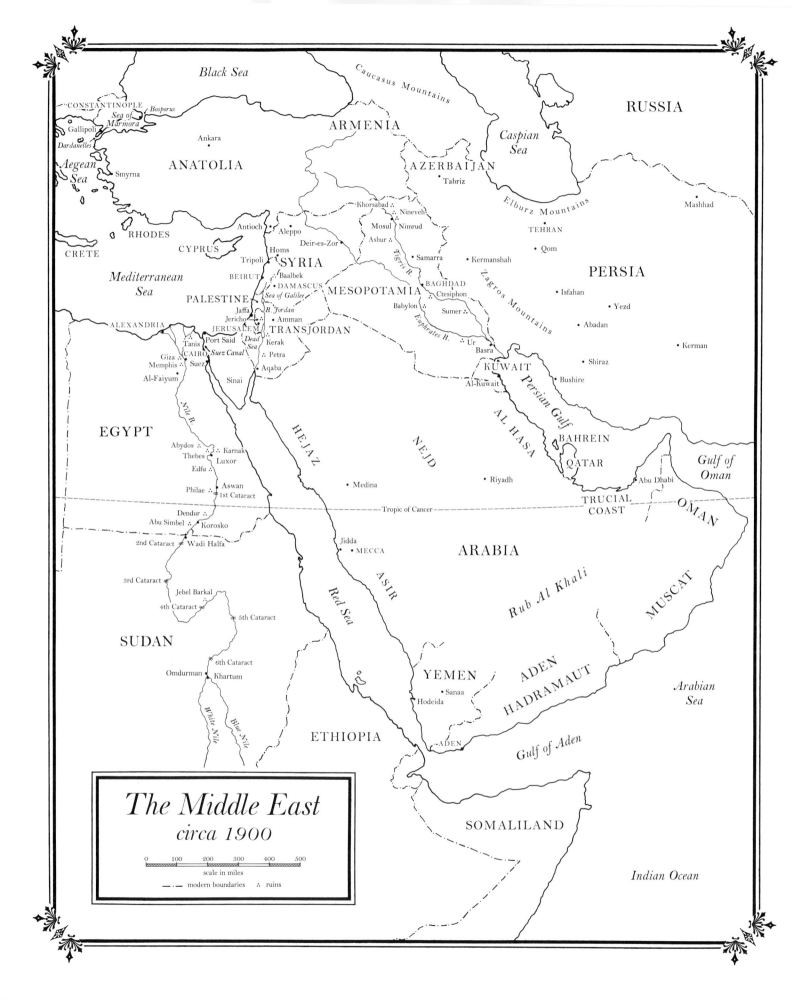

Black Sea

CONSTANTINOPLE
Bosporus
Sea of Marmora
Gallipoli
Dardanelles

Aegean Sea

RUSSIA

Caspian Sea

ARMENIA

Caucasus Mountains

AZERBAIJAN

Ankara

ANATOLIA

Tabriz

Elburz Mountains

Mashhad

Smyrna

RHODES

Khorsabad
Nineveh
Mosul Nimrud
Ashur Samarra
Deir-es-Zor

TEHRAN

CRETE

CYPRUS

Antioch Aleppo

Qom

Kermanshah

PERSIA

Tripoli Homs
SYRIA
BEIRUT *Baalbek*

Tigris R.

BAGHDAD
Ctesiphon

Isfahan

Yezd

Mediterranean Sea

PALESTINE
DAMASCUS
Sea of Galilee
R. Jordan

MESOPOTAMIA

Babylon

Sumer

Abadan

Zagros Mountains

ALEXANDRIA

Jaffa
Jericho
JERUSALEM

Amman

Euphrates R.

Ur

Kerman

Tanis
CAIRO
Giza
Memphis
Al-Faiyum Suez

Port Said
Dead Sea
Suez Canal

TRANSJORDAN

Kerak
Petra

Aqaba

Sinai

Basra
KUWAIT
Al-Kuwait

Shiraz

Bushire

Nile R.

EGYPT

HEJAZ

NEJD

AL HASA

Persian Gulf

BAHREIN

QATAR

Gulf of Oman

Abydos
Thebes Karnak
Luxor
Edfu

Medina

Riyadh

Abu Dhabi

TRUCIAL
COAST

OMAN

Philae Aswan
1st Cataract

Tropic of Cancer

Dendur
Abu Simbel Korosko

2nd Cataract Wadi Halfa

Jidda
MECCA

ARABIA

3rd Cataract

Red Sea

ASIR

Rub Al Khali

MUSCAT

Jebel Barkal
4th Cataract

5th Cataract

SUDAN

Arabian Sea

Omdurman
6th Cataract
Khartum

YEMEN

Sanaa
Hodeida

ADEN

HADRAMAUT

White Nile
Blue Nile

ETHIOPIA

ADEN

Gulf of Aden

SOMALILAND

Indian Ocean

The Middle East
circa 1900

0 100 200 300 400 500
scale in miles

— · — modern boundaries   ∴ ruins

FOREWORD

From 1839, the very year when the technology of photography was announced, foreigners began to take pictures in the Middle East. Both Europeans and Americans bought them in uncountable numbers because the West had always been fascinated by those exotic lands on its borders.

Travelers in Ancient Lands begins with a brief history of the Middle East—the first villages in the world, the first conquering civilizations, the Muslim empires, all of which left architectural ruins to be photographed. Events of the nineteenth century are brought into sharp focus, with photographs of the people in the living cities and on the land, to explain how the Ottoman Empire began to disintegrate from its own weaknesses and from European imperialists, commercial interests, and foreigners streaming in. Then text and camera move to the vast deserts in which the history of the Middle East is embedded, the caravans and the bedouin without whom no civilization could have maintained itself there, the village farmers without whom no civilization could have begun, and the towns and great cities that played vital roles in world history. Altogether we have attempted to create a portrait of the Middle East between 1839 and 1919 as the greatest melting pot of all time, before nationalism awoke fiercely patriotic rulers who after World War II walled off their communities from one another.

The term Middle East in this book refers to the region occupied by the modern sovereign nations, with former names in parenthesis, of the United Arab Republic (Egypt), Sudan (partly Nubia or Kush or even Ethiopia), Jordan (Transjordan), Israel (Palestine), Lebanon and Syria (Syria), Turkey (Anatolia or Asia Minor), Iran (Persia), Iraq (Mesopotamia), Saudi Arabia (Arabia), northern Yemen (Yemen or Sanaa), Southern Yemen (Aden and part of the Hadramaut), Oman (part of the Hadramaut and Muscat), the United Arab Emirates (Trucial Coast), and Qatar, Bahrein, and Kuwait.

This is a land mass of 3,700,000 square miles, somewhat larger than the United States. It is bordered by Greece, the Black Sea, the Caspian Sea, the U.S.S.R., Afghanistan, Pakistan, the Persian Gulf, the Arabian Sea, the Red Sea, Ethiopia, the countries of central Africa (Kenya, Uganda, Zaire, Central African Republic, Chad), Libya, and the Mediterranean.

The borders follow natural frontiers through Europe, Asia, and Africa and encompass all the land bridges and waterways connecting the three continents, a geographical situation that is one key to the history of the immense area. The other characteristic feature of the Middle East is that less than 10 percent of the area receives enough water from rain and irrigation systems to bear crops. The rest offers only desolate mountains and deserts.

The total population in 1920, the first year when a serious attempt was made to count heads, was estimated at fifty million, give or take a few million. Using worldwide population growth rates, a census count during most of the span of years dealt with here would have been around twenty-five million at most.

In the seventh century the Middle East was conquered by tribes out of Arabia and converted to Islam, and Arabic became the official language of the Arab empire that eventually included all of North Africa, Spain, Sicily,

Afghanistan, and parts of India, and reached deep into Asia. But the leadership passed to Persians and finally to Turks. In 1453 a dynasty of Turkish sultan-caliphs, the Ottomans, became the rulers, and they extended the Ottoman Empire to include present-day Greece, Bulgaria, Albania, and Romania, and parts of Yugoslavia and Hungary. By 1839, however, when photography was announced, all the lands except the Middle East as defined here had either broken away from the Ottoman Empire or were only loosely allied to it, and even in the Middle East most of the provinces had a great deal of autonomy under local governors, who were sometimes self-appointed.

During the nineteenth century Europeans and Americans began to travel extensively in the crumbling empire, which they called the Near East or, loosely, the Orient. The term "Middle East" became popular following World War I after the empire was dismembered by the victorious Allies. Today it is convenient to speak of an Arab world, and sometimes "Middle East" is meant to include the countries of North Africa and Afghanistan, making an uninterrupted flow of desert lands from the Atlantic to India, inhabited by a mixture of peoples who share a history of thirteen hundred years under Muslim rulers claiming to be Mohammed's representatives, and who acknowledge a cultural heritage that stems from the first Arab Empire. But in this book "Middle East" refers only to the countries listed, to preserve its identification with the Near East, during the period when the photographs in this book were made.

Although for over a thousand years dialects of Arabic had formed the common language of the Middle East (except in the Ottoman Empire, where Turkish was the official language, and in Persia, where the Indo-European Parsi or Pahlavi was the written language and Persian was spoken), and although Islam was the common religion (though bitterly split into Sunni and Shiite sects, each having many internal schisms), there also lived throughout the Middle East segregated communities of Greek Orthodox, Roman Catholic, Coptic, Maronite, and other Christian sects; Jews; Zoroastrians; pagans; and various semisecret tribal cults. Culturally an even greater diversity existed: Egyptian, Arab, Turkish, Iranian, Syrian, Iraqi, Kurd, Druze, Armenian, Jewish, Assyrian, Yemenese, Maltese, Greek, Cretan, Cypriot,

and Italian. But the list does not hint at the very strong tribal differences within each overall group; some estimates number a thousand and more such subcultures, each with distinctive speech and cultural expression. Thus in one sense it is as convenient to speak of Middle Easterners today as it is to speak of Europeans, and just as misleading to call all the inhabitants Arabs as it would be to call the European people Romans because long ago Rome had ruled most of them and Latin had been the language of literacy through which Christianity had become their common religion. In fact, the common name for European Christians in Arabic is *Frank* because most of the Crusades were led by French kings. But only the people indigenous to Saudi Arabia are truly Arabs, and as *Arab* also means nomad, really only the bedouin of Saudi Arabia can claim to be pure Arabs.

The tourists, photographers, scholars, soldiers, and merchants who went to the Middle East in the nineteenth century found a civilization ruled from Constantinople by Ottoman sultan-caliphs. Arrested and sealed up in the fifteenth century, it knew almost nothing of the European Renaissance, the explorations of the sixteenth century, the growth of scientific knowledge from the seventeenth century, or the eighteenth century's political revolutions, beginnings of the industrial revolution, and colonialism. The Westerners actually looked at a mummified Middle Ages, which they then set about destroying. World War I wiped out the ancient political structure and introduced the machine age and the concept of nationhood. Until World War II Western imperialism tried to keep a firm hand on the new Middle East that it had created, but the hand shook more and more and at the end of the war it was flung off by the fledgling nations. Since then a cataclysmic sequence of events in the Middle East has changed irrevocably and dramatically not only the Middle East but the whole world.

It is quite impossible to search for an understanding of what is going on in the Middle East today without knowing something about the region in the nineteenth century, when Europeans and Americans eagerly photographed its cities, its people, and its antiquities; and it is fortunate that so much of their work has been preserved in collections. We have tried to combine a mini-history of the Middle East and a description of life there during the years 1839 to 1919, with photographs of that life in the

Syrian desert, on the streets of the big cities, in village cafés, Turkish harems, along the Nile and the Euphrates, of Arabian caravans, Crusader fortresses, Persian workshops, Egyptian shepherds, bazaars, Sudanese boatmen, mosques, tourists in Luxor, bedouin guerrillas, veiled women, dancing girls and prostitutes, dervishes, beggars and porters, shahs and khedives, and more. Life for most people did not change much between the two world wars, and therefore leaders in the Middle East today spent their youth in that way of life.

During those years, the gulf separating the Middle East and the West seemed to everyone too wide and deep ever to be bridged. This book suggests why the bridges that are now being designed do not suit the purposes of the industrialized world. It is ironical that the people who control these crossroads linking Asia, Africa, and Europe, where civilization was born, have once again seized a dominant role in world history, this time based on the needs of the machine.

A Note on the Photographs

There are, in collections, hundreds of thousands of photographs of the Middle East, most of which have not been studied since they were assembled. How many honestly reveal the culture and the people? Surprisingly few. It turns out that often the most startling image was expertly faked to supply a commercial market. One must search hard to find pictures that portray the Middle East before World War I with depth, sensitivity, and truthfulness. The concept of "Orient" provided photographers with the same liberties that it gave writers and painters for fictitious reporting. We have kept to a minimum the work made to fit myths of the time and have favored photographs that contain genuine information and insight about the people and their way of life in the landscapes of the Middle East.

But gathering historical photographs for a portrait of a complex geographical area also poses the problem of balancing the beautiful against the best documentation, against the importance of a unique though unprofessional photograph of a significant subject, against the demands of the text. Our judgment was guided by the plan of the book as a whole rather than by the visual appeal of a lovely image. Yet it is amazing how more often than not the lovely coincides with the important.

Travelers in Ancient Lands draws from all categories of photographs: artfully designed or slick commercial studio scenes, informal personal snapshots, precise daguerreotypes, grainy calotypes, professional stereographs, magnificent wet-collodion negatives, and bromide prints taken under difficult conditions with box cameras by adventurers. We have not relied on the artistry of only two or three great masters but have included the work of many kinds of travelers whose relationship to the camera and to the Middle East differed enormously. Thus, this book can be viewed as if it were a collection of quotations by various authors about what they saw and found poignant or poetic or fearful or beautiful or symbolic in these ancient lands.

Panels between the chapters provide historical notes about photography in the Middle East. Biographies of the photographers appear at the end of the book.

1 TEN THOUSAND YEARS OF HISTORY

In the Name of Allah, the Compassionate, the Merciful!

When the sun ceases to shine; when the stars fall down and the mountains are blown away; when camels big with young are left untended and the wild beasts are brought together; when the seas are set alight and men's souls are reunited; when the infant girl, buried alive, is asked for what crime she was slain; when the records of men's deeds are laid open and the heaven is stripped bare; when Hell burns fiercely and Paradise is brought near: then each soul shall know what it has done.

—THE KORAN

CIVILIZATION BEGAN in the Middle East where, in an area slightly larger than the United States, only one tenth of the land gets enough water to be farmed. The rest is baked mountain and blazing desert with wild pastures brought to life here and there, for a month or so at most, by a few days of rain. Although some of the developments leading to the first civilization have been identified by archeologists, their causes remain theoretical. Of great importance, however, was the geographical situation of the Middle East.

Many hundreds of millions of years ago a single landmass, named Pangaea by geologists, rose out of the

On Jebel Barkal, the holy hill in Napata, Kush (also called Nubia), these pyramids were built for kings in imitation of Egyptian funerary edifices. The photograph was taken from the top of the hill.

Horst Schliephack, Breasted expedition, 1906.

shallow sea covering the world. On this motherland evolved and flourished the ancestors of our familiar animals and plants. About two hundred million years ago Pangaea began to break up into large pieces that slowly drifted apart to become the continents that we know. But as the oceans opened between future Africa, Europe, and Asia, the Arabian peninsula with its adjacent land- and waterways remained a bridge linking those three continents.

Less than a hundred thousand years ago Neanderthal hunters appeared throughout the Old World, followed by Cro-Magnon societies. And then about ten thousand years ago, hunters discovered in the Middle East how to domesticate plants and animals, and lifted themselves from wanderers scrounging on the environment to independent farmers creating their own food supply. Some of the steps in this first cultural revolution have been worked out from archeological remains; one was the domestication of bread wheat. The revolutionaries had to evolve a never-before-dreamed-of technology for planting,

Village scene on the Tigris indicates the tropical climate near the river.

Anonymous, after 1900.

About 8000 B.C. the first farming villages in the Middle East appeared where rainfall was adequate. The original Jericho was one of the earliest settlements. Many different towns have been built one on top of the other above the original. Possibly one of these towns worked out one of the world's first systems for irrigation. References to Jericho in the Bible abound, beginning with its destruction by Joshua's army. In the Ottoman Empire it had no importance. The excavation shown here reveals the walls of houses.

D. D. Luckenbill or assistant, 1908–1909.

tending, harvesting, and preserving crops, and a technology for selective breeding of flocks and herds, as well as technologies for building villages and for brand-new village crafts. They had to develop rules for private ownership, leadership, specialization in labor, and they had to find new gods who were concerned with fertility and with every family hearth. Later on, whether they were hunters or farmers tired of tilling the land, some people chose to live as tented nomads shepherding animals from one meager pasture to another. These ancient manipulations of nature, and the ways of life dependent on them, were perpetuated in the Middle East unchanged through the millennia into the early twentieth century, linking villagers and nomads in their struggle to cope with the desert, and nourishing a long list of exuberantly different civilizations.

The first villages seem to have been created on the rain-catching slopes of the Zagros Mountains, which separate the deserts of Mesopotamia from the deserts of Persia. As the villagers accumulated knowledge they began to migrate into more productive regions of what has been named the Fertile Crescent, especially along the Tigris and Euphrates rivers and along the Nile. Because the Nile floods its banks annually to deposit fertilizing mud, while the Tigris-Euphrates valley maintains vast marshlands and shallow lakes, two different systems of irrigation were invented. They are followed to this

day. Digging out the record of a place like Jericho, where thirty villages were built, each on top of the ruins of its predecessor, one feels that nothing much seems to have changed culturally and technically for about five thousand years. One can imagine a slow growth in the number of settlements and a slow growth from settlement to village to embryonic town, but something more mysterious was shaping for the next great transformation of society, as great as that from hunter to farmer.

About 4000 B.C. among some of the peasant engineers on the Tigris and the Euphrates, a still unknown sequence of technological and social innovations suddenly burst the timeless traditions to create Sumer, the first city civilization in the world. A few centuries later, perhaps emulating Sumer's revolution, the villages of the upper (southern) and lower (northern) reaches of the Nile coalesced with a similar metamorphosis to create the civilization of Egypt.

In Mesopotamia a bewildering history of civilizations followed, acknowledging Sumer as ancestor. The Akkad-

· 2 ·

Nº 76 Karnak Vue prise du Nord-Est   H. Béchard

ian, Babylonian, Hittite, Assyrian, and Persian empires are the most familiar; they overlap, vanish, reappear in new trappings with new gods and new frontiers and glorious new cities as they conquer and reconquer one another or are destroyed by waves of barbarians hurtling on them from lands beyond the Middle East or out of its own deserts.

In Egypt, on the other hand, a single civilization outlasted various invasions, revolutions, and disintegrations from 3500 B.C. to 30 B.C. Instead of incessant rivalries among racially and culturally diverse peoples, the record presents an amazing continuity through Old, Middle, and New Kingdoms, during which a succession of thirty-two dynasties, with several periods of transition, ruled the whole of Egypt.

Thebes, about four hundred miles south of Cairo on the Nile, became the capital of Egypt during the 11th Dynasty, circa 2000 B.C. Temples and monuments were built on sacred ground known by the name of a village as Karnak, on the flat east shore of the Nile in the northern section of Thebes. The southern section was Luxor. The tombs of the kings, queens, and nobles were in the barren mountains on the west shore. In this view, the columns, pylons, and obelisks of the Great Temple of Amon-Ra, the supreme deity, rise from the fallen stones.

H. Béchard, before 1878.

· 3 ·

From 1567 to 1085 B.C. *pharaohs and nobles were buried at Thebes on the west bank of the Nile. Entrances to a few of the sixty tombs can be seen here. All but Tutankhamen's were plundered many centuries ago.*

R. M. Junghaendel, ca. 1890.

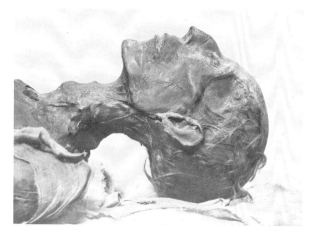

The refined features of the mummified head of Ramses II do not suggest the megalomaniac whose fallen statue inspired Percy Bysshe Shelley's "Ozymandias."

Anonymous, before 1900.

*The Tomb of Seti I, who died in 1304 B.C., was the
most beautiful in the Valley of the Kings, though its
contents had been plundered long ago. Several magnesium
flares seem to have lit the scene for the unknown photographer, C. S., who made this picture, probably before 1880.*

*The two colossi of Memnon, nearly seventy feet high,
each cut from a single block of stone, guard a vanished
temple in Thebes. They and several others that have disappeared depicted Amenhotep III, whose reign ended in
1372 B.C. Ancient Greeks believed the statues were of
Memnon, a mythical being of Abyssinia. The one on the
right was the famous singing statue, visited by countless
tourists and monarchs in ancient times until the Romans
restored the deteriorating outside and thereby silenced it.
The accepted theory is that, as the rising sun heated the
stone, expansion caused the sounds.*

A. Beato, after 1862.

The Great Temple of Amon-Ra at Karnak, composed of several structures, is the largest temple in Egypt and one of the largest in the world. This hypostyle hall (in which two rows of columns support a flat roof) was erected by Ramses I (19th Dynasty) in the fourteenth century B.C. The floor area is 5,800 square yards, about the size of a football field, and the columns are 78 feet tall with a second row of smaller columns flanking the first; altogether 140 were raised.

A. Beato, after 1862.

A panorama that suggests the monumental magnificence of the Great Temple and other structures at Karnak includes for contrast the village of Luxor, once part of Thebes, to the right.

Maxime Du Camp, 1849–1850.

The temples and shrines on the island of Philae above Aswan on the Nile were begun in the fourth century B.C. by the last Egyptian pharaoh, Nectanebo II, and were added to by the Greek Ptolemies and then the Romans through the first century A.D. The island was sacred to the goddess Isis, but there are also two churches built later by Copts. The first dam at Aswan, 1902, flooded part of the structures, but the High Dam, 1970, upstream, lowered the Nile and they emerged again.

Francis Frith, 1857.

Many animals of Egypt figured in the complex religious beliefs that were woven together through the millennia. The crocodile god, Sebek, was associated with fertility, death, and burial. He was especially venerated in the Faiyum and Thebes.

Francis Frith, 1857.

A view of the Temple of Isis on Philae, showing the delicacy of the bas relief.

R. M. Junghaendel, ca. 1890.

Giant figures of Isis (left) and her son Horus decorate the walls of the Great Temple of Isis on the island of Philae.

Francis Frith, probably 1857.

Breathtaking in grandeur as the Mesopotamian cities must have been, judging from descriptions of ancient travelers and from their ruins today, the architecture of Egypt was even more overwhelming, as are its ruins. Along both river systems, however, the same unrelenting force challenged the builders: empty deserts surrounding their farms and separating their cities by hundreds of miles.

About 2000 B.C. pastoral Israelite tribes in the desert around the Sumerian city of Ur, near present-day Baghdad, began to worship Yahweh, revealed in visions to the patriarch Abraham. A stern tribal god, Yahweh stayed with his chosen people wherever they wandered, turning them gradually against other gods and evolving with cultural change through nomadism, serfdom, and nationhood into One God for all mankind, to whom King Solomon built the First Temple of Jerusalem in the tenth century B.C. And though the Israelites left very little architecture, they preserved in the Old Testament the vivid dialogues between Yahweh and their prophets and kings.

In the seventh century B.C., when the Persian Empire of the Achaemenids was the strongest in the world, Zoroaster founded in Bactria a new religion with a supreme deity, Ahura Mazda, which spread through the Middle East. Its monotheistic principles and concern with good and evil influenced Judaism and later on Christianity and Islam.

*The Western (or Wailing) Wall is all that is left of the
Second Temple of the Jews, destroyed by the Romans
in* A.D. *70. Prayers are chanted here for the restoration
of the Temple.*

Peter Bergheim, ca. 1864.

The creativity of those early civilizations is overwhelming. They invented the wheel, chariots, sailing ships, mining and metallurgy, the alphabet, maps, paper, law, mathematics, geometry, medicine, monumental architecture and sculpture, jewelry, money, finance, trade, the basic handicrafts and techniques for mass manufacturing, the training of engineers, artisans, clerks, priests, soldiers, the whole apparatus of bureaucracy and management, the institutionalization of religion, the strategies of war, the fundamental notion of empire and government, and more.

Yet village life and the farmer's tools that delivered food to the great cities and the armies never changed. Of the several theories of how the social organization necessary for civilization came about, one suggests that the mutual dependence of peasant and nomadic herdsman developed the procedures of trade, and also encouraged the nomads to loot when they could. This forced the villagers into developing techniques for military defense, which produced an idle warrior class. Eventually genuine warfare evolved. The complicated division of labor demanded by warfare and the possibilities of amassing loot and subjecting conquered people to serfdom laid the ground for civilization. Another theory is that river irrigation projects demanded collaboration among the villages using the river; a central authority was needed to direct the engineering and to oversee land titles and the distribution of water. Thus, large-scale irrigation and not warfare could have generated the complicated weave of professions necessary for a civilization. Neither theory can be proved and neither can be applied to civilizations in the Americas or in Asia. They explain only what happened in the Middle East, and they are contradictory as well.

In any case, barbarians on the periphery of the Middle East and in its deserts were a constant menace with hit-and-run raids. And sometimes they actually conquered with a superior technology, as did the Hittites, who, having discovered how to domesticate the horse and how to smelt iron from ore and beat it into swords, chopped up bronze-armed foot soldiers as they galloped into the lands of milk and honey. Occasionally, instead of conquering, barbarians merely took away knowledge and established derivative civilizations, as in Crete and Greece. About 600 B.C. the rural, mercantile Greeks with their small cities and colonies on the shores of Anatolia began to assimilate what they had learned traveling in Egypt and Mesopotamia, specifically Babylon, with their own amazingly different insights and view of nature. And they produced, for the first time in history, a civilization that celebrated the individual citizen of a political democracy, whose philosophers argued for understanding natural events through study rather than by inventing supernatural forces, whose artists idealized the human body and represented life in terms of everyday values. But the initial impact of Greek culture on the rest of the world came with the armies of Alexander the Great, who set out to conquer the Middle East and everything else beyond. In 332-331 B.C. he founded Alexandria at the mouth of the Nile; it gradually replaced Athens as the center of Greek

In this daguerreotype of about 1845, Alexandria is still a humble town, although Mohammed Ali had already enlarged the harbor and linked it by canal with the Nile. On the left an obelisk, called Cleopatra's Needle, rises above the old fishing town that is being transformed into a modern city.

Jules Itier, 1845–1846.

culture, which force of arms carried into India before Alexander died. It was in Alexandria that the first great university and library were established and alchemy was born — that fascinating mixture of logic, myth, magic, religion, and experimentation from which the modern laboratory sciences evolved two thousand years later.

Not long after Alexander's conquests another agricultural people in Europe, the Romans, having civilized themselves by emulating the Greeks but having acquired a more pragmatic and technologically ambitious orientation, conquered Greece, most of Europe, and the Middle East as well. With their no-nonsense militarism and engineering, and a constitutional form of government, they also changed the Middle East dramatically and in turn

were themselves changed. Roman laws made sense and could be enforced, Roman coins stabilized commerce, a centralized government maintained fast communications throughout the empire, knitting together the Middle East, North Africa, and Europe. For the first time in history the status of "citizen" was as meaningful as it is today.

Just after Egypt fell to the status of a Roman province

Baalbek in Lebanon, near Damascus, was a Phoenician city where Baal was worshipped, but Alexander the Great renamed it Heliopolis. When the Romans came they built this temple to Jupiter and another to Bacchus. After the Arabs conquered it Baalbek never rose above the status of a provincial town. Excavations began in 1898.

Maxime Du Camp, 1849–1850.

This fallen seraph, or celestial being, found at Memphis was not Egyptian but of later Greco-Roman workmanship.

Théodule Devéria, ca. 1858.

Gateway to the Temple of Jupiter in Baalbek.

Taken by a photographer working for the Palestine Exploration Fund, ca. 1875.

(in 30 B.C. with the suicide of Cleopatra), Jesus, a Jew, was born in Roman-ruled Bethlehem, grew up as an unknown carpenter, meditated in the desert, and began preaching one God for all humanity. Following his crucifixion, his disciples became missionaries against paganism and Rome's emperor worship. Carrying the teachings of Jesus, eventually collected in the New Testament, throughout the Middle East and into Africa and Asia, they founded congregations that survived persecution by going underground. Arguments over dogma and leadership established several centers claiming primary authority. But the strongest bishop resided in Alexandria, even though it was believed that Peter, chosen by Jesus as "the rock," had founded a cell in Rome and was martyred there.

During those early centuries in the Christian calendar, the Roman Empire began to suffer from the incursions of barbarians on all sides and eventually it was decided that four emperors would divide the lands for better defense. One of them, Constantine I (the Great), vanquished two of the others, left Rome and the Western Empire to the fourth, and set up his own court in the Eastern Empire, in a city he had built and in 330 dedicated as his capital from which to rule both East and West. Constantinople rose on the site of Byzantium, an ancient trading town on the western shore of the Bosporus, the waterway con-

A woman of Bethlehem.

Anonymous, before 1877.

The Via Dolorosa ("Way of Sorrows") in Jerusalem, along which Jesus carried the Cross to Golgotha and his crucifixion. (Detail.)

Anonymous, before 1877.

Jesus liked to preach on the Mount of Olives; it was on its slope in the Garden of Gethsemane that Judas Iscariot betrayed him to the Romans, and the mount is believed to be the place from which he ascended to heaven. Here a monk tends the garden.

Probably Frank Good, ca. 1860.

During the third and fourth centuries after the Crucifixion, when Christians were struggling to survive against Roman persecution, hermits and then monks retreated into the deserts, where they built monasteries and convents with towering walls against raiders. The monks were tough farmers and fighters; one of their functions was to shelter and feed travelers. This is a corner inside the monastery of St. Catherine at the foot of Mt. Sinai, founded by Greek Orthodox brothers about A.D. 250.

James McDonald, 1868–1869.

The first Church of the Holy Sepulchre in Jerusalem was formerly believed to mark the site where Jesus was entombed and resurrected. It was erected by Constantine the Great in 335. But Jerusalem was destroyed several times, and in rebuilding the city and its walls the exact locations of the tomb may have been lost. The present building, constructed in 1810, incorporates remnants of previous edifices but is no longer thought to mark the tomb. The Greek Orthodox, Roman Catholic, Armenian Orthodox, Syrian, Ethiopian, and Coptic churches share the administration.

James McDonald, 1864–1865.

This Roman pedestal is the base for the obelisk of Theodosius I in the Hippodrome, Constantinople.

James Robertson, ca. 1854.

A scene in Constantinople clearly shows wooden houses in the Balkan tradition. The obelisk is the Kiz Tash (meaning Column of the Virgin); it is one of the few monuments remaining from third-century Byzantium.

Anonymous, before 1877.

The pilgrim to Mecca wears two pieces of seamless cloth and does not shave or cut his hair or nails. He begins the ceremony at the sacred mosque, kissing the Black Stone inside the building called the Kaaba, walking seven times around the Kaaba, and then running seven times between Mt. Safa and Mt. Marva, two elevations outside Mecca. Next he goes to Mina and Arafa 15 miles away, where he listens to a sermon. He spends the night at Muzdalifa near Arafa, and on the last day he offers a sacrifice. After he has performed all these and several more rituals during the last month of the Arab year, he can call himself a hajji. Women follow the same rituals but their prescribed dress covers the body.

Taken by an Egyptian quarantine doctor, ca. 1912.

necting the Black Sea and the Mediterranean that had more than once stopped Middle East conquerors from invading Europe. Pagan Rome was soon engulfed by Nordic and Mongol tribes and the Western Empire collapsed. But Constantinople, the capital of the emperors who made Christianity the state religion, survived and continued to rule most of the Mediterranean and the Middle East, except for the Sassanid Persian Empire, where Zoroastrianism dominated, and Mesopotamia, which the Persians had conquered. Constantinople became the magnificent center of a new civilization, the Byzantine, compounded of Roman, Greek, and Middle Eastern elements but speaking Greek and establishing what came to be known in its rivalry with the Roman Catholic Church as the Greek Orthodox, or Eastern, Church. (The bishops of Rome had earlier assumed the title of pope and throughout the decline of the Western Empire and during the Dark Ages maintained their claim that only the Roman pope, who was also Patriarch of the West, could be the Vicar of Christ. The Patriarchs of Constantinople disputed the claim.)

A century and a half after the founding of Constantinople, in 570, in the Arabian market town of Mecca, a son named Mohammed was born to a well-to-do merchant family of the Quraysh tribe, whose leaders ruled Mecca. Although the city harbored many pagan beliefs, there

The night spent in the vast encampment around Mt. Arafa always awed pilgrims by the sheer numbers of the faithful gathered from all over the world to worship in the desert.

Taken by an Egyptian quarantine doctor, ca. 1912.

were also flourishing Jewish and Christian settlements nearby, and Mohammed learned about the Old and New Testaments. He spent a great deal of time alone in the desert, and in that empty wasteland there was revealed to him the same God that Hebrew prophets and Jesus had preached but with this difference: Allah had picked Mohammed to be His final and greatest prophet, empowered to lead Arabia into the true faith of Islam, meaning submission to God's will.

Historians and theologians agree that the great bonding force in Islam from the very beginning was the simplicity of the basic tenet that whoever abides by the Five Pillars, or duties, is a good Muslim and pleases Allah. They are: one, he must fully understand and accept the statement, "There is no god but God and Mohammed is his prophet"; two, he must pray five times a day at the appointed hours; three, he must be generous with alms; four, he must keep the fast of Ramadan; five, he must make the pilgrimage to Mecca, if he can, once in his life.

Mohammed's followers accepted their mission, but

The pilgrims rent their mounts in Mecca.

Taken by an Egyptian quarantine doctor, ca. 1912.

*The Dome of the Rock in Jerusalem was completed in 691
by Caliph Abd al-Malik ibn Marwan as a Muslim shrine
on the site from which Mohammed ascended to heaven.
This is also the place where Abraham prepared to sacrifice
Isaac. The shrine is one of several buildings in a walled
area called the Harim ash-Sherif, which incorporates the
ground where the First and Second Temples (including
the Western or Wailing Wall) of the Jews were built.
Thus this land is sacred to both Jews and Muslims.*

James McDonald, 1864–1865.

A section of the wall inside the Harim ash Sherif, south-west corner.

James McDonald, 1864–1865.

from the outset he was opposed by the ruling merchant class. Armed hostility in Mecca drove him to Medina. His supporters drew together into a military organization that soon developed a fanatical drive for conversion through conquest. By 750 the armies of Islam, led by Arab tribes, had seized the Middle East from Byzantium, conquered North Africa, Spain, Persia, and part of India, and were adventuring toward China. Only Constantinople and its surrounding lands held out.

How this incredible sweep of victories was achieved by former nomads and how they consolidated that enormous mosaic of cultures has fascinated historians. One of their methods was to recruit converts as equals before Allah to fight with them, share the loot, staff the bureaucracy of

Ctesiphon on the Tigris River near Baghdad was one of the capitals of the Parthian Empire in the third century B.C. and later of the Sassanids. Greeks, Romans, and Persians occupied the city, but after the Arabs made Baghdad their capital, Ctesiphon declined. This stereograph shows the ruin of the Parthian palace Taq Kisra.

Underwood & Underwood, 1915.

government, and rule as their representatives in a network of multiracial loyalties to Islam. But the original tribesmen from Arabia and their descendants kept special privileges. They maintained a military aristocracy that non-Arabs could not join and they formed a power elite in the empire. Thus, leadership was always in the hands of Arabs who really did believe that they were on a mission ordained by God. The desert was also of key importance in their strategy: principal garrison towns were on the edge of deserts for a last-ditch stand if need be before retreat into the wastelands where no enemy could follow. But most important, perhaps, was the title of caliph, which signified the deputy or successor of Mohammed. As it could be claimed only by the secular ruler of the Arab Empire, the sultan, all religious, political, and military powers were united in a single leader.

Inevitably, quarrels over the succession created both political and religious rivalries. The first three caliphs after Mohammed's death had been given the title by acclamation, but the third, a member of the Omayyad family, was murdered. Ali, the prophet's cousin and son-in-law, husband of Mohammed's daughter Fatima, was now acclaimed caliph, but for complicated reasons he was eventually opposed by Mohammed's widow, Aishah, and others. After putting down several rebellions Ali was assassinated, as were his two sons. The Omayyads now reclaimed the title and held it until 750, moving the capital from Medina to Damascus in 661 for more centralized, efficient administration.

A rebellious sect, the Shiites, argued that the Omayyads were usurpers, that only Mohammed's descendants — through Fatima or Ali — were legitimate, for they were divine like Mohammed, and that the twelfth in this succession would appear before the Day of Judgment as the Mahdi, a redeemer who would restore the true faith. In their adherence to mystical tenets such as these, the Shiites opposed legitimated authority and also broke away from the orthodox beliefs of the majority of Muslims, the Sunnis, who followed the interpretations of the Koran and the record of Mohammed's sayings together

This group of dancing dervishes in Constantinople was wealthy, judging by the clothes and well-fed faces. Dervishes have been compared to Christian monks, although Islam does not allow religious orders or monastic seclusion. Dervishes believe in versions of Sufism, a movement that grew from Shiite mysticism. It is concerned with the union between the individual and God, but is more literary and philosophical than theological, and found its most lyrical expression in poetry. The movement spread from Persia throughout the Middle East and generated dervishes who taught as well as sought ecstatic or hypnotic states through dancing, howling, whistling, or whirling exercises. The costumes of some sects were strictly prescribed: a black outer cloak symbolized the grave, a tall hat the headstone, white undergarments resurrection.

Anonymous, before 1877.

The Day of Treading in Cairo was an annual religious ritual of the dervishes. They lay face down in a row and their sheikh rode horseback across them. Those whose bones broke under the hooves were assumed to have been sinners. After 1881 the sheikh dismounted for the walk.

J. Pascal Sébah, after 1868.

This mysterious photograph without a caption possibly shows a dervish and his disciples. A dervish could be a holy man, or a scholar-teacher, or a healer, or a wandering beggar who had devoutly given up the world. Thieves and charlatans often pretended to be dervishes, playing the role of pious men to take money from the faithful.

James Robertson, ca. 1854.

with traditions called the Sunna. The Shiites spread through Persia and Mesopotamia and fostered several messianic schisms, such as the Assassins and the Ismailis, which in turn diverged into offshoots. The Sunnis also fathered new sects from time to time, such as the Wahabis, but these tended to be puritanical. Mohammed had not allowed orders, yet the Sufi movement, mostly among Shiites, generated a kind of brotherhood and from it came what may be called sects like that of the various dervishes, special pleading, and practices. (Sufism is a philosophical concern with the personal relationship between a soul and God.) It is commonly said that Islam's two main streams have branched a thousand times, and even if this is a figure of speech, it suggests one reason for the unend-

It is believed that Damascus is the oldest continuously inhabited city in the world, because antiquities dating to 3000 B.C. have been found there. Every ancient conqueror occupied it and most of them built something or other, fragments of which are still standing or the site of which is commemorated. Greek and Roman influence is clearly visible, but the Byzantine style is prominent from the time when Damascus was a Christian city. It was on the road to Damascus that Saul was converted and took the name of Paul. Around 635 the Arabs made it the capital of their empire, but after the caliphate was moved to Baghdad, in 762, Damascus fell on hard times and was occupied by a variety of armies. Occasionally it prospered as a manufacturing and caravan center, at other times it was almost deserted, but it was always the most important city in Syria and usually the capital. Refugees sometimes turned Damascus with its large oasis into a hodgepodge of ethnic enclaves, but Christians, Jews, and Muslims managed to share the city's life peacefully whatever happened. Damask and swords were only two of its famous manufactures.

In 1400 the Mongols under Timur destroyed the city and shipped the renowned sword-makers and armorers to Samarkand. Under the Ottomans after 1516, Damascus regained its reputation as the loveliest of the desert cities and a center for industries and the caravan trade. Here the largest caravans were assembled for the pilgrimage to Mecca.

Damascus has lived its 5,000 years off the ample food it grows in its own gardens and on the surrounding farms in the Ghouta oasis, seen here stretching beyond the roofs, watered by the Barada River, which springs out of the Anti-Lebanon Mountains — at top of picture — and then vanishes into the sand. It was a city of inner courtyards with fountains hidden from shaded streets, though this view does not show them. The domed building at upper left is the Great Mosque. Only fifty miles away across the mountains was Beirut with its Riviera climate, Christian population, and Parisian style of life. But Damascus remained Muslim and Arab in every way, its face to the great Syrian desert. (Detail.)

Francis Frith, 1857–1858.

ing restlessness in the Muslim world — which at the same time has maintained a coherence through the five daily prayers, the pilgrimage to Mecca, and the ethos of Islamic law, to win more converts worldwide than any other religion can boast.

In 750 a descendant of Mohammed's uncle, therefore an acceptable alternative to the direct line from Fatima and Ali, won the caliphate and established the Abbasid dynasty. His support came mainly from the Shiites, and though he made conciliatory compromises with the Sunnis, he later moved the capital from Damascus to Baghdad, emphasizing the shift from the Mediterranean and Western lands toward the East. The Egyptian, Syrian, and Turkish populations, overwhelmingly Sunni, rejected the Abbasids, and various military tyrants claimed to be rival caliphs in different parts of the empire. But Baghdad retained its primacy and became the cultural center, the wealthiest and most sophisticated of the several worldly cities of Islam, outshining Christian Byzantine Constantinople itself. The sultan-caliph Harun al-Rashid of *The Thousand and One Nights* in the eighth century and the mathematician-poet Omar Khayyam in the tenth are only two of the many famous Persians of this period. It was under the Abbasids that the exiled Omayyads of Córdoba, as rival caliphs in Spain, created a stunning culture with its glorious architecture and universities, while other leaders conquered southern Italy, raided France, and vanquished India.

Inevitably Arabs gradually became less important in the army and administration. Many acquired lands and settled permanently, giving up privileged status. A great many returned to Arabia. From the beginning however, they had been successful in recruiting loyal troops from conquered peoples. One of their most successful methods was a system of buying slaves, largely from Turkish tribes, training them to be Muslim soldiers and officers, and rewarding them handsomely after battles. These slave armies, called Mamelukes, became increasingly important in the military machine of the empire and began to vie with the sultan for power in the provinces entrusted to them. As they could demand freedom according to Islamic law, here and there former slaves became actual governors. Later, other Turkish tribesmen like the Seljuks and Circassians flocked into the army as volunteers, and they also began to press for power in bailiwicks of

A temple of Jupiter (or Rimmon) from Roman days in Damascus was converted under Byzantine rule into the Cathedral of St. John the Baptist. Arabs in 705 bought the cathedral, tore down most of it, and transformed it into the Great Mosque of Damascus. They did not disturb the crypt where the head of St. John was supposedly buried. This same adaptability led them to retain the Byzantine towers and use them as minarets. The repeating columns and their shadows create an effect of geometric unity, yet every column has different decorations, asserting the uniqueness of each element in the overall pattern.

Bonfils, after 1867.

that immense territory.

The Catholic Church naturally viewed the spread of Islam with horror, not as a new religion but as a heresy because Mohammed had recognized Christ as a prophet and had even accepted the Virgin birth. Heretics roused greater hatred than pagans. The papacy and the European

kings launched nine crusades, from 1095 to 1291, against Islam to liberate Jerusalem and the Holy Land for the true church. The enemy in the Middle East was called Saracen, whether Arab, Syrian, Turkish, Persian, Egyptian, or whatever, while Berbers, Arabs, and all other Muslims in North Africa and Spain were called Moors. Both Christians and Muslims called each other infidels.

During those two centuries the feudal armies of the West were in direct contact with the two greatest Middle Eastern civilizations, far superior to any in Europe at that time: the shrunken but still powerful Christian Byzantine Empire that sometimes helped and sometimes hindered the Crusades, and the dominant Muslim empire. The First Crusade conquered the shores of Syria and Palestine and in 1099 established a Latin kingdom in Jerusalem that lasted until 1187 when the great Kurdish general Salah al-Din (Saladin), later sultan of Egypt and Syria, drove them out. All the other Crusades were failures in one way or another. The Fourth Crusade sacked Constantinople while on its way to the Holy Land in 1203 and remained to rule it as a Latin kingdom for half a century before Greek armies managed to overcome quarreling leadership and recapture the city.

The energy of the Crusaders was phenomenal. The logistics of marching thousands of miles through hostile lands, or of packing invasion forces into little square-rigged ships belonging to rapacious Italian traders (whose captains sold the "Childrens' Crusade" into slavery) boggles the imagination. Then when they reached the Muslim world they erected fortresses, dug out harbors, maintained a communications network, and fought better trained, better fed, better equipped armies who were protecting their own lands against the motley invaders serving wrangling lords. In fact, Christian armies sometimes battled each other. On top of this they established permanent settlements in several cities, occupied the islands of Cyprus, Rhodes, and Malta, and conducted lucrative trade between Europe and the Middle East. Military-religious orders, like the Knights Templars and the Hospitalers, acquired lands and wealth and meddled actively in politics at home. And yet Arab chroniclers described the Crusaders as barbarous and ignorant, with repulsive habits and capable of shocking inhumanity, including the slaughter of prisoners and occasional cannibalism after battles.

And, indeed, generally speaking, when the knights went home, usually as remnants of beaten armies, they found the same barely domesticated barbarism and hardships into which they had been born, the shadow of pagan

Bonfils

961 ... Forteresse de Kérak, prise de l'est

The fortress of Krak des Chevaliers (Kerak, Al-Karak) in Syria is on the site of a walled hill town that was a Moabite trading center in Biblical days. In 1136 the Crusaders seized the town from the Arabs and built this magnificent fortification, which Saladin retook in 1188. It was captured by the Mamelukes in 1271.

Bonfils, after 1867.

worship inside every church, illiterate robber barons, murder a commonplace in the struggle of weak kings against the nobles, and the grinding poverty of serfdom. Their memories of the incredible intellectual, artistic, and sensual extravagances of Byzantium were impossible to describe to stay-at-home rustics whose largest city, Paris, was a hamlet compared to Constantinople. Even more impossible to describe was the vast empire of the Arabs from Spain into India with its endless variety, color, pomp, scholarship, and sumptuous beauty. For during periods of truce some Crusaders journeyed in the Middle East as tourists, or as prisoners of war waiting to be ransomed. Back home they could only dream of the tangy foods, lilting music, erotic dancers, the brawling, racy street life of semitropical cities, the perfumes of exotic flowers and fruits, the sparkling fountains in the gardens, the thronging bazaars, the palaces. Civilization, the Crusaders knew, was far, far away under a flaming desert sun and bewitching desert moon. The haunting call of the muezzin echoed faintly against the tolling church bells.

In fact, after the ancestors of the Crusaders had torn up the Roman Empire in the fifth century, very little learn-

Minaret d'El Azhar avec muezzins

Bonfils

· 28 ·

ing was preserved in Europe, and that only in parchments salvaged by churchmen shivering in monastic isolation here and there. The manuscripts wore out, literacy faded, and the tribal peoples forgot what they had known about the glories of Rome. The paved highways, the bridges and aqueducts, the forums and temples became mysterious, decaying ruins of some golden age long ago, and the stones cut by Romans were dragged away to buttress village walls. The continent sank into the Dark Ages while Byzantium flourished and Islam burst out in brilliant fireworks created from the best of all the cultures the Arabs had conquered. They had an unusual passion for knowledge and they imbued their subjects with the same passion. Although they never managed to break the defenses of Constantinople, they discovered an immensely rich reservoir of Greek manuscripts in the surrounding territories, and they were inspired by it all—Plato, Aristotle, Archimedes, Ptolemy, Euclid, and the other giant intellects of Hellenic civilization. Arab as well as Persian, Hindu, Jewish, and Christian scholars, who happily converted to Islam and took Arab names, translated everything into Arabic. Sometimes the original Greek versions had been lost but early translations into Syriac, Aramaic, or Hebrew were found, and so these were translated. Latin, Chinese, Hindu, Persian, and Sanskrit manuscripts were just as stimulating. And, escaping from its tribal confines, the Arabic language itself expanded steadily under the pressure of scholarship, research, and the administration of a hundred-tongued empire; it adapted to new concepts and adopted what it needed, becoming the most poetic and richest language in the Middle Ages anywhere.

Islamic scholars were not content merely to translate. Whatever interested them was elevated, improved, added to. They treated with sensitivity and depth literature, art,

A daguerreotype of Cairo shows the city's many minarets and the density of housing.

Jules Itier, 1845–1846.

The University of Al-Azhar with its mosque was established in Cairo in 973. To this day it is the world center for Islamic studies in law, religion, language, and philosophy. Parts of the original mosque have survived numerous invasions. The muezzins seen here chanting the call to prayer have been replaced by a recorded broadcast.

Bonfils, after 1867.

music, history, geography, philosophy, and they prized fresh views and originality. Men with Arabic names became masters of the practical arts and technologies like navigation, optics, architecture, engineering. Natural philosophy (science), mathematics, and medicine inspired them, and their contributions to these fields and to alchemy were brilliant. Baghdad was transformed into a glittering center for a wholly new civilization rivaling all its predecessors, yet its language and religion were rooted in Mecca and its ideals in the tribal ethic of the desert nomad.

Love of knowledge insists on teaching, and Islamic scholars, whether Arab or not, shared what they were doing with the only literate class left in Europe, the churchmen. About the year 1000 the lonely, pious, rustic priests of Rome began to venture abroad to learn Arabic, to study at Islamic educational centers and later at the first universities that flourished in the Middle East and Islamic Spain long before universities appeared in Christian Europe, and to translate from the living Arabic into resurrected Latin what they felt the Catholic Church, so fearful of heresy, could safely absorb.

In such strange fashion, pagan Greek classics—preserved in Eastern Christian Byzantium, augmented significantly by Islamic researchers and poets and scientists, adapted to Roman Catholicism, taught in Latin church schools—became the nucleus for still another new civilization: the European of the Middle Ages. It in turn generated the Renaissance, out of which emerged the Age of Reason, the political, industrial, and scientific revolutions, and the modern West whose soldiers have been sent to the moon. In that original nucleus were folded all the things the people of the Middle East had invented or discovered and all of it acquired a wholly European form and style, as deeply dyed by Christianity as it had been by Islam.

Throughout the Crusades the Abbasids retained the caliphate in Baghdad. Rival caliphs of the Fatimid dynasty, an offshoot of the Ismailis, one of the strong Shiite sects, had conquered Egypt and ruled unchallenged there, until Saladin drove them out with his Mameluke army and established the Ayyubid dynasty in Cairo, rivaling the Abbasids and putting the Mamelukes in charge of Egypt.

Then about 1200 there rode out of Asia on swift ponies the most terrifying barbarians of all, the Mongols under Genghis Khan, who called himself the Scourge of God. Muslim armies defeated detachments of Mongols—later called Tatars—in a few battles in Asia but nothing could stop the stupefying determination of the Mongols to conquer the world. In 1258 they destroyed Baghdad, slaughtered the inhabitants with their caliph (down whose throat they poured melted gold from his treasure house), let the irrigation system fall into ruin, and annexed Mesopotamia to Persia, where they had set up headquarters. Not until 1401 would the Mongols, under Timur (Tamerlane), abandon Baghdad. After its destruction the Abbasid Caliphate reappeared in Cairo, but there the succession of caliphs was merely a parade of puppets set up by the Mamelukes, who now governed Egypt as a hereditary class, an oligarchy of landed gentry descended from slaves. They maintained their army with the same old system of buying fresh slaves.

Now volunteers from the Ottoman, or Osmanli, Turkish tribe began to dominate the Muslim armies, defeating rivals for power in this province and that and taking on the burden of defending the empire. At long last in 1453 they captured Constantinople, which had held out against all attackers for so many centuries, and moved the caliphate there from Cairo, leaving the Mamelukes as governors of Egypt.

This transfer of the caliphate from Cairo to Christian Byzantium on the edge of Europe marked the beginning of the Ottoman Empire. At once it became involved with European affairs to a far greater extent than any previous Muslim power. Suleiman I the Magnificent in the sixteenth century led the empire to its peak of glory, conquering most of what are now Greece, Bulgaria, Yugoslavia, Albania, Romania, Hungary, while his admiral Khaireddin, nicknamed Barbarossa by Italians, ruled the Mediterranean with lateen-rigged ships that could sail circles around any square-rigged European. Piracy and raiding Christian shores became games they could not lose.

The Ottoman sultan-caliphs controlled absolutely all, the land and sea routes between Europe, the Middle East, Africa, and Asia. But instead of encouraging and protecting trade, they chose to exploit it at key points, leaving the policing and regulations to regional satraps, who naturally also wanted their share. Furthermore, religious and tribal strife, rebellions, raids by uncontrollable bedouin, and dislocations following the Mongol withdrawal made journeying hazardous anywhere in the empire. The risks and cost of both caravan transport and shipping rose enormously. The stunned Europeans, who had become dependent on luxuries, silks, and spices from the Orient, found in their deprivation the ambition, greed, adventurous spirit, and energy to finance searches for a westward route to Cathay and a southern one around Africa. Only forty years after the fall of Constantinople Columbus discovered America, six years later Vasco da Gama rounded the Cape of Good Hope and reached India, and the next generation of explorers circumnavigated the globe. Europe had escaped from the Old World.

This tremendous expansion of knowledge of the earth, its races and civilizations, fauna and flora, the importation of new edible grains and plants, and the avalanche of gold and silver from South America created the first major cultural revolution since the Roman Empire. Yet nothing of that Renaissance affected the Middle East— not just because the Ottoman sultan-caliphs had the power to seal off their empire, but because they were quite simply not interested in learning. Their first loves remained war and government. And the learned men of Islam who had once had no peers for discovery and creativity gradually fell in love with tradition, with poring over the works of the past, refining and redefining what was already known instead of changing, adding, synthesizing the new. And so the Ottoman Empire settled down to live comfortably on its own resources for the next four hundred years, decaying slowly until it finally fell apart in World War I and was eliminated from history.

During those four hundred years Europe put together the social, religious, scientific, technical, commercial, political, and governmental revolutions that just before 1800 delivered the steam engine, the first alternative to the power of wind, water, and muscle. It created the industrial revolution of the nineteenth century — as fantastic a metamorphosis of the human condition as were the agricultural revolution of ten thousand years ago and the birth of civilization five thousand years ago. Almost nothing that one can think of relates industrialized twentieth-century life to life during the Renaissance. And the Middle East knew nothing about it in 1839 when the first photographers went out there. The only important events in the Ottoman Empire during those centuries were the wars the sultans' armies won and lost in Europe and the subsequent jockeying with European governments that by 1800 were dedicated to imperialistic expansion in Africa and Asia and were looking at the Middle East as an increasingly valuable stretch of territory in the geopolitics of colonization. Only at the very top levels of society in the Ottoman Empire were there a very few potential leaders aware of the profound gulf that four centuries of isolationism had deepened between their domain and the Western world.

OVERLEAF

This panoramic view indicates the strategic power Constantinople on its seven hills holds over the Bosporus, which links the Black Sea, the Sea of Marmora, and the Straits of Dardanelles to the Mediterranean. Throughout history migrations, traders, and armies have crisscrossed the narrow waterway between Asia and Europe.

While the Roman Church barely survived against barbarians, the Eastern Church flourished in Constantinople, developing sumptuous rites and converting the pagans of Anatolia, Syria, Mesopotamia, Palestine, Egypt, Arabia, Ethiopia, and Persia to Christianity. Byzantine civilization became legendary for its splendor and culture, and for five centuries Constantinople was not only queen of the Mediterranean but the most important city in the world. By the tenth century, however, most of its empire had fallen to the Muslims, who absorbed Byzantine knowledge and passed it back to Europe through Spain, thereby helping to revive the Roman Church to launch the Crusades. In 1453 the Ottoman Turks captured Constantinople.

In their characteristic way the Turks adapted what they found, converting churches into mosques by adding minarets, into schools, baths, and hostels by adding domes. They allowed Europeans, segregated in various quarters, to carry on a Mediterranean trade. And they made the Byzantine way of life even more extravagant and sensuous, elaborating intrigue into ferocious brutality, backed by the military might of Islam, more powerful on land and sea than any other before or since.

Attempts at Westernization in the nineteenth century did not change the city or its polyglot life-style. In a sense Constantinople was the oldest of all melting pots. For the nineteenth-century tourist the power of an enormous empire was overwhelming. Signs were everywhere of incalculable wealth gathered from defeated nations for fifteen hundred years. Constantinople's uninterrupted European heritage, far away from the deserts that surrounded its Middle East satellites, gave the sultan a tremendous distance from his Muslim subjects. At the same time it brought about the chaotic system of government that relied on military despotism and intrigues in the imperial seraglio.

This panorama was taken from the European heights looking down on the Golden Horn and its two bridges; Galata Bridge is on panel D, with shipping on the Bosporus to its right. The railroad station with its tracks is on panels E and F, on the water. At the extreme left, panel A, is the Suleymaniye Mosque; Topkapi Palace, in the center of panel F, faces the Sea of Marmora, which narrows into the Bosporus; the Osmaniye Mosque to its right stands closer to the camera; the many small domes are the roof of the great bazaar; near the point, on panel H, rise the minarets of Hagia Sophia and, to its right, closer, the Blue Mosque.

G. Berggren, ca. 1870.

A

B

E

F

C

D

G

H

The First Photographers in the Middle East

On January 7, 1839, the Frenchman François Dominique Arago rose in the chamber of the Académie des Sciences in Paris and made the first public announcement of the invention of photography. Louis Jacques Mandé Daguerre had, Arago reported, succeeded in using the camera obscura to make lifelike pictures on a metal plate — without himself drawing or painting on the plate. Arago said the discovery had many marvelous applications, and one he mentioned on the very first day when the world learned that "the sun could draw" related to photography and the Middle East: "To copy the millions and millions of hieroglyphics that cover (even on the outside) the great monuments of Thebes, Memphis, Karnak, etc. one would need twenty years and legions of draftsmen. With the daguerreotype, one single man could do this enormous work by himself. Give the Institut d'Égypte two or three of Daguerre's cameras . . . [and] these drawings will surpass on all counts the fidelity and local color of the most skilled painters; and the . . . [photographic] images, abiding by the rules of geometry, will allow us, with the help of a small number of given facts, to reveal the exact dimensions of the highest, most inaccessible parts of these edifices."

The camera was not a new optical instrument. Arab scholars of the eighth century understood the principles of the camera obscura, the precursor to the photographic camera, and a complete description of it was first recorded in the tenth century by Hassan ibn Hassan, sometimes called Ibn al-Haitham al-Hazin or Alhazen. Nine hundred years later, Westerners brought cameras back to the lands of Islam, as early as they traveled with them any-

A rare daguerreotype shows the temple at Edfu (modern Idfu), between Luxor and Aswan. Dedicated to the god Horus, the temple was begun by Ptolemy III Euergetes in 237 B.C. It is still standing.

Jules Itier, 1845–1846.

where else.

Painters and draftsmen had been busy in the Middle East since 1798 when Napoleon led an army into the area. The campaign opened the whole of the Ottoman Empire, not just Egypt, to scholars and adventurers and then to the tourists who started to come in steamships in the 1840s.

The painter Horace Vernet, his nephew Charles Marie Bouton, and Frédéric Goupil-Fesquet went to Egypt and the Holy Land in October 1839, carrying daguerreotype equipment and an instruction manual. The daguerreotypes dazzled Mohammed Ali, Khedive of Egypt, but he called them the work of the devil, sometimes used as a synonym for the Frankish infidel (just as "devil" was a European appellation for Arab). Their and others' daguerreotypes were copied by engravers and served as the basis of the illustrations in N. P. Lerebours' *Excursions daguérriennes: Vues et monuments les plus remarquables du globe* (1840–1844).

On the boat going up the Nile, Goupil-Fesquet was surprised to meet another Frenchman with a camera. Pierre Gustave Joly de Lotbinière was there on a commission from the architect Hector Horeau, who needed accurate pictures of the condition of Egyptian antiquities for his reconstruction of the palaces and temples of the pharaohs. Lotbinière's daguerreotypes became the basis of the color aquatints in Horeau's *Panorama d'Égypte et Nubie* (1842).

In 1842 the first Oriental scholar arrived with a camera. Joseph-Philibert Girault de Prangey, an expert on Islamic architecture, made daguerreotypes of details of buildings in Egypt, Syria, and Palestine. These were copied into engravings for his book *Monuments arabes d'Égypte, de Syrie et d'Asie Mineure* (1846). Of the other daguerreotypists who followed, not all were as successful in getting an image on their copper plates.

Except for some examples of Prangey's work, all the daguerreotypes by the artists mentioned above have disappeared or were destroyed when copied by engravers. One of the most exciting finds in recent years has been an actual set of daguerreotypes dating from 1845–1846 of cities and sites in Egypt. The daguerreotypes on pages 10, 29, 34, 43, and 101 are from this group by Jules Itier and show the mysterious quality of these early plates, a quality that is lost in engraved copies. The sands piled against the Temple of Edfu seem real and heavy and one wants to push them away to discover what lies beneath. The picture of Alexandria is like a setting for a fairy tale, where all the characters are very small and can disappear along with their city in a flash.

A daguerreotype, to be properly seen, has to be held in the hand. The number of people in the nineteenth century who could experience its richness of detail was therefore limited to but a few. It was not until the first calotypists—those photographers who made paper negatives that could be printed in unlimited quantities—arrived in the Middle East that significant numbers of people actually saw photographs of the ancient lands.

The Reverend George W. Bridges, C. G. Wheelhouse, and Maxime Du Camp were all in the Middle East in the year 1849–1850 making calotypes, but only the work of Du Camp became well known. He traveled with his friend Gustave Flaubert, and both recorded their impressions. About seeing the Sphinx Du Camp wrote: "Gustave gives a loud cry, and I am pale, my legs trembling. I cannot remember ever having been moved so deeply," and "When we reached the Sphinx . . . Flaubert reined in his horse and cried, 'I have seen the Sphinx fleeing toward Libya; it was galloping like a jackal.'" And elsewhere Flaubert added: "We don't have emotions as *po-hé-tiques* as that every day, thank God; it would kill us." He also mentioned, "No drawing that I have seen conveys a proper idea of it—best is an excellent photograph that Max has taken" [page 165].

Du Camp published 125 of his photographs in his book *Égypte, Nubie, Palestine et Syrie* (1852), printed at Blanquart-Evrard's establishment in Lille, France. (Blanquart-Evrard, by modifying the calotype process, was able to print paper negatives easily and permanently in large editions.) The first photographically illustrated travel book, it is a masterpiece of subtlety and refinement, the images revealing their beauty and power only after careful study. The book was expensive, 500 gold francs, and yet it sold well and received much publicity. A critic in *La Lumière* wrote: "Mr. Maxime Du Camp's publication . . . opens a new pathway for investigation for orientalists, and a new horizon for studies." Du Camp's images started what we today take for granted—the shadowy experience of faraway places through photography.

2 THE BREAKUP
OF THE OTTOMAN EMPIRE

Two days later I received the following laconic intimation from the War Office.

"You have been attached as a supernumerary Lieutenant to the 21st Lancers for the Soudan Campaign. You are to report at once at the Abassiyeh Barracks, Cairo, to the Regimental Head-quarters. It is understood that you will proceed at your own expense and that in the event of your being killed or wounded in the impending operations, or for any other reason, no charge of any kind will fall on British Army funds."

. . . The movement of the regiment 1,400 miles into the heart of Africa was effected with the swiftness, smoothness and punctuality which in those days characterised all Kitchener's arrange-ments. We were transported by train to Assiout; thence by stern-wheeled steamers to Assouan. We led our horses round the cataract at Philae; re-embarked on other steamers at Shellal; voyaged four days to Wady Halfa; and from there proceeded 400 miles across the desert by the marvellous military railway whose completion had sealed the fate of the Dervish power. In exactly a fortnight from leaving Cairo we arrived in the camp and railway base of the army, where the waters of the Atbara flow into the mighty Nile.

—WINSTON S. CHURCHILL,
A Roving Commission (1930)

THE EIGHTY YEARS OF PHOTOGRAPHY in the Middle East that this book is concerned with, 1839 to 1919, portrays the final step-by-step breakup of the Ottoman Empire from internal conflicts and from the commercial and imperialistic ambitions of Russia, Britain, France,

The mayor of Jerusalem, Hussein Hashim el-Husseini (with cane), is shown surrendering the city to the British, who had defeated the defending Turkish forces, ending thirteen centuries of Islamic rule. Palestine became a British mandate.

Lewis Larson, 1917.

Italy, Germany, Austria-Hungary, and Greece. World War I snuffed out the Ottoman Empire, but that war toll-ed for the victorious European empires as well, even if very few people heard the ringing. In fact, Queen Victoria and her son and grandson, who ruled the largest of those empires, were believed by their subjects to have provided them with the most prosperous and stable of all times, and this feeling was shared by the upper classes through-out Europe, in regard to their own monarchs.

For much of the century, every country in Europe had a king or queen, the royal families were related by blood or marriage ties, and never had their thrones seemed so secure, especially when compared to the sultan's. The Ottoman Empire was called the "sick man of Europe" because of financial and treaty entanglements harassing the Sublime Porte, as the government was referred to, and because of rebellions throughout the empire. The first task of Western monarchs was to preserve the hereditary privileges of the aristocracy and land-owning nobility, without whose support they could not continue to sit on their thrones. Thus, though the kings or queens ruled through favorites, it was the hidebound nobles who held real authority and manipulated the machinery of government. Occasionally advisory assemblies debated and rubber-stamped royal wishes. Few political parties existed in the modern sense. Murmurs of dissent were suppressed. Confiscation, execution, mass jailings, torture, censorship, and quasimilitary police action were considered necessary techniques. They were not much different from those that sultans used to eliminate rivals, except that in Europe they were backed by legal procedures, whereas the sultans didn't care what anybody thought. The fiercely competing Europeans had the trappings of constitutional government, and the concept of "nation" was paramount.

The Ottoman Empire, on the other hand, was an immense conglomerate of cultures and races that had never known more than tribal coherence after the Arab conquest. There was not even an idea of constitution, for no electorate could be imagined and the notion of political parties divorced from fanatical religious tribal partisanship was inconceivable. Literacy was below 5 percent, and probably 80 percent of the population was peasantry tied by tradition, debts, and taxes to villages and oases, or to nomadic herding in the desert. Every sultan, however he assumed the title, was also named the caliph and was accepted as the supreme ruler by his subjects. But in reality his authority depended completely on military action against or appeasement of governors who commanded their own armies in territories as large as Egypt or Mesopotamia, entrusted to them by the sultan but often wrested from him by self-appointed satraps. By 1800 his authority in North Africa had dwindled to the merest recognition that he existed, the Sudan was charting its own course, and Persia remained unconquered by the Ottomans, harassing the Empire sporadically.

In contrast were the tightly controlled sovereign nations of Europe. Yet European royalty was just as involved in bitter intrigues against one another as the sultans were against their rivals. More importantly, the Europeans sought the sultans' aid as much as they sought theirs in a century of continuously shifting alliances so complicated that only the broadest outline can be sketched here.

Britain, France, Russia, Italy, Austria-Hungary, and Germany were set on colonial expansion. The Ottoman Empire was fair game, but nobody wanted it dismembered for fear that the others would get a better share. Having been isolated since the Age of Discovery, the Middle East had become again a crossroads because colonialism demanded the shortest routes into Africa and to Asia. After 1830, steamships competed with sail, not so much in speed as with smaller crews, greater cargo space, and more reliable schedules. The need for coaling stations on the long passage was new and vital. The ancient dream of a canal connecting the Mediterranean with the Red Sea became more important than ever.

But the key to nineteenth-century history in the Middle East was the industrialization in northern Europe that created a mechanical cornucopia — the camera being perhaps as important as the machine gun — of enormous profit and power to the ruling class as long as it could control sources of cheap raw materials and could monopolize large markets for its manufactured goods. So the Middle East was not just of strategic value to the imperialists; it was also a virgin market for factory goods.

But the industrial-scientific revolution also created entrepreneurs who became millionaires overnight and demanded the privileges of nobility, a fast-swelling middle class that demanded political representation, and a burgeoning factory-labor class, which had never existed before, that demanded humane wages, decent housing, and safe working conditions. Rebellious peasants emigrated to America. In sum, growing literacy and general prosperity based on the machine instead of muscle was rousing longings that had never before confronted rulers.

Visitors from the Middle East saw both aspects of the revolution. They wanted only loans to buy specific money-making machines like railroads and water pumps. The last thing they wanted back home was the social upheaval of industralization. So xenophobic pashas with armed attendants and bevies of veiled women on shopping sprees, and diplomats with colorful entourages negotiating private deals, flattered by Westerners who owned steamships, had no intention of importing Western ideas. The only other Middle Easterners in the West were a very few students idling at famous universities, knowing they could never take home what they learned. So it was from the steadily expanding flow of visitors to the Orient that the people of the Middle East learned about the West: the tourists, explorers, archeologists, soldiers and officers, consuls and diplomats, scholars, pilgrims, writers, painters, and photographers.

Europeans in the nineteenth century, on the other hand, had several other sources of knowledge — or popular myth — about the Middle East besides travel and the stories of travelers. There was the literature of ancient Greek and Roman historians, some writings by the Crusaders, and the experiences of pilgrims and of commercial outfits, mostly French and Italian, that had maintained representatives in the ports and caravan cities for centuries. After the Crusades, relics and fragments of antiquity kept trickling into European collections and later into the new national museums. Intrepid explorers and artists in surprising numbers before 1839 kept vanishing through Ottoman gates to return unharmed with tales and sketches of teeming cities as old as time and ruins older still, lost in the deserts. Most illuminating was firsthand experience with the "terrible Turk" as the despotic ruler of the Balkans for four centuries, and in warfare with Muslims on land and sea for a thousand years.

European historians downgraded the cultural debt owed to the Arab world, and focused on unpleasant matters such as the Barbary pirates and the Janissaries. In the fourteenth century the Ottoman Turks had started kidnapping Christian boys and raising them as fervent Muslims and celibate warriors, who took orders from the sultan only. These Janissaries, monkish fanatics, fought with a disciplined ferocity so famous that at news of their coming the enemy sometimes ran from the battlefield, and no one faced them with much hope of winning. Their cruelty to subject peoples was notorious (and was an important factor goading the Balkans into rebellions after 1800). Long before the nineteenth century, they began to marry. Their sons entered the elite corps as privileged recruits and thus dynastic forces emerged to vie with one another and with viziers at the sultan's court. Eventually Janissaries deposed or murdered sultans to set other favorites on the throne. Complicated intrigue, torture, spying,

A minaret in Cairo.
C. G. Wheelhouse, 1849–1850.

assassination, and even pitched battles among the factions destroyed continuity in government except when the sultan was a ruthless tyrant who could command loyalty from his palace guard and outsmart the Janissaries. European rulers, with a genealogy preserved in the *Almanach de Gotha*, were fascinated by this Turkish system of letting the most determined nobodies fight their way to power.

And, of course, another aspect of the sultan's palace, the harem or seraglio, was even more fascinating. Muslim law allowed a man at any one time four wives, who had to be treated equally, and any number of concubines and slaves. The harem fired the imagination of the West, with very little to go on beyond tales brought back by ambassadors' wives or the gossip of the bazaar.

The stark differences between Christians and Muslims

A young groom in his finery, Cairo.

Anonymous, before 1889.

These Turkish dancers posed in the photographer's studio. They must have been popular, judging from their expensive clothes and carefully coiffed hair.

Zangaki, after 1860.

were exaggerated, both in the West and in the Middle East. Christian churches are holy places visited by congregations for services mostly on Sundays; they have worldwide affiliations and obey central powers on matters of dogma. Preachers and priests are ordained: that is, empowered to administer sacraments. They are intermediaries between the faithful and God. Even in the most Catholic countries there is a clear-cut demarcation between church and state. In contrast, the mosque is a public place — a town meeting hall, a school, a hostel for travelers, a refuge for the poor and dispossessed, often with a bathhouse attached. Open day and night, only one part of it is reserved for prayers. The muezzin climbs the minaret and calls the faithful five times a day in a quavering singsong that carries miles across the rooftops. Most of the faithful stop and pray wherever they are — in their shops and offices, on the street, at home, anywhere. Peo-

ple kneeling and bowing in public, unimaginable in the Christian world, are a normal sight. In Islam there are no ordained intermediaries between the individual and Allah. There are teachers of the Koran and scholars — sheikhs and mullahs, ayatollahs — who ponder theological questions at Islamic universities, creating an expanding body of Islamic law. These laws are not church laws only, for there is no separation between church and state. The laws of Islam are derived from interpretations of the Koran, which is the record of Allah's conversations with Mohammed, and Hadith, which is the record of the Prophet's sayings and interpretations, from which comes the tradition, or Sunna, that sanctions it all. Islamic law ruled the Ottoman Empire, but non-Muslims who were citizens by birth had various degrees of freedom granted

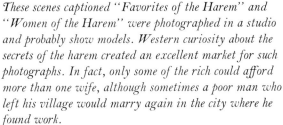

These scenes captioned "Favorites of the Harem" and "Women of the Harem" were photographed in a studio and probably show models. Western curiosity about the secrets of the harem created an excellent market for such photographs. In fact, only some of the rich could afford more than one wife, although sometimes a poor man who left his village would marry again in the city where he found work.

Underwood & Underwood, 1900.
Anonymous, no date.

them; their treatment varied in the same place at different times from complete tolerance to persecution as in mid-nineteenth-century Lebanon.

For all these reasons and more, the concept of Orient had connotations to Europeans of the heathen (i.e., non-Christian), chaotic, dangerous, despotic, piratical, lawless; corrupt, deceitful, cunning, vengeful; erotic, exotic, lascivious, depraved. The word *oriental* was also consonant with wisdom, serenity, unworldliness, fatalistic submissiveness; chivalry, suicidal courage, fanaticism, religious ecstasy, humble devotion. The Orient was a maelstrom of races and cults, freaks, fakes, feuds, palaces and mud huts, hordes of beggars, holy men, nomadic horsemen, poets, dancing girls, whores, numberless servants to jump at the clap of a hand, and oases flowering in the desert.

Before the ninteenth century it seemed that the Middle East and the West could have only nodding acquaintanceship. But with the intensification of colonial rivalry, Napoleon Bonaparte, who was to become the most modern ruler of his time, attacked in 1798 the oldest, richest, most populous, and most famous province of the Ottoman Empire — Egypt. Before losing a naval battle at Abukir to the British, the French had defeated the medieval cavalry of the Mamelukes at the Battle of the Pyramids. Napoleon's primary purpose was to seize the route through the Red Sea to India, where the British had driven out the French thirty years before. He planned to dig a canal from the Mediterranean to the Red Sea and with it control world shipping between Europe and the Far East. The Nile would become a French avenue into still unknown Africa, and to begin Frenchifying Egypt he took along nearly 170 scientists, scholars, and artists — referred to as the Scientific and Artistic Commission — to study both ancient and contemporary cultures. Among them was

A mummy case.

A. Beato, after 1862.

The Temple of Dendur in Nubia, between the First Cataract at Aswan and the Second Cataract at Wadi Halfa, was built between 23 and 10 B.C. and dedicated to Isis, the Egyptian mother goddess and enchantress. The cult of Isis and her consort Osiris, ruler of the underworld, had become popular throughout the Roman Empire. When the plan for the Aswan High Dam was announced in 1961, a procedure was worked out to dismantle the temple and save it. It was reassembled in the Metropolitan Museum of Art, New York City. This photograph, taken a century before, shows villagers in front of the temple. (Detail.)

J. Pascal Sébah, after 1868.

Comte Claude-Louis Berthollet, probably the most famous chemist in the world since Lavoisier, Étienne Geoffroy Saint-Hilaire, a zoologist whose ideas on evolution later on helped shape Darwin's theory, and the artist Baron Dominique Vivant Denon, who became a specialist in recording the ruins as well as contemporary life. In 1799 Napoleon hurried back to France, but the Commission remained, measuring, studying, collecting, and sending to the Louvre a flow of ancient statues, sarcophagi, jewelry, mummies, funerary artifacts, furniture, tools, and even obelisks. This wealth stunned European imagination and started a massive looting spree that became the foundation of modern archeology.

A joint British and Ottoman attack in 1800 and 1801 drove out the French, and among other things the little Rosetta stone, the key to hieroglyphics, fell into British

The Nile is navigable for a thousand miles from Alexandria to the First Cataract at Aswan, shown in this daguerreotype, but irrigation is sparse above Cairo because the riverbanks are often rocky or rise in high cliffs.

Jules Itier, 1845–1846.

hands though a Frenchman had found it. Decoding was begun by Thomas Young, the famous British physicist, but completed only in the 1820s by the French historian Jean-François Champollion. It added fuel to the European passion for things Egyptian, already aroused by the 24-volume publication, between 1809 and 1822, of the Commission's report, *Déscription de l'Égypte*, which contained thousands of illustrations by Denon.

Soon after the French had left Egypt, the British also withdrew, and in 1805 Mohammed Ali, an officer of obscure origin leading Albanian troops who had helped the British, maneuvered to force the sultan, Selim III, into appointing him viceroy, or khedive, of Egypt. Ambitious, ruthless, and brilliant, he modernized his army and bu-

reaucracy, built schools, expanded irrigation, and introduced Western industries. Six years later he invited the several hundred remaining Mameluke officers to a banquet, where he slaughtered them all. Meanwhile the Wahabis, a puritanical sect in Arabia led by the Saud family (ancestors of the King Abdul Aziz ibn Saud who a century later would unify Arabia), seized Mecca and Medina from the Turks and threatened further expansion. In 1818 Mohammed Ali, at the sultan's behest, sent his son

The history of Egypt begins at Memphis, south of present-day Cairo, when it became the capital circa 3000 B.C. The three most ancient pyramids in Egypt were built near Giza, north of Memphis, by pharaohs of the Old Kingdom (2686–2160 B.C.): Khufu (Cheops in Greek), Khafre, and Menkaure. This is Khufu's, the largest and oldest. To this day visitors are awed by its immense size and perfect geometry, while the numerical dimensions and orientation still fascinate scholars of the occult. The photographer's tent and equipment can be seen in the center of the picture, to the right of the pyramid's corner.

J. Pascal Sébah, before 1877.

Ibrahim with a crack army to drive the Wahabis back into the desert, and now the khedive contemplated further conquests to the east and south. He sent another son, Ismail, to conquer the Sudan. Next the sultan promised Mohammed Ali more territory if he would put down a rebellion in Greece. Mohammed Ali sent Ibrahim, who again was successful until combined British, French, and Russian forces defeated him in the late 1820s. The sultan reneged on his promise. Mohammed Ali ordered his army into Syria in 1832, defeated an Ottoman force sent against him, and prepared to march into Turkey itself. This time the shaky sultanate was rescued by a combination of European armies that swept the Egyptians out of Syria. But in 1841 the sultan made Mohammed Ali hereditary governor of Egypt (and it was his descendant King Farouk who was forced to abdicate in 1952). Mohammed Ali went mad in 1847 and died in 1849. Most of his schemes were unrealized or were too hastily set up, so that they soon fell apart, but he was the first ruler in the Middle East to attempt Westernization. (Others who followed his goal, whether in Turkey, Persia, or Iraq, made the same mistake of importing the products of industrialization, like railroads, without understanding that a profound social revolution, far more drastic than the one going on in Europe, had to precede any machine-powered economy.) His career also illustrated the turmoil created by a steadily weakening sultanate, the increasing rebelliousness of long-suffering subjects, and the growing aggressive meddling of Western imperialism.

In fact, by 1800, just as Mohammed Ali began his career, all the Balkans were being stirred by Western ideas and agents. The Serbs were the first to revolt, in 1804, unsuccessfully, but the Greeks, who last had been their own rulers in Byzantium, drew more sympathy and even volunteers from the West. One of them was George Gordon, Lord Byron, the impetuous, romantic, and gloomy poet who had exiled himself from England some years before. In 1824 he died of fever in the midst of plans to raise money for an army against the Turks. Eight years later Greece became a monarchy and won its first step toward independence.

Byron's gesture was symbolic of two cultural movements, which had begun in the second half of the eighteenth century and which inspired many Europeans to visit the Middle East. Both were tangles of contradictions, which is perhaps why they were so stimulating. One, Romanticism, valued individuals and discovery rather than institutions and tradition, and the other, Neoclassicism, sought to revive the esthetic of a long-ago golden age. Intuition, said the Romantics, is a better guide to truth and beauty than formal debate and learning, while awareness of death melts the illusions of life to uncover the sublime. The ruins of the Middle East, the medieval traditions that still ruled there, and ancient Egyptian worship of the dead, dazzled the Romantics. The Neoclassicists were awed by the magnitude and power of ancient Egypt that had civilized the Greeks, who then civilized Europe so long ago. To both movements the Sphinx seemed to symbolize the mystery of life and the pyramids the search to understand that mystery; and the deserts that made islands out of habitable places seemed a perfect expression of man's fate since Adam and Eve were driven into the wilderness. Both movements rejected the violent transformation of society by industrialization, the horrors of factory pollution and workers' slums, and elevated the ancient civilizations to heights no machine age could dream of.

Painters went to the Middle East in amazing numbers,

The ancient Biblical city of Sela in present-day Jordan was renamed Petra by the Greeks; in 312 B.C. it was captured by the Arab Nabataeans, who lived in northeastern Arabia as traders, and became the capital of a then prosperous kingdom and the center of the spice trade. Petra was conquered by the Romans, who built this tomb entrance and many other buildings. Then Muslim Arabs swept it into their empire, then the Crusaders took it, and eventually it was abandoned and forgotten until the Swiss explorer Johann Ludwig Burckhardt discovered it in 1812. The city, again inhabited since World War II, is surrounded by colored sandstone cliffs, which led John William Burgon to call it the "rose-red city."

L. Vignes, photogravure by Charles Nègre, ca. 1874.

Abu Simbel, a village just below the Second Cataract at Wadi Halfa, is the site of two temples built by Ramses II, who reigned from 1304 to 1237 B.C. These four colossi, 67 feet tall, portray him with his wife Nefertari, and his children, not as tall as his knee. When the second Aswan dam was planned, an international committee was formed to save the figures from the lake that would drown them, and they were sawed up and reassembled on higher ground.

Friedrich Koch, Breasted expedition, 1906.

and in 1839 photographers with cameras, the product of scientific and technological research, admired by both Romantics and Neoclassicists, joined the rush to capture the Orient. The role of painters, photographers, and

other Western travelers in the deterioration of the Ottoman Empire was not minimal for they quarreled with officialdom, held it in contempt, and showed it to be corrupt, arbitrary, stupid, and cruelly indifferent to everything except bribes. Everyone knew this, but foreigners were unafraid to combat it. And because they spoke in so many different tongues in the universally Arabic world, they introduced the idea of independent nationhood.

The first foreigner in the nineteenth century to write at length about the Middle East, to an awed audience, was Johann Ludwig Burckhardt (1784–1817), a Swiss scholar who learned Arabic and was hired by an association in England to explore the Sahara. He became side-tracked in the Middle East and in 1812 found forgotten Petra in Transjordan, journeyed up the Nile and discovered Abu Simbel, and finally, disguised as one Sheikh Ibrahim ibn Abdullah, completed a pilgrimage to Mecca, the first Christian known to have done so.

Perhaps the most famous visitor was Sir Richard Burton (1821–1890). A dazzling linguist, he began his career in the army in India on a spying mission in bazaars disguised as a Muslim merchant. He wrote brilliantly about the Indian subcultures he lived in. In 1853, disguised as an Afghan doctor, or dervish, he joined pilgrims to Medina and Mecca. The next year he and John Hanning Speke (1827-1864) were the first Westerners to visit and return alive from the holy city of Harer in Somaliland. The pair, later setting out to find the source of the Nile, discovered Lake Tanganyika. Burton's translations of the *Thousand and One Nights* and *The Perfumed Garden* were best-sellers.

Charles Montagu Doughty (1843-1926), a scholarly product of Cambridge, devoted himself to describing the life of the desert and desert cities in Arabia. In 1876 he joined a caravan in Damascus and for two years wandered about, recording everything he saw and learned. His *Travels in Arabia Deserta* was published in 1888.

Among nonscholarly Westerners who recorded their adventures in letters and diaries and then in published work, was the novelist Gustave Flaubert (1821-1880). Hardly an adventurer or explorer, he was fascinated by the harlots, courtesans, and homosexuals who made a living in Egypt quite openly. The photographer who accompanied him, Maxime Du Camp, some of whose work is reproduced here, also wrote his impressions of the scandalous tour in 1851. Another novelist, Mark Twain (1835-1910), in 1867 joined a group of Americans who chartered a whole ship for a Mediterranean cruise. Out of it came his *Innocents Abroad*.

More disturbing than the photographers and writers were the archeologists, whose endeavors acquired a scientific bent only toward the end of the nineteenth century. Archeology was not even a profession when Napoleon's commission began its investigations; it was concerned primarily with ransacking tombs and temples. Agents commissioned by European governments and museums, dealers and private collectors, hired laborers and guides

The head of an unfinished granite colossus at Napata in Kush.

Horst Schliephack, Breasted expedition, 1906.

whose ancestors had been robbing graves from the day they were sealed, and with them dug out and transported to Europe everything they could find. Most flamboyant of the early hunters was Giovanni Battista Belzoni (1778–1823,) a physical giant and circus strong man who eventually became an expert in discovering tombs, blasting into them with dynamite, and hauling away the treasure to shipboard with ingenious engineering techniques. Forged papers, fists, cudgels, even guns were used to establish claims, on top of the hardships and dangers of travel into remote places, because of the amazing profits that could be reaped. In 1820 Belzoni, now world-famous but still poor, left Egypt to his enemies, the brigands and the British and French consuls, who continued battling over shiploads of mummies and statues for their governments. The government did not interfere with the noisy, frantic treasure hunt. Egyptians were accustomed to plundering and liked being paid by crackpot foreigners, and the Khedive Mohammed Ali was not interested in preserving the past. Not until 1857 did the French engineer Ferdinand de Lesseps persuade the Khedive Said — son of Mohammed Ali — to invite Auguste Edouard Mariette (1821–1881), a self-taught archeologist like the rest, who had become wealthy digging for

The capital of Kush was Napata, below the Fourth Cataract. Egyptian influence dominated the religion and architecture as can be seen on this wall in the temple of Amon. Cush eventually occupied Egypt, 712–663 B.C.

Friedrich Koch, Breasted expedition, 1906.

Ashur (present-day Sharqat) on the Tigris in Mesopotamia was founded about 2500 B.C. and about a thousand years later became the religious capital of Assyria, Ashur being the name of the king of the gods. The city was later overshadowed by Nineveh and Nimrud, and in 614 was destroyed by Babylon. A German archeological expedition began excavations in 1903.

Gertrude Bell, ca. 1910.

the Louvre, to formulate a conservation policy. Hiring a successful thief to keep an eye on other thieves worked well. Mariette gradually stanched the flow and founded the Egyptian Museum in Cairo.

By then all the great sites along the Nile as far upriver as Abu Simbel had been rediscovered, but none had been excavated or even studied in an orderly manner. Not until the 1890s did the English archeologist W. M. Flinders Petrie (1853–1942), working industriously at Memphis, Thebes, Abydos, and a dozen sites in Palestine, develop a systematic technique for excavating, a forerunner to modern methods. Early in the twentieth century the American James Henry Breasted (1865–1935) studied antiquities in the Sudan and Egypt and wrote popular histories as well as scholarly works on hieroglyphics.

Digging for treasure in the ruins of the Tigris-Euphrates civilizations attracted many fewer adventurers because there were far less gold and fewer jewels or art objects to be found. Also, Baghdad, the center of communications, was remote and provincial and the nomads controlled the deserts of Mesopotamia. Shipping out through the Persian Gulf and around Africa was another problem; the only alternative was camel transport to the Mediterranean, which drastically limited the size of objects that could be moved. (On Nile barges even towering obelisks weighing hundreds of tons could be floated to ships in Alexandria.) And then the Mesopotamian ruins had suffered more from wars than those of Egypt and were more deeply buried, harder to find. Still, by the 1840s Nineveh, Khorsabad, Nimrud, and other sites were being

This seems like a bit of archeological humor, but the sign marks the stop on the Baghdad railroad where the Breasted expedition excavated the ruins of Babylon. Its walls are visible on the horizon beneath the board. The flivver was far from being the first car in the deserts of the Middle East.

James Henry Breasted, 1919.

Over 8000 years ago Nineveh was a village on the Tigris River, facing present-day Mosul in Iraq. In the third millenium B.C. it was the capital of Assyria. The biblical rulers Sargon, his son Sennacherib, and Assurbanipal brought the city to its peak of importance. It was destroyed forever by Persians, Medes, and Scythians in 612 B.C. The first explorations of the ruins were made in 1820, and in 1845 Sir Henry Layard began to uncover the palace of Sennacherib. Others continued to dig out the now familiar sculpture and artifacts. In this picture the village of Kuyunjik sits on the mounds that still cover the remains of Nineveh.

Anonymous, no date.

A desert city, probably Baghdad. Seven storks are perched on buildings and minarets.

Gertrude Bell, ca. 1910.

The Ottoman sultanate was not interested in shrines or antiquities but allowed whoever was concerned to maintain them. Because of hostilities among the Christian sects, the Holy Sepulchre itself fell into decay, as shown here.

Auguste Salzmann, 1854.

excavated by French and English teams.

At the end of the century a forgotten civilization that predated the first Babylon, the Sumerian, was discovered near Baghdad and awed the world, forcing a rewriting of history. Beginning in 1898, Sir Arthur John Evans gradually dug out the Minoan civilization in Crete, which then belonged to the Ottoman Empire, and these ruins helped spark in both Europe and America a fascination with ancient styles. The climax, however, was the long labor of Howard Carter and Lord Carnarvon that began in 1906 in the Valley of the Kings near Luxor and ended in 1922 with the discovery of King Tutankhamen's tomb. Architects designed private homes, banks, government buildings, warehouses in imitation of Egyptian temples; jewelry and clothing were designed after pharaonic fashions; tableware and furniture copied the finds in tombs. Popular fiction was filled with stories of early civiliza-

tions, as well as of contemporary Egypt. Millionaires steamed up the Nile on their private yachts, admitting that the marvels of antiquity equaled their own creations—they were the peers of those ancient sun-kings.

Thus did life in the oldest cities of the world enchant the inhabitants of the newest cities. Unfortunately this enthusiasm for the past relegated the flesh-and-blood people of the Middle East, in the eyes of Western visitors, to natives of little consequence.

Still another invasion was that of Christian pilgrims. Although the Turks did not interfere with pilgrimages, they took no responsibility for the holy places: it was up to the infidels to look after them. And they, of course, depended on contributions from their various churches and governments. As travel to Palestine became steadily easier, bitter fights broke out among Christians of different sects worshipping at the same sites where long-ago events usually involved the beliefs of Jews and Muslims as well. Muslims watched the fights bemused. But pilgrimages were as old and familiar as the ruins, and they did not really affect the Middle East politically; even the annual flood of Muslims from all over the world to Mecca was of commercial import only to the people who supplied the caravans. The increasing number of Christian pilgrims in the nineteenth century also was a significant source of income around Jerusalem.

Concern for Christian citizens of the Ottoman Empire was another matter. Occasional persecution by local authorities or outbreaks of fanatical violence against them caused quarrels between the sultan and European powers. Russia felt a special responsibility for the large number of Orthodox Christians in the Balkans and for the upkeep of the holy places in Palestine, and this was one of the many excuses for the Crimean War (1853–1856), in which the allies of Sultan Abdul Medjid I—in this instance England, France, and Austria—supported him against Russia. When the terrible fighting stopped they agreed that Russia had lost.

The religious issues of the Crimean War did not really involve the Middle East. But a few years later complicated frustrations inflamed the Druze, a hill people in Syria belonging to a secretive Muslim sect, to massacre Maronite Christians. The French, using this as an excuse they had been looking for, in 1861 landed an army and quelled the strife, with the sultan's cognizance. On one

In 1800 B.C. Beirut was a Phoenician port serving both land and sea routes between Europe and the East. Armies and earthquakes destroyed it more than a few times, but always the inhabitants rebuilt it into a thriving trade and cultural center. Beirut flourished in the Byzantine Empire, and after it fell to the Arabs in A.D. 635 it remained the largest community of literate Christians in the Muslim world.

When the French occupied Syria in 1860 the city with its adaptability began to acquire a French orientation. French became the second language, the wealthy sent their children to schools in France, new houses and restaurants were built in the French style, more or less. Horses and buggies, kiosks, and sidewalk cafés all imitated the boulevards of Paris. Yet Westernization mingled casually with the Arab style, and the Old Town remained the center of commerce: camel caravans continued to wind into the marketplace, the alleys smelled of open fires and spicy cooking and at night were lit by torches. Muezzins called from the minarets, the bells of a chapel rang modestly.

Throughout its history — between wars — Beirut enchanted inhabitants and visitors alike with its beautiful settings and sophisticated fun. The seaside climate is moist and breezy; in the olive groves and orchards anemones bloom; the slopes of the Lebanon Mountains behind the city rise green, dotted with white villages, and on their peaks snow glistens through the winter. The American University of Beirut sheltered the largest American colony in the Middle East until oil was discovered in Saudi Arabia.

Anonymous, before 1900.

Nasr ud-Din Shah, King of Kings, the Shadow of God, the Center of the Universe, the Well of Science, the Foot of Heaven, Sublime Sovereign Whose Standard is the Sun, Whose Splendor is that of the Firmament, Monarch of Armies Numerous as the Stars, sits in his palace. Frustrated by rival British and Russian encroachments, fanatical religious clashes, and staggering corruption, he tried to introduce Western technology but ruled as a despot. The centuries-long decline of the Peacock Throne's authority and increasing foreign imperialism created chaos in Persia, and the shah was assassinated in 1896.

Sevruguin, ca. 1890.

pretext or another the French remained the dominant power in Syria and Lebanon until World War I, though local affairs were left, more or less, to the wealthy landlords. Part of Beirut became a delightful Frenchified seaport and summer resort with shaded boulevards, cafés, and European-style villas. Only fifty miles inland on the other side of the Anti-Lebanon Mountains, Damascus remained the poetic garden city of Islam, a major caravan center at the edge of the great Syrian desert.

Just as important in the long run, perhaps even more than French military presence, were the American, English, and French religious missions, both Catholic and Protestant, that clustered around Beirut, where the Christian population was the largest in the Middle East. Schools and colleges were founded with foreign mission-

ary money, and in 1866 a joint effort by American Protestant missionaries established the Syrian University of Beirut, which after World War II became the American University of Beirut. Here instruction was given in English by a largely American faculty, and in the whole of the empire with its many famous, ancient Islamic universities, only here could a Middle Eastern student acquire a degree acceptable to the Western World in medicine, engineering, or science. Nowhere in Islam did Christian missionaries make converts, not even in Syria, but Muslims did attend the Christian schools and the university. Robert College in Constantinople, founded in 1863 also by American Protestant donations, gave degrees in both humanities and engineering, and most of the instruction was in English.

In Mesopotamia, for centuries after the Mongol devastation that had destroyed irrigation systems, Persian and Turkish armies vied for power. Finally descendants of the Mamelukes took over until 1831, when Sultan Mahmud II reestablished Turkish authority and his appointees began a slow reconstruction of the country. European commercial interests, especially British, were granted resident status in Basra and Baghdad under consuls who had considerable influence with the government. They used their influence to get favorable trade agreements and concessions. The desert nomads, however, defied the Ottoman authority and pursued their habits of tribal feuding, raiding villages, and plundering caravans. In 1914 an English force landed at Basra; after some reverses it captured Baghdad, and the Turks gave up Mosul in 1918. "Mess of Pottage" (in reference to the Old Testament tale of Esau and Jacob) was what the English called Mesopotamia from then on.

Persia, not a part of the Ottoman Empire in the nineteenth century but always an integral part of the Middle East, was a disturbing presence on the border of the empire. Many of its problems went far back to the long Mongol occupation, which had ended in the fifteenth century. But there were also deadly Sunni-Shiite clashes, pressure of intransigent Kurds and other warrior tribes along the Afghan border, fiery wars among claimants to the throne followed by cruel punishment of the losers' supporters. The Shiite teachers, the mullahs and exalted ayatollahs, had far more power than mullahs in Sunni lands, and the grip of the land-owning families on the villages and on the whole economy of the country was far more exploitive than elsewhere in the Middle East, more pitiless toward the peasants, more corrupt in government. One difference between Persia and the rest of the Middle East was obvious in a glance at a map: many more Persian

The ruling elite of Persia often lunched in the palace in Tehran. The lovely dishes here all look like sweets. The chairs were used for Western-style occasions.

Sevruguin, after 1880.

The photographer cast his shadow on this public hanging of the man who had assassinated the shah of Persia, Nasr ud-Din. (Detail.)

Probably Sevruguin, 1896.

cities famous in the past were still important centers of trade—cities like Tabriz, Kerman, Shiraz, Mashhad, Kermanshah, Isfahan, Khorasan, whose names were woven into the legendary rugs that the people loomed.

The shahs of Persia during the nineteenth century made feeble attempts to establish commercial ties with Europe. The English, fearful of French, Afghan, and Russian ambitions to push into India, had obtained trading concessions and permanent representation in 1800, and were the dominant foreign influence. They were bitterly challenged by Russians, who had seized Azerbaijan in 1806 as a first step toward the Persian Gulf and India. In the 1860s the English started to plant a line of telegraph poles from one end of Persia to the other, connecting India with the Mediterranean and England. German commercial firms, determined to catch up with the English, sought concessions in the latter half of the century, especially to build a railroad. But the shahs and the nobles squandered the considerable payments that came to them from concessions, and there was little development of any sort until the discovery of oil in the first years of this century. The formation of what was later known as the Anglo-Persian Petroleum Company, the details of its agreement with the government, the completion at Abadan in 1913 of the then largest refinery in the world, and of pipelines and harbor facilities, set the pattern for post-

World War I oil exploration and development through similar concessions in Iraq, Saudi Arabia, and the Persian Gulf sheikhdoms.

In the Persian Gulf, the influence of British India was unchallenged. The principalities of the Arabian coast, after being menaced by Wahabis and then Egyptians in the early nineteenth century, had accepted the suzereignty of the Ottoman sultan, but as their trade was with India they were willing to enjoy British protection. The southern shores of Arabia, called the Hadramaut, were inhabited by truculent desert tribes who recognized no overlord. In 1841 England simply claimed the Hadramaut, and Aden at the entrance to the Red Sea. Aden was turned into a coaling station, naval base, and citadel guarding the seaways from Europe to India and maintaining a watch on Yemen to the north and, more especially, on the East African coast, the Somalilands and Ethiopia.

Yemen, just north of Aden, remained closed to outsiders, although nominally it was claimed by the sultan. With the highest mountains in Arabia and with the heaviest rainfall, from the beginning of time it had been fruitful farmland. In Biblical days when its Sabaean civilization

Medina, once the ancient town of Yathrib, is the second holiest city for Muslims, and most pilgrims to Mecca visit Medina as well. Mohammed's flight here from his enemies in Mecca, an event called the hijrah or hegira, in 622, begins the dating of the Islamic calendar, which, like the Jewish one, is calculated by the moon: 1981 translates into 1401. The tomb of Mohammed and the mosque of Quba, the first mosque built, are in Medina. These and other holy places there are forbidden to non-Muslims. Medina was the Prophet's base for converting Arabia to Islam and for the preparation of the first surge of armies into foreign lands. It was the capital of the caliphate from 622 to 661, when the capital was moved to Damascus. It lies in a rich oasis about 120 miles from the Red Sea, served by a small port, Yenbo. The farmers' market is in the foreground, outside the fortress-like walls.

Probably T. E. Lawrence, ca. 1917.

Riyadh was the capital from which the Saud dynasty ruled the Wahabi tribes after 1821. In 1891 a rival family, the Rashids, captured it, but in 1902 ibn Saud retook the city. In 1932 Riyadh was named the capital of Saudi Arabia. This photograph is taken from the east gate.

W. H. I. Shakespear, 1914.

was the equal of any, its Queen of Sheba, or Saba, visited King Solomon. The name Yemen was mistakenly thought by Europeans to mean happiness, hence their term for the area, Arabia Felix. The Wahabi invasion early in the nineteenth century and the Egyptian retaliation were the most important events until World War I, which drew Yemen closer into international affairs but never to the vital extent of its relationships with Africa. In fact, it was

from Ethiopia that Christianity had invaded Yemen.

Arabia proper had long been divided into four regions: the Hejaz along the Red Sea, with Mecca, Jidda, Medina, and several small seaports, and the giant oasis of Taif; the upland interior called the Nejd, with a few towns like Riyadh, the capital; the Persian Gulf territory, Al Hasa, with pearl-fishing villages and oases; and, in the south, the terraced mountain farms of Asir and the uninhabitable Rub Al Khali. In 1902 Abdul Aziz ibn Saud, descendant of the Wahabi leaders who had been ousted from Riyadh by their rivals, the Rashid family, recaptured Riyadh and was soon master of the Nejd. He next seized Al Hasa from the Turks and prepared to lead his tough, seasoned Wahabi tribes (allied through the Ikhwan, a fanatical religious organization) against the Hejaz, where the Hussein

The most impressive leader in the Middle East after World War I, other than Kemal Atatürk, was King Abdul Aziz ibn Saud (ca. 1880–1953), who united Arabia. He was a desert sheikh who obeyed the tenets of tribal government while gradually leading the bitterly feuding tribes into accepting nationhood. His success, apart from winning battles, was due partly to his immense physical size (six feet five inches), majestic bearing, courage, and charm. Partly it rested on blood alliances; he never had more than three wives at once, so that he could always marry for political reasons, immediately divorcing one. The palace in Riyadh was a small town of ex-wives, each with her own household and children. It was rumored that he had over fifty sons binding him to the tribes. But he also had an extraordinary understanding of Western culture, which won him the respect of foreign governments. Here, in white headpiece, he is surrounded by sons and brothers.

W. H. I. Shakespear, 1911.

family ruled under the Ottomans as sherifs of Mecca, tracing their ancestry to the Quraysh tribe to which the Prophet had belonged. Ibn Saud promised the British, for subsidies, not to attack the sherif when World War I broke out. In 1916 Colonel T. E. Lawrence, an amateur archeologist, persuaded British Headquarters in Cairo to give him gold and arms with which he and the sherif's sons, Feisal and Abdullah, would unite the tribes of the Hejaz against the Turks. Their guerrilla force skirmished with Turkish garrisons and defeated a force near Aqaba as the war was ending. The deadly enmity between the Husseinis and Ibn Saud, held in check by further subsidies from the British, now broke into the open, and Ibn Saud, after vanquishing dissidents and rivals in Nejd and in the south, finally captured Mecca and the Hejaz in 1924. As king, Ibn Saud unified Arabia for the first time in centuries, gave it his name, and made the pilgrimage to Mecca safe for the poorest and the richest.

We have circled back to Egypt. Cairo was a worldly city with a huge foreign population, financially muscular and independent of Constantinople. It was also, as it always had been in the Ottoman Empire, the center of Is-

A crowd in Aqaba, on the Sinai peninsula, is awaiting the entry of the army led by King Hussein and Colonel T. E. Lawrence.

Goslett (from T. E. Lawrence's photographic collection), 1917.

lamic studies. The first real symbol of Westernization in the Middle East appeared there in the 1850s — the railroad from Alexandria to Cairo and then to Suez. And probably the single event with the greatest effect on Middle East Westernization was the construction of the Suez Canal — the dream of the pharaohs. It was finished in 1869 after dramatic conflicts involving several governments and agents, with intricate loans mostly by English and French financiers and carpetbaggers. The French architect Ferdinand de Lesseps and his staff of largely French engineers directed Egyptian laborers conscripted from farms. The planners had calculated that tens of thousands of fellahin carrying away sand in baskets on their heads would be cheaper than steam-powered machines, but before the digging was finished the ghastly mortality rate forced them to import dredges. To celebrate the opening of the canal an opera house was built in Cairo in European style and Giuseppe Verdi was commissioned to compose a suitable opera. It was *Aida*, a story of pharaohs and slaves.

By midcentury tourism was big business in Egypt. Thomas Cook and Son offered package deals, dahabiyahs left Cairo on schedule for Aswan, and Shepheard's Hotel

A canal connecting the Nile (near Cairo) and the Red Sea (near Suez) was begun by the Pharaoh Necho II about 600 B.C. Persian, Egyptian, and Roman emperors finished it. In A.D. 641 the future caliph Huawiya I reopened the canal, which had silted up, but after a few generations the sand flowed back into that one, too. Throughout the centuries various European and Middle Eastern monarchs proposed building a new canal, and in the nineteenth century colonial rivalry and the development of the steamship made a sealane between the Mediterranean and the Red Sea inevitable. The concession to build a Suez canal was granted in 1854 by the khedive of Egypt, Mohammed Said, to a French diplomat and engineer, Ferdinand de Lesseps. He raised the money and supervised the construction, which took ten years, ending in 1869.

Anonymous, ca. 1865.

Ismail (1830–1895), the khedive or viceroy of Egypt from 1863 on under sultans Abdul Aziz and Abdul Hamid II, continued to negotiate the concessions with foreign entrepreneurs for digging the Suez Canal. In keeping with his goal to modernize Egypt, he established an assembly of delegates, mostly village sheikhs, to counsel him. But because he squandered enormous sums of money on his schemes, running up the national debt, the sultan gave in to foreign pressure and deposed Ismail in 1879. Ismail's son Mohammed Tewfik (1852–1892), here a little boy, succeeded to the title. An Egyptian nationalist party, by far the strongest such party in the Ottoman Empire and opposed to European influence, continued to grow under Tewfik.

Anonymous, ca. 1860.

was known the world over for its elegance, comfort, trained personnel, and distinguished guests. Thousands of wealthy Europeans lived in Egypt, enchanted by the expatriate life in a setting far more exciting than Paris or London.

The Nile had been mapped long ago as far as Khartum, where the Blue and White Niles meet, and the search for their sources attracted the explorers Burton and Speke, the Scottish missionary David Livingstone, and the American journalist Henry Stanley. One can say that this mixture of Victorian gentleman's passion and missionary zeal in Africa and Asia always accompanied imperialism, the White Man's Burden, abolition of the slave trade, and an odd sense of ownership, in this case of the whole Nile itself. In fact, the Nile traversing the Sudan was increasingly important for colonialism in Africa. The conquest of the Sudan was begun in 1820 by Mohammed Ali, and further military action increased the territory claimed by Egypt — nominally a province of the Ottoman domains. In the 1860s the Khedive Ismail, to secure loans from Europe for modernization and expansion into Ethiopia, agreed to extinguish the Sudanese slave trade, which, with the ivory trade, provided the main income for a vast equatorial region. Its rulers were the slave merchants, who kept garrisons of their own armies and who controlled all the routes to east and west Africa. To show his sincerity, Ismail appointed the English explorer Samuel Baker to establish Egyptian authority and end the slave traffic. Baker was successful in setting up an administration, but it could do nothing about the traffic. Next the khedive appointed Colonel Charles "Chinese" Gordon, military hero of Britain's war in China, as governor of the Sudan in 1873. But he, too, resigned after a few years, leaving a muddle of forces vying for power that included imperialists, slave traders, nomadic tribes, local aristocrats, and foreign merchants. In 1881 Mohammed Ahmed ibn Abdullah proclaimed himself the Mahdi, descendant of the Prophet and the divinely inspired leader who would bring about a glorious revival of Islam before the Day of Judgment. With an army of fanatical supporters, he began a war for Sudanese independence.

A year later British forces invaded Egypt to help the bankrupt Khedive Tewfik suppress a popular uprising against foreigners and to prevent any other European power from edging into the disorder along the Nile; the

British showed every sign of settling in permanently, sultan or no sultan, khedive or no khedive. Gordon was sent back to Khartum. The Mahdi's army besieged the city and in 1885 destroyed it, slaughtered the inhabitants, and paraded Gordon's head and others' on their spears. After the Mahdi's death a few months later, his deputy, or khalifa, Abdullah el Taashi, succeeded him and continued the holy war until he had established a strong administration for the whole Sudan. The English general Horatio Herbert Kitchener, who had been sent to relieve Gordon but had arrived too late, was eventually made commander-in-chief of the Egyptian army.

In 1898 the French, determined to seize territory throughout Central Africa to connect their holdings in East and West Africa, decided to oust the British from Egypt by sending an expedition from West Africa through the jungle to Fashoda, a village on the Nile in southern Sudan, there to build a dam and shut off the Nile, thus ruining Egypt. The British were even more determined to conquer a wide passage for trade and communication all the way from Cairo to South Africa. London

Tribal warriors like these tormented the British lion in the Sudan, gateway into Africa via the Nile. Rudyard Kipling eulogized their courage when they were finally wiped out by machine guns in the battle of Suakim.

> So 'ere's to you, Fuzzy-Wuzzy, at your
> 'ome in the Sowdan;
> You're a pore benighted 'eathen but
> a first-class fightin' man. . . .

A. Beato, after 1862.

These disciplined Egyptian troops parading in the ruins of Karnak may have been under General Horatio Kitchener, en route to Khartum, where General "Chinese" Gordon was besieged in 1884 by the Mahdi Mohammed Ahmed and his Sudanese followers.

A. Beato, possibly 1884.

ordered Kitchener to eliminate the French at any cost and, on the way to Fashoda, to do something about the Mahdists. Kitchener met the Sudanese at Omdurman, the capital they had built across the river from the ruins of Khartum. In a few hours his 25,000 men, using the newest rifles and machine guns, slaughtered almost three times as many incredibly reckless Mahdists armed with flintlocks and spears. Winston Churchill, a young officer acting as a correspondent with Kitchener's army, described the carnage in his dispatches — the might of the machine age against moral and physical courage. He was bitingly critical about Kitchener's treatment of the wounded and the very few captured. From Omdurman Kitchener struggled on to Fashoda. The French, waiting for supplies and reinforcements, had little choice. After parleying they withdrew. Germany and Italy, each scrambling for African territory, had already formally agreed to keep out of Egypt and the Sudan, so the whole of the sumptuous Nile, the trackless deserts, and the burned-out mountains of the Red Sea coast became a British protectorate under a so-called consul-general in Cairo, who told the khedive exactly what to do.

And how was the Sublime Porte reacting to all this? One of the eroding forces in the empire was the Capitulations, which were treaties signed with European powers beginning in the sixteenth century, in which the sultan granted diplomatic and commercial representatives immunity from Islamic law, taxation, and tariff regulations, and gave them freedom to establish residential quarters where their security was guaranteed. These extraordinary privileges were, of course, exploited in various ways. For example, Christian citizens of the empire were granted passports by European powers in return for special advantages in the marketplace that subverted monopolies held by the Ottoman government. European goods were sold without taxes or import duties, making the foreign merchants automatically wealthy at the expense of local merchants, and steadily increasing their power through bribery of officials, an integral part of Ottoman rule. By the mid-nineteenth century, when Western nations were competing fiercely to sell manufactured goods (clothing, kitchenware, etc.), a maze of extensions to the Capitulations froze the Ottoman government and Muslim merchants out of the import-export business. The Porte tried many times to get the Capitulations trimmed

Sikhs trained in India fought in the Sudan with the Suakim Field Force under British officers against the Mahdi.

Royal Engineers, 1885.

or have them abolished but was always met with adamant refusal. It could not unilaterally ignore them. Yet the importation of manufactured goods was ruining the handicraft industries of the Middle East, throwing out of work artisans and small merchants, who joined the floating population of beggars, unemployed servants, destitute peasants, and criminals in the big cities. It also effectively changed, toward the uniformity of the European style, the ancient tradition of styles that varied from district to district.

The more the sultanate's grip on taxation weakened, the more loans it contracted in Europe, where bankers eagerly complied, demanding and getting steadily rising interest. Speculators in Constantinople made fortunes in the complicated discounting of bills at exorbitant rates. Finally in 1875 the national debt was so enormous that the Porte announced semibankruptcy. Bureaucrats were not paid salaries and became even more corrupt, peasants were reduced to starvation, and businesses were ruined by taxes.

In Anatolia itself, a movement toward modernization of the government, army, and schools, later called the Tanzimat, had begun in 1808 under Sultan Mahmud II. Its first effect was a clash with the Janissaries. Perhaps

Sultan of the Ottoman Empire from 1876 to 1909, Abdul Hamid II (1842–1918) hoped to modernize his realm, but continuous intervention by rival European governments left him little freedom. In 1877 he set aside the constitutional government he himself had created (the first in Ottoman history) less than a year before. As a complete autocrat, with help from German interests to combat the British, Russians, and others, he managed to get railroads built and to create new systems of schools, courts, and community services. But he could not slow the disintegration of the sultanate's power, which resulted in several disastrous wars with Russia and the Balkan countries. Even though the sultan restored the constitution in 1908, the Young Turks, a militant group dedicated to hasten modernization and end corruption, started a revolution that in 1909 deposed him.

W. & D. Downey, ca. 1880.

inspired by Mohammed Ali's treatment of the Mamelukes in Egypt a few years before, in 1826 Mahmud slaughtered the Janissaries in their own barracks and hunted down those stationed in the Balkans. Centralization of power against the ancient feudal system was perhaps his primary goal. But by the time he died in 1839, Greece had won its freedom and Egypt was on its own, dominating Arabia, the Sudan, and Syria, and plotting to

attack Anatolia itself. The Crimean War in the 1850s was soon followed by renewed uprisings in Serbia, Bosnia, Herzogovina, and Bulgaria, which Ottoman armies put down. This action in turn brought the Russians to the defense of the revolutionaries. The outcome of the Russo-Turkish War in 1877–1878 was that most of the Balkans became either independent or autonomous, while some Turkish territories were ceded to Austria-Hungary and Russia. The reluctance of European powers to destroy the empire was very clear from the way they pruned Russian demands, and it was equally clear that they controlled the sultan's future.

Several groups were involved after 1850 in the Tanzimat, or reform movement, although with conflicting goals. Under Sultan Abdul Hamid II (1876–1909) some reforms continued, others stagnated or were abandoned. Perhaps most dramatic as a symbol were the stretches of railroads built in the 1880s by English and French firms. Then German interests shouldered in and finished a line from Constantinople to Ankara in 1893. The concessions were extremely profitable to the builders and several more short lines were laid in Anatolia, Syria, and Palestine. The sultan's ambition was to link them and extend the network to the Persian Gulf. A consortium of German, British, and French capitalists won the concession in 1902 and finished most of the railway from Constantinople to Baghdad by 1914, with a spur running to Medina.

The concept of Turkish nationalism gradually grew out of the frustrations of trying to imagine Westernization in the empire. Clearly it had to be a revolution of some kind, but the only name for it broad enough was Pan-Arab, which excluded the Turks! The notion of "Anatolia" or "Turkey" simply did not exist. In any case, the five centuries of occupying Christian lands and the recognition that Europe was the model for any future that included industries, constitutional government, literacy, and freedom of speech drew Turkish intellectual movements toward the European model of nationhood rather than toward a revitalization of the Islamic world. By 1900 the sultanate and its grand viziers, generals, and governors — the whole medieval apparatus that had been so successful for so many centuries — had become an immovable obstacle to the aspirations of those who came to be called the Young Turks. Thus, modernization, instead

One of the dreams before World War I of the German imperialists, led by Kaiser Wilhelm II, was to build a railroad from Berlin to the Persian Gulf, to tap the Middle East and challenge the British in India. The Baghdad Railroad was part of the famous Drang nach Osten. *The first leg was completed in 1896 from Constantinople to Angora (Ankara); another part, Eskishehr to Konia, in 1896. French and English protests to the sultan delayed further concessions, but in 1911 German engineers resumed the work. World War I stopped them again. The British laid a few sections during the war, but many years passed before the whole Berlin-Baghdad-Basra line was finished. Shown here is a third-class coach.*

Stereo-Travel Company, 1908.

of pulling the empire together, became a divisive force of increasingly threatening proportions. When World War I broke out, the government wanted to remain neutral and would have done so except for rather peripheral events. German influence was strong, and the first German victories against Britain, Belgium, Russia, and France were impressive. Russia was a long-hated enemy, and Britain and France repeatedly missed chances to persuade the sultan to stay neutral. Enver Pasha, leader of the Young Turks and minister of war, for obscure reasons tipped the scales to join Germany. Turkish armies at once became a significant factor against the Allies and at Gallipoli — brainchild of Winston Churchill — they thrashed the British terribly.

Before the war ended, the Allies arrogantly agreed that Britain would keep Egypt and the Sudan and receive Cyprus and southern Mesopotamia, including Baghdad; France would keep Lebanon and Syria and add half of Mesopotamia and a piece of Anatolia; Italy would win Izmir and other territories in Anatolia, and the Dodecanese Islands; and Russia would receive Constantinople, the Dardanelles, and large sections of Anatolia. Palestine would be governed by an international committee that would allow Zionists to create a nation for Jews in Palestine. Arabia's sheikhdoms would be left alone to work out their own future. But, as always in the Middle East, very few of these agreements were realized in the way they were planned.

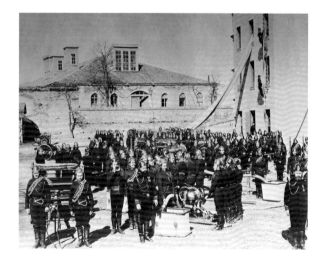

Sultan Abdul Hamid II gave Abdullah Frères, the court photographers, the task of documenting life in Turkey under his reign, with special emphasis on institutions in Constantinople, hoping to prove to the world that he was pulling the Ottoman Empire into the twentieth century. Fifty-one albums containing the Abdullah Frères photographs were presented by the sultan to the Library of Congress in 1893. The fascinating range of ethnic types — Nordic, Mediterranean, Balkan, Slav, Semitic, Mongoloid — seen in the photographs shown here from these albums suggests that the Turks had been marrying their conquered subjects for centuries. The pictures reproduced show medical students (outdoors), children who attended different types of schools, and a fire department.

The Photographic Surveys

Two members of the Ordnance Survey of Jerusalem at the Ecce Homo arch, where Pontius Pilate is said to have presented Jesus to the Jews, saying, "Behold the Man!"

James McDonald, 1864–1865.

To map the Holy Lands became important to two groups in Great Britain in the 1860s. Growing skepticism about the literal truth of the Bible inspired church circles to identify precisely the places where events in the Old and New Testaments took place. At the same time the strategic importance of Palestine to British imperialism made good maps of the area necessary for military purposes. But this reason was kept secret, cloaked in the first, and the surveyors appealed to reverence for the Bible, Jerusalem, and antiquities.

The first official survey of Jerusalem was made in 1864–1865 under the direction of the Ordnance Survey in Southampton, England. Captain Charles Wilson of the Royal Engineers, who had just spent much of the past four years freezing in western Canada while surveying the 49th parallel, was put in command. The survey had been the brainchild of Angela Burdett-Coutts of the banking family, who wished to provide Jerusalem with an improved water supply system.

Wilson and his team of Royal Engineers, including Sergeant James McDonald, who turned into a brilliant photographer, worked in Jerusalem from September to June. The Turkish governor, Izzet Pasha, contrary to what had been feared, ordered that the group be assisted and thus they worked easily almost anywhere. Wilson even obtained permission from the sheikh of the Harim, whose family had been in charge there since Saladin, for his men to photograph and survey the Muslim sacred area that includes the Dome of the Rock, from which Christians were previously barred.

The team also excavated near the site of the first Jewish Temple and around the Church of the Holy Sepulchre, where for fifteen centuries Christians had been building shrines one on top of another. Wilson wrote bluntly:

The whole building is the most puzzling and

curious that I have ever seen; the possessions of the five sects, and also the Turks, being mixed up in the wildest confusion, as if they had been put into a bag and shaken up together. Over the Latin chapel there is a large Turkish stable; at the end of a Moslem mosque a Franciscan monk has his cell; side by side on Calvary, Greek and Latin chapels rise up, the latter being shown as the place where our Saviour was nailed to the Cross, and the former over the hole in the rock where the Cross stood; while the Syrians have pushed in between the Greeks and Latins . . . whilst high above all, on the very roof, ensconced between the two large domes, live the veiled beauties of a Turkish hareem.

The publication in 1865 of the survey consisted of maps of Jerusalem and the surrounding region, large-scale plans of the Harim and other major buildings, and eighty-five photographs of the most ancient structures in and near the city. Even before the team returned home, the success of the survey stimulated others to systematic study of the Holy Lands.

The Palestine Exploration Fund, which still exists, was specifically founded in 1865 to encourage research in the Middle East and was the model for many other such societies throughout the world. It invited Wilson to be on its board and to lead another mission to Palestine, this time with only two others. But again, one was a photographer, Sergeant H. Phillips of the Royal Engineers. Their job was to survey specific regions, to verify a French map of Lebanon, blueprint more than fifty synagogues, churches, temples, tombs, etc., and choose sites for possible excavation.

The fund's commitment to photography in the nineteenth century was quite exceptional. Sergeant Phillips made 164 wet-collodion negatives in 1865 and 1866 and then another 179 in 1867. After Phillips, the Palestine Exploration Fund commissioned Lieutenant H. H. Kitchener, R.E. (later on of Khartum fame), to photograph in 1876 and 1878; a Captain Mantell, R.E., in 1882; and Gottlieb Schumacher in 1890. The high proportion of Royal Engineers on these missions was the result of the fact that the Sappers taught photography from 1856 on as part of military training.

The next development was a move among Biblical scholars and others, including Sir John Herschel, the astronomer and early experimenter in photography, to raise money for a thorough survey of the Sinai peninsula. Wilson was again asked to lead the expedition, and this time was accompanied by an explorer, a scholar, a naturalist, and five Royal Engineers, including, once again, James McDonald. Their instruction from Sir Henry James, head of the Ordnance Survey, was to produce a map of the Sinai for:

> . . . Biblical scholars and the public, to illustrate the Bible history, and to enable them, if possible, to trace the routes which were taken by the Israelites in their wanderings through the wilderness of Sinai, and to identify the mountain from which the Law was given, some writers contending that the mountain called Jebel Musa on the existing maps was the Mount Sinai of the Bible, whilst others contend that it was Jebel Serbal, and others that it was Jebel Ajmeh.

The survey team worked in the desert through the winter of 1868–1869. Their feverish activity in the broiling sun caused their attendants to conclude that these Englishmen were possessed of the devil.

While the others measured and calculated, McDonald went through all the incredibly difficult operations of wet-plate photography. (Francis Frith recorded that the temperature in his dark-tent when he was in the desert reached 130° F. and the collodion boiled.) That his negatives were dust-free and his exposures perfect is remarkable. It is astonishing, too, how McDonald, out of misty-green England, instantly grasped the power of the desert. Rather than thinking about himself as an artist or an entrepreneur or a hired technician, he made documentary photographs that, like those made on U.S. Geological Surveys in the western United States in the 1870s, were much more telling than maps, plans, or statistics could ever be. The discipline seemed to free McDonald. He looked at tiny figures in the glitter of sand under a scorching sun, mountains all around, and saw that these people could do anything if they could move about there so casually. These photographs, along with maps and plans, were published in 1869 in three parts (with the photographs in three volumes) in the *Ordnance Survey of the Peninsula of Sinai*.

3 THE DESERT

It shall not be quenched night nor day; the smoke thereof shall go up forever: from generation to generation it shall lie waste; none shall pass through it for ever and ever.

But the cormorant and the bittern shall possess it; the owl also and the ravens shall dwell in it: and he shall stretch out upon it the line of confusion, and the stones of emptiness.

They shall call the nobles thereof to the kingdom, but none shall be there, and all her princes shall be nothing.

And thorns shall come up in her palaces, nettles and brambles in the fortresses thereof: and it shall be an habitation of dragons, and a court for owls.

The wild beasts of the desert shall also meet with the wild beasts of the island, and the satyr shall cry to his fellow; the screech owl also shall rest there, and find for herself a place of rest.

Say to them that are of a fearful heart, Be strong, fear not: behold, your God will come with vengeance, even God with a recompense; he will come and save you.

Then the eyes of the blind shall be opened, and the ears of the deaf shall be unstopped.

Then shall the lame man leap as an hart, and the tongue of the dumb sing: for in the wilderness shall waters break out, and streams in the desert.

And the parched ground shall become a pool, and the thirsty land springs of water: in the habitation of dragons, where each lay, shall be grass with reeds and rushes.

—ISAIAH 34: 10–14, 35: 4–7

Most cemeteries are in the desert, for watered land is too precious to use as a burial place. The graves are marked by one or two steles, sometimes with a carving that represents a turban, but without symbols of veneration. In this City of the Dead outside Cairo, however, many famous men are commemorated by actual houses with gardens. Today, hundreds of thousands of villagers who have thronged into Cairo live in the crypts.

Gaston Braun, 1869.

THE ALL-PERVADING CHALLENGE to all the empires of the Middle East, including the Ottoman, was the desert. It never changed, and it ruled virtually all of the stupendous area. Because it was a given, it was seldom discussed by the inhabitants.

But whenever a stranger entered the Middle East, whether five thousand or one hundred years ago, and wherever he traveled, he was at once gripped by its presence. In the thousands of villages nestled among their

This is the view from the foot of the mesa of Masada, a
huge rock rising almost 1,500 feet, toward the Dead Sea.
The Jewish inhabitants of Masada held out for two
years, until A.D. 73, against a Roman army, and all but a
few of the garrison of more than 900 chose suicide to capture.

D. D. Luckenbill or assistant, 1908–1909.

Each desert has its own character. Some are beautiful,
others are gloomy, exhilarating, terrifying, boring, or
mysterious. An area like this at Ascalon (Ashkelon) in
Palestine, with dunes and a surprising patch of vegetation
drinking from a subterranean formation that holds rainfall, is a profound delight for the traveler.

D. D. Luckenbill or assistant, 1908–1909.

crops and orchards along the banks of the three mighty rivers, or under the date palms of an oasis, he saw that a mile or so away the heat-shimmering green fields ended in sand. In the cities he found that the streets began and ended in sand. If he asked about that wasteland beyond, he was told that only the bedouin knew the wells scattered many days' camel-march apart. He realized for the first time that life begins with water.

The sand drifted down the bowered avenues of the cities, rasping his cheek and building yellow hummocks around corners, in doors and windows, in pockets of walls. The people never seemed to notice. The grains floated up, up, dazzling micro-mirrors that flashed the sun. The people did not squint, nor remark on how black the shadows were and how they moved with astonishing speed to keep pace with the fireball sliding overhead. At nightfall suddenly all was transmuted as velvet darkness filled with glittering stars closer to earth than any star the stranger had grown up with. No one seemed to look up at the stars. A breeze blew off the empty space, no longer scorching but smelling faintly of frankincense, perhaps, or water, or the pitch of thorn trees, or flowers that bloomed one day a year. When the moon rose, the visitor could read in its light letters from home. It floated so close that he could study with naked eye its own desert mountains and valleys. And it moved as fast as the sun.

The traveler understood that the empty desert, the empty sky, and the city with its water were one. He wondered if the people ignored the desert because they were born in its embrace, or if they refused to recognize its power over them, or if they were wedded to it secretly night and day. But never did he see anyone walk to the end of a street or field and keep on walking into the desert. When he prepared to cross the desert for the first time, he asked: what is it like? Hell, was the reply. He wondered why no one could tell him what it was like and suspected, having studied it furtively from a housetop, that the whole earth was enslaved by it. He did not want to leave the city's defenses. The blazing light out there, in which he could not imagine surviving, blinded him. And then after his first journey across the desert the foreigner either hated and feared it beyond anything he had ever felt about nature, and never returned, or he loved it in a way he could not understand. He realized that without in the least caring about him the desert had

put her hand upon his soul. He would carry that secret mark wherever he went.

Then the newcomer discovered that there were many kinds of desert, different and yet always the same, that time was meaningless and yet the whole universe was a clock, that he had fallen in love, it seemed, with empty sand and gravel. He learned to move about in that trackless space. One day when he got off his lurching camel to stretch, flapping the sweat-soaked clothing from his body and looking around, something unexpected happened. As far as he could see in all directions: nothing. Until this moment that *nothing* had made him anxious about his animal breaking down, about losing his water skin, about becoming lost. Suddenly it overwhelmed him that he and his camel were the only living creatures in a sea of yellow sand and black rocks and glistening pebbles and glittering salt flats. Nothing else breathed. Only the air sighed along his feet, rolling the grains and rising in trembling curtains skyward. As far as he could see he was alone.

Now for the first time in his life he realized that he could not be an accident of nature. With dismay, dizzily, he saw that he could not be just a statistic and no more, or merely a fleeting shape, an incidental point. He was not just a tiny, brief swirl of energy. He was not a meaningless cipher in the cosmic order. Senses reeling, he raised his eyes and looked into the empty sky above the empty desert. And he felt at home.

He wasn't an accident and he wasn't without meaning for the simple reason that nothing else moved as far as he could see. There had to be a purpose in his being there, on that spot. And he opened his mouth and spoke to thank the Lord, or Yahweh, or Allah, or to shake his fist and curse One or the Other, or to sink to his knees and beg forgiveness. But One God for all was watching His son whom He had brought alone into the desert for a purpose. Perhaps to speak to him.

The former stranger, now married forever to the desert no matter where he went in the world, did not become more religious than was his wont. This may seem strange. But he knew that the desert was not interested in religion. Or in him. The grains of sand merely told him that he was not a grain of sand. He had a soul. That was enough.

Now, mystical feelings may be generated anywhere, even in a closet. But what seems so unusual about the

Few deserts are as dramatic as the Sinai, part of which is seen here, where Yahweh chose to give Moses the Ten Commandments. The peaks are, from left to right, Ras [promontory] Sufsafeh, Aaron's Hill, Jebel [mountain] Rabbeh, Jebel Triniyeh.

J. McDonald, 1868–1869.

A wadi is a dry river bed that can carry off a torrent during a winter cloudburst and yet store moisture for a year or more to keep life in the shrubs till the next winter. This is Wadi Iram, northeast of Aqaba.

W. H. I. Shakespear, 1914.

where moisture was held beneath the glittering sand to keep sap in bushes, pouched mice leaped twenty feet as if on wings, doves roosted on aromatic trees and wheeled above the rocks, hawks circled higher, kites and buzzards higher still. Lizards and snakes hunted droning, rustling insects; butterflies fluttered. Gazelles leaped into view as if transformed that instant from the yellow billows. Even short-snouted wolves and muscled apes showed themselves confident, masterful inhabitants of the desert, sharing it with foxes, bats, and owls. Cheetahs, lynxes, jackals, hyenas, and porcupines were not uncommon. As for birds, they came in vast clouds migrating between Europe and Africa: songbirds, waterfowl, storks, grouse, bustards, plovers. Everything was in its place, including the lonely rider, whether stupefied by the summer sun or racked by the freezing winter winds.

Even in the most fearful desert of all, the Rub Al Khali, or Empty Quarter, in southern Arabia, where sand dunes three hundred feet high marched for a hundred miles, where no bedouin could survive, there lived the oryx, the ostrich, a kind of wild goat, and the famous wild ass that kings rode.

If water was trickled daily into a ditch meandering through the sands, there were conceived and delivered from the seed wheat, barley, berries, peppers, tomatoes, radishes, beans, corn, mangoes, tobacco, rice, parsley, dates, grapes, apricots, oranges, limes, melons, figs, plums, alfalfa, okra, basil. . . .

There were not many oases where water bubbled from the ground; most were nourished by underground lakes from which water had to be raised. But if the reservoir lay too deep, then not a blade of grass told the passerby that a deep well was there. Water was lifted from river or well by a variety of methods: bucket and rope, derrick, Archimedes' screw, and water wheels, which were turned by harnessed animals.

Every desert was different—in appearance, in flora and fauna, and in its impact upon the senses. Some were shunned by all, crossed only when necessary; in others animals and men found pleasure most of the year. But to an outsider all were equally forbidding, even terrifying, and never to be entered without first being expertly outfitted and then guided by those who lived in the desert, the bedouin—also the scourge of caravans and villager.

Middle Eastern desert is that the four monotheistic religions began there, with numerous prophets who saw visions and heard voices, and that to this day prophets are born in those deserts who have visions and who relate what the voices command. But it is useless to analyze this apparent correlation between the desert and the adoration of one God. And that is its power: either the prophets are believed or are not believed. What seems to be indisputable is that in the desert ultimately a single creator sufficed.

But all deserts do bear life although it would be invisible to the newcomer for some time. Rain came randomly in early winter, yet within hours, wherever it fell, seeds that had been waiting sometimes many years began to sprout. Within days the sand was carpeted by grass and plants a few inches high, sometimes barely visible when seen from above, but green and exuberant at eye level. The carpet had designs, clusters of small colored flowers with honeyed smells. Desiccated bushes and thorny trees swelled and put out leaves, but only where it had rained. By spring some pastures that had bloomed were drying up, and the others soon would dry. But all year hares ran

Photography and Archeology

In the nineteenth century any visitor could kneel before an edifice thousands of years old and push away the sand to uncover one more inch of ancient history. If he photographed the site, it often helps researchers today because the ruins were sometimes raided by local residents as well as collectors, and they continue to deteriorate. Or the terrain may have changed in the last hundred years. A riverbank could crumble, a sand dune cover up telltale stones.

To the gradually developing science of archeology, the camera was indispensable. From the start archeologists used photography to investigate: to focus on specific detail, the shape of an arch, a single hieroglyphic, or on overall patterns, hoping to uncover secrets to the past. Charles Breasted wrote in the biography of his father, the famous archeologist James Henry Breasted, that "the meticulous recording of long-known, steadily perishing, and largely unpublished historical monuments *above* ground had about it almost none of the excitement and fascination popularly associated with digging for *buried* treasure. But he [James Henry Breasted] was more than ever convinced that however much the excavations of men like [Sir Flinders] Petrie, [Theodore M.] Davis, [James Edward] Quibell and others might contribute to Egyptology, he himself could render it no greater service than to copy while they were still legible the historical records in the ancient monuments of Egypt."

Undoubtedly more photographs have been taken in the Middle East of inscriptions, pots, mummies, tombs, or chambers than of peasants, princes, or holy men. As early as 1846 a pamphlet containing three original photographs of hieroglyphic text titled *The Talbotype* [Calotype] *Applied to Hieroglyphics* was printed at Fox Talbot's Reading Establishment and distributed to scholars.

One of the first men to make a thorough study of a specific subject was the French painter Auguste Salzmann. In 1854 he photographed for six months in Jerusalem on behalf of the archeologist Louis Félicien de Saulcy. Saulcy was dating Jewish, Christian, and Islamic architecture and needed pictures to confirm his theories.

Salzmann's eye became quickly attuned and his intensive study of ancient stones at very short distances resulted in richly textured images that seem imbued with sacred meaning. Similarly, John B. Greene, who studied archeology and went on an excavation in Thebes in the 1850s, sought intimate relationships between human constructions and their environment. He could blend a pyramid's angles into the soft rolling dunes or reveal more about an obelisk's function than its height, shape, and hieroglyphics could possibly tell.

Most archeological expeditions took along someone who could use a camera. Théodule Devéria, for example, accompanied Auguste Mariette, later director of the Egyptian Museum in Cairo, to Egypt in 1858 as a copyist and photographer. Vicomte Henri de Banville, an archeologist himself, photographed all the artifacts found on the 1863–1864 expedition to Egypt led by the curator of the Egyptian wing of the Louvre, Olivier Charles de Rougé. Johannes Dümichen, professor of Egyptology at the University of Strassburg, in 1870, like Professor Breasted of the University of Chicago thirty years later, photographed, with the help of colleagues, inscriptions and texts, which they translated on returning to their universities. Breasted, on two trips in 1905 and 1906, traveled with his wife, son, and assistants two thousand miles up the Nile and photographed all the monuments relating to Nubia as an independent nation.

Many of the early photographers took outstanding pictures of the antiquities. Although they were not scientific in their approach and tended to be romantic, their work can be used by contemporary archeologists. Maxime Du Camp's pictures are important not only esthetically but because they are often the earliest we have of many sites. Félix Teynard's softly focused photographs of antiquities, made in 1851–1852, are some of the most striking of desert views. They look almost as if taken under water, and this contradiction between what we know and what we feel, when we see the shimmering light reflected at oblique angles from the parched surfaces, is moving. Much more than a talented artist, Fran-

The statue, at Karnak, of Amenhotep I, who reigned 1546–1526 B.C., *is of colossal size.*

Félix Teynard, 1851–1852.

cis Frith, who went to the Middle East three times in the 1850s, was a true explorer and adventurer who wrote lively commentaries on his pictures, which were then published together in numerous albums. On his third trip, in 1859, he followed the Nile to the Third Cataract, one of the few Westerners to have traveled that far. One feels that Frith had a theory of composition that centered the picture so as to produce a lovely balance and sense of peacefulness. Each is a complete image; nothing extends beyond the borders so that everything that could be interesting to the viewer, were he at the site himself, is present. Louis de Clercq, an amateur archeologist who traveled alone throughout the Orient in 1859–1860, made some of the most stunning photographs of the period. He could focus upon a small detail in such a way as to give it monumental importance, and make panoramas that were large and mysterious; looking at them, one feels indeed like a traveler in an antique land.

Perhaps the most curious cameraman in search of scientific truth was the Astronomer Royal for Scotland, Charles Piazzi Smyth. A mathematician as well as an astronomer, he was determined to find something significant about the proportions of the Great Pyramid. After making exact measurements and photographs inside and out in 1865, he concluded the pyramid was divinely inspired, that the ancient Egyptians used the same "sacred cubit" as had Noah to build his ark, and that the British inch was based on it. Although his measurements were accurate, his conclusions were not well received by the scientific community.

In order to photograph within the Great Pyramid, Smyth needed a solid, relatively small camera and designed one that made one-inch-square wet-collodion negatives. He used magnesium wire for the newly discovered "flash" photography. Under the most difficult conditions, he succeeded, and these pictures of the interior of the Great Pyramid do have a place in archeological as well as photographic history.

Groupe de Bédouines syriennes   Bonfils

4 THE BEDOUIN

The land of Idumea lay before me, in barrenness and desolation; no trees grew in the valley, and no verdure on the mountain-tops. All was bare, dreary, and desolate.

But the beauty of the weather atoned for this barrenness of scene; and, mounted on the back of my Arabian, I felt a lightness of frame and an elasticity of spirit that I could not have believed possible in my actual state of health. Patting the neck of the noble animal, I talked with the sheikh about his horse; and, by warm and honest praises, was rapidly gaining upon the affections of my wild companions. . . .

In the evening, while making a note in a little memorandum-book, and on the point of lying down to sleep, I heard a deep guttural voice at some distance outside, and approaching nearer, till the harsh sounds grated as if spoken in my very ears. My Bedouins were sitting around a large fire at the door of the tent, and through the flames I saw coming up two wild and ferocious-looking Arabs, their dark visages reddened by the blaze, and their keen eyes flashing; and hardly had they reached my men, before all drew their swords, and began cutting away at each other with all their might. I did not feel much apprehension, and could not but admire the boldness of the fellows, two men walking up deliberately and drawing upon ten. One of the first charges Toualeb gave me on my entrance into the desert was, if the Arabs composing my escort got into any quarrel, to keep out of the way and let them fight it out by themselves; and, in pursuance of this advice, without making any attempt to interfere, I stood in the door watching the progress of the fray.

—JOHN LLOYD STEPHENS,
Incidents of Travel in Egypt, Arabia Petraea, and the Holy Land (1838)

NOMADIC CULTURES HAVE EXISTED throughout history in environments that could nourish neither hunters nor farmers. In the Middle East one kind of nomad raised sheep and goats for a living, though they used donkeys, horses, and camels for transport, and the other raised camels or horses for a living, herding some sheep and goats for their own use. The cultural differences between them were profound, although all were bedouin, or *badawi* (meaning desert dwellers), with the connotation of nomads who live in black tents. The ancient name for them is *Arab*, people of the desert. The bedouin were a significant part of the Middle East population, perhaps one-tenth overall, and in Arabia and Mesopotamia considerably more, and they inhabited immense areas according to hereditary tribal claims. They domesticated the desert in a marvelous way, moving about in single-family groups or as a small clan, visiting with other clans,

The caption reads: A Group of Syrian Bedouin Women.
Bonfils, after 1867.

This looks like a cold winter's day in northern Mesopotamia when the bedouin shiver in their threadbare clothing.

Gertrude Bell, ca. 1910.

and attending tribal gatherings where pasture and wells could sustain hundreds of families and their thousands of animals for a few weeks.

Blood lines traced every individual to ancestors reaching back to the time of the Prophet. A clan consisted of families closely related in the present. Clans were associated through more extended kinship to form a tribe. Large tribes were comprised of subgroupings of clans. Sheikhs — headmen — of clans belonged to families that had inherited the title but the incumbent sheikh held his position at the will of clan members; sons were often passed over when a new sheikh was chosen. This system held in the tribe, too. Clans and tribes had names, and everyone knew who was friend or foe of the year because loyalties shifted as a result of feuds, marriages, and other considerations. The reality was not as simple as this outline, of course, and most bedouin lived with complicated loyalties.

Deserts that were uninhabitable, like the Rub Al Khali, were nevertheless visited from time to time, so knowledge of the whole Middle East was common coin in the form of tales constantly circulated and updated, giving an outsider listening to them the conviction that the bedouin felt completely at home in their wanderings. But because their technology appeared so fragile and minimal, so utterly inadequate in the waterless sand and gravel, they were always seen by villagers and townsfolk as mysterious people. At the same time their very ease with the mysteries and disasters out there, their fierce pride and quarrelsomeness, their grave hospitality, as if they were grand masters of it all, gave them an air of nobility, impoverished though they were. Balanced against this was their readiness to beg, steal, and loot.

The bedouin's thousands of years of success with an unchanging technology yet a variety of cultural traditions depended on four factors. First was the nature of their animals and the symbiotic relationship between beasts and masters; second was the nature of the terrain and their knowledge of it, constantly refreshed to allow long-range planning; third was the economic and social relationship between the bedouin and the settled population and among the tribes themselves; and the fourth factor was the traditions and beliefs by which private and family needs were met. Clearly, the rewards had to seem greater to those who grew up as nomads than the rewards held out to them by town or village. No one, however, can explain adequately how so many times in history illiterate, pastoral nomads in the Middle East and Asia were suddenly transformed into world-conquering people.

The camel was wonderfully strong, satisfied for months with withered shrubs and a drink twice a week during the dry season, and no water at all during the few weeks when the pastures were green. Year round it gave wool for clothing and tents, and milk, which was the sta-

Bedouin in the Biblical land of Moab, now Jordan, show off a treasured pet mare. On the Arab horse the Muslim armies conquered the Roman, Byzantine, and Persian empires and rode as far as China. Only mares were ridden, often without a saddle and always with a halter.

Bonfils, after 1867.

Armed bedouin on the march in northern Arabia have stopped for a rest and coffee. The grazing camels will have to be rounded up, usually a scene of great pandemonium.

W. H. I. Shakespear, 1911.

At a gathering in Arabia, perhaps in a sheikh's tent, rugs and camel saddles serve as furniture. Falcons and salukis, graybeards and little girls are commonplace, but the shoes in the lower right show that a nonbedouin is visiting inside.

Gertrude Bell, c. 1913.

ple of the bedouin diet; when it died, it gave meat and leather; in the camel markets it sold handsomely for money that bought everything a family needed: rice, dates, clothing, utensils, harness, coffee, trinkets, weapons. A few camels could carry a family's possessions and a few more all the family, and driving unburdened animals with a few sheep and goats, a little train could vanish from the vicinity of an oasis over the shimmering horizon, meet no one for months, then rendezvous with others for political news, for gossip about friends, relatives, and enemies, the latest rainfall, the condition of wells and pastures, and for games and love matches. One topic of conversation was a favorite camel — her superb anatomy,

strength, endurance, disposition, loyalty, speed, quality of milk, and so on. Everyone in a tribe that bred better camels was socially superior to everyone in a tribe that was heedless of breeding lines; and freight camels were one thing, racing camels another.

As for horses, they could be bred only by tribes that claimed certain regions, like the north central part of Arabia, where rain was more plentiful and grazing more reliable. But the social prestige of these tribes, too, depended on the excellence of their stock. The Arab is the oldest pure breed of domesticated horse in the world, appearing in records before 400 B.C. All other light breeds have been derived from it through selective crossbreeding. Pure Arabs were rated according to five anatomical points, but the common characteristics were beauty, intelligence, spirit, endurance, and companionableness. Mares were jealously guarded, and only stallions were put on the market. Bloodlines were recorded in the phenomenal oral tradition that illiterate people develop as a history of the past; even the names of the horses the Prophet rode have been preserved. Into the twentieth century various tribes raised horses for sale to racing and polo stables all over the world. Almost every sheikh owned a few horses for pleasure, but only the richest could afford a string. For either, the prized possession was the favorite mare, who walked into the tent, was fed dates and milk, and let children play with her.

The other animals attached to the bedouin were two breeds of dog and the falcon. One dog was a mongrelly but powerful guard animal, the other the carefully bred saluki — sacred in ancient Egypt — which resembles a greyhound and was trained to hunt. It can hit fifty miles an hour in spurts and maintain over thirty for miles chasing gazelles. Because the saluki does not salivate and has other aristocratic habits with food and defecation, it was the only dog the bedouin allowed inside the tent. Exceedingly friendly and yet not a pest, it grins and hisses when it greets visitors and made a great pet for children and women. Everyone could afford a saluki. Falconry, however, was an expensive sport and not every sheikh could buy the equipment and hire a specialist to trap wild falcons and then train and handle them.

The camel herders were the social elite; the sheep herders stood markedly lower on the list. Their love of sheep was as old as the Bible and dictated an unwarlike attitude, a greater need of reliable pasturage, and a much slower, less adventurous pattern of migration with the seasons. Below even them were the nomads — still bedouin — who spent much of the year in the vicinity of villages, perhaps doing odd jobs or scrounging, reluctant to face the dangers of year-round dependence on what the desert offered. And at the bottom of the list, socially, were the families of general handymen who did the work of tinkers, blacksmiths, veterinarians, toolmakers, harness menders, who bartered their craftsmanship for food and everything else, and for freedom of passage through the feud-infested deserts so that every tribe could hire them.

Dry wells and sandstorms threatened them all. One year of rainless skies along a herding route and the pastures still grew green, for the desert's substratum in those regions held water tenaciously. Even two rainless

The general poverty of the bedouin is indicated by this picture. Travelers commented on it with profound wonder: why should people choose a way of life guaranteed to keep them destitute? But the same travelers often became enchanted by that way of life. The caption identifies these people as bedouin in the land of Moab, but in the nineteenth century few Westerners knew much about the tribes and their territories. (Detail.)

Bonfils, after 1867.

years were bearable because there were always alternate routes, and if the last rains had been unusually abundant, three years of unwatered land could still support the families that used them. After that all pastures vanished. Thus the pattern of last year's rains controlled the strategy of migration. The bedouin never saw themselves conquering nature. Like plants and animals, they could only fit into the ecology where the balance between life and death was poised on a hair's breadth of stamina, courage, and luck. And yet, though forced to keep on the move, they relished the state of wandering and created a comfortable existence out of nothing, as far as the stranger

682. Chef de bédouins pasteurs

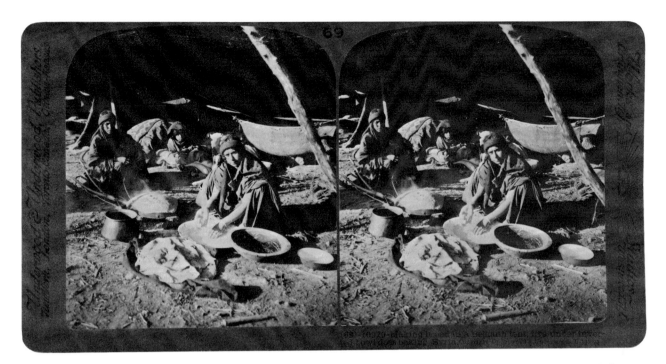

From one end of the world to the other, wherever fuel is scarce and ovens are rare, bread is made in pancake shape by spreading a thin layer of unleavened dough, or sometimes sourdough, over a hot surface where it can bake fast. The fire under the inverted bowl, here with a bread over it, is of shrubs when available, and dry camel dung when they are not. Bedouin tribes living far from wheat-growing regions ate boiled rice instead of bread. Wheat or rice, dates, coffee, clothing, and gear were bought in towns where the bedouin sold camels, stallions, sheep, the tribe's only source of income.

Underwood & Underwood, 1911.

An alleged "chief of bedouin shepherds" posed for this portrait before a painted backdrop. Perhaps he was; the heavy sheepskin cloak and boots suggest a mountain man, but the face and hands seem rather too citified.

Bonfils, after 1867.

In Abu Dhabi, Arabia, on the Persian Gulf, this executioner was probably a former slave. The man to be executed is holding the pan into which his head will fall.

W. H. I. Shakespear, 1911.

could see. Westerners who lived with bedouin — Doughty, Burton, Lawrence, Harry St. John Philby, Gertrude Bell, and some others — described how their songs, tales, and gossip declared an ecstatic love for their nomadic life, their camels and horses, the pure air, the clean sands, the very emptiness. The desolation itself made them sing.

Occasionally, a tribe gathered a wild crop. One of the most interesting was a species of barley that grew about six inches high in Egypt's western desert near the Mediterranean. Once a year the tribe that claimed the area appeared out of nowhere to harvest it on hands and knees, using a sickle and collecting the handfuls into pouches. It supplemented the rice they had to buy. Then it was discovered that this barley provided a malt that could not be surpassed in making scotch whisky. Agents came out from Alexandria to buy as much of it as the tribe would sell and shipped it to Scotland's best distilleries. Ambitious farmers tried to grow the strain under controlled conditions elsewhere, but it lost the special flavor created by the wild desert and sea air.

But the idea of settling forever in one place and plowing, raising, and harvesting crops was abominable to bedouin sensibilities. They despised physical labor. The cramped, stifling villages with heavy barnyard smells, garbage dumps, and stinking latrines revolted them. They held their noses there in plain disgust and shouted for joy when they escaped again into the pure desert. The farmers, on the other hand, were horrified by the very idea of riding into the desert with no more than a camel could carry. The permanent deprivation — all bedouin were small, bone and sinew, and looked half-starved, which was more or less the case — seemed terrible enough, but worse were the threats of wells running dry, sandstorms, drought years that killed most of the camels, hit-and-run raids. Only madmen would choose such a hell. But to the bedouin true hell was the farmers' serfdom under landlords who seized everything the fields produced and left the peasants only enough for survival, with debts that generations could not pay off. Government agents poked and commanded, imposed ruinous taxation, and conscripted young men into lifetime service in the army. Even more horrible were the hysteria, greed, and corruption of cities.

The differences in tribal cultures were hallowed. People spoke of one another in terms of the legendary attributes of their tribes and reacted in encounters as if every individual were first and foremost a reflection of his or her tribe's image. Someone from a clan known to be frugal was automatically considered mean and stingy no matter how average his generosity might have been. If the women were reputed to be quarrelsome, every bride from that clan carried the label, and her husband's clan read cantankerousness into her every whim. A plain girl from a tribe proud of the beauty of its women had a bad time of it.

Unexpected variations in the desert could be fatal, so children began to learn the environment, to pick up signals so faint that even years of association with the bedouin could not teach an outsider how they did it. And this subtlety of experience in that harsh setting created a society rich with nuances within traditional rules that outwardly seemed to tyrannize over behavior. For example, the patriarchal authority of the sheikh was balanced by the duty of the patriarch to be just, clever, and generous, and by the right of the community to replace him. There could never be an apparatus of government, with a bureaucracy, but neither could a dictatorship last for very long. Tents also imposed a practical democracy, but the separation of the sexes by a curtain and by rules that defined which male relatives and friends could visit the women, maintained a necessary privacy. It also domesticated the enormous pleasure both sexes looked for, and attained, in sanctioned lovemaking, while it inhibited rape and adultery. Romances probably outnumbered all other types of tale in the repertoire of storytellers and in gossip. Communal sharing meant profound respect for the community's needs rather than for one's own. To be a specialist was impossible. All the girls learned how to do the men's work, and all the boys helped the women. The social techniques that to an outsider at first seemed harsh and meaningless had worked for thousands of years without blunting the bedouin's determination to feel free.

One aspect of desert life that seemed to non-bedouin almost harder to bear than the anxieties he imagined was boredom. But the bedouin overcame boredom by plumbing to its depth the human potential for companionship, trust, generosity, loyalty, love, hate, jealousy, celebrations, trials of nerve, physical challenges, and so on. Everyone played, sang, and danced. Gregarious and gossipy within their tribe, though silent and evasive with outsiders, the bedouin lengthened greetings and formalities with an artfulness that made any encounter exciting. Bragging and flattery were spun to heights that would seem ridiculous to Westerners.

The bedouin's great burden was the blood feuds that sparked raids and ambushes and sometimes cruel slaughter. No bedouin male went anywhere unarmed, unprepared to fight for his life in the desolation where stalking an enemy, or fleeing one, needed all his cunning, hate, and courage. What made the feuds bearable were the rigid rules concerning pillage and the sanctity of women and children, who were never molested. News of a clash spread like the wind, and all the details were remembered and set the course for future tests. Those who broke the rules were universally condemned. Thus, even warfare was contained within the larger community's sense of right and wrong, related directly to ultimate survival. At the same time, nothing equaled the thrill of plotting and carrying out a raid for camels.

But the bedouin was never much of a soldier in the Western sense, whether under his own, Turkish, or other banners. His tradition of hitting and running back into the desert where the enemy could not follow and where there was no town or fortress to store loot, made large-scale warfare impossible. More to the point, hit-and-run depended on clansmen fighting together with personal loyalty to a trusted leader who was kin to all, and who was followed because he manifested heroic qualities as well as cunning, accepted responsibility for failure, and had the ability to weld quarrelsome clans into collaboration, wheeling and dealing and threatening, exhorting them as if they were prima donnas. Payday was loot shared according to a complicated pecking order; it came after every skirmish and often in the thick of battle when the dead were stripped and mutilated. Every bedouin reserved the right to quit a battlefield anytime, regardless of anyone's grand plan. Because death was a personal tragedy for all in the blood-linked troop, shooting it out until the last man dropped was impossible. None of these habits was compatible with the idea of an army marching in drill formation on orders from officers no one in the ranks had ever met, would ever speak to, or owed a shred of personal loyalty to. And in any case, it was impossible to catch the bedouin, force them through military training in a barracks, and then hold on to them for years and years. And yet there were those extraordinary times when nomads with their kinship discipline destroyed the barracks-disciplined conscript armies of empires.

The bedouin lived from the sale of their animals, from working in, guiding, and protecting caravans, and from raids. But they contributed something deeply spiritual to the history of the Middle East. They chose perpetual penury in an empty land, and this fact, which everyone in towns and cities grew up knowing, was a constant reminder that possessions were not the only way to happiness, that the Koran's ethic, based on brotherhood, was not a philosophical ideal but the reality of desert life that the Prophet himself had enjoyed. Without tribes inhabiting the deserts and transforming them into avenues of communication, no Middle Eastern civilization could have grown beyond village technology.

Arabists with Cameras

It is ironical that the four Europeans who knew the Arab lands best and had the most to do with raising Arab hopes for independence before World War I ended were English. W. H. I. Shakespear, product of Sandhurst and service in India, was sent to report on activities in the interior of Arabia, where Abdul Aziz ibn Saud, the Wahabi leader, was consolidating his rule over the tribes. Shakespear became his advisor on foreign affairs. After Shakespear's death, Harry St. John Philby, another English Arabist and explorer also sent from India, became Ibn Saud's advisor. Thomas Edward Lawrence, the Oxford-educated bastard son of an aristocrat, went to Syria as an amateur archeologist, became liaison officer between the British army in Cairo and Prince Feisal of the Hussein family, rulers of Mecca, and helped organize the Arab revolt against the Turks along the Red Sea. Gertrude Bell, wealthy Oxford graduate, went to Persia and Mesopotamia as a private scholar, then became an advisor to the British in Baghdad during the war and an influential friend of the same Prince Feisal, future king of Iraq.

These four—like Charles Doughty and Sir Richard Burton before them—fell in love with the desert and the bedouin and were considered masochistic by other Westerners because they were happy to live with nomadic hardships. They were also enthusiastic photographers, and it is amazing how well they managed to solve the difficulties of packing on camel-back not just cameras and gear but also glass plates, unexposed and exposed, and of photographing under all sorts of hostile conditions. Bell and Shakespear each had two cameras, one large for panoramic views, and Shakespear carried the apparatus and chemicals for developing plates in the desert. Shakespear and Lawrence took pictures of men on the march and go-

ing into battle. No one before these three had ever photographed the bedouin's life deep in the desert, or remote towns in Arabia and Mesopotamia.

Their photographs were never taken for or put to any specific purpose. They were made apparently for personal delight, as a diary of what they saw and whom they met. Because they were photographing the bedouin as close friends, the pictures reveal intimate and rich details of life that no one else could capture. Most of them are necessarily of snapshot quality, but some have a composition that adds esthetic dimension. Bell and Shakespear were concerned with translating the feel of the desert and the sky and the shape of habitation in the emptiness, and the panoramic camera was the best instrument to achieve this. Their aim was never purely artistic, however; always they were aware that no one else could document or record the things that they knew. A sense of history is apparent in the photographs, and so is their love for what they believed were noble and wonderful traditions, older than any other in the world.

It is fair to ask: must a photographer know the culture and the language of the people he freezes on a negative in order to achieve more than a memorable image? The answer seems to be yes. These three were enormously handicapped in the number of pictures they could take, which forced them to consider carefully each shot, and it was their knowing eye that told them where to look. Today a competent professional can jet to any spot in the world and in a few days take a hundred rolls of film with sophisticated equipment and artificial lighting, jet out, develop under optimum conditions, and select five for publication. The five might be startlingly beautiful, yet not one might tell much about the land and the culture.

Aqaba, an ancient fortified seaport in the Sinai, was cap-
tured from the Turks in 1917, without a battle, by the
Arab tribes under King Hussein and T. E. Lawrence.
Lawrence took the picture of this triumphant charge into
the town.

5 CARAVANS
AND SAILING SHIPS

The appearance of the Caravan was most striking, as it threaded its slow way over the smooth surface of the Khabt (low plain). To judge by the eye, the host was composed of at fewest seven thousand souls, on foot, on horseback, in litters, or bestriding the splendid camels of Syria. There were eight gradations of pilgrims. The lowest hobbled with heavy staves. Then came the riders of asses, of camels, and of mules. Respectable men, especially Arabs, were mounted on dromedaries, and the soldiers had horses: a led animal was saddled for every grandee, ready whenever he might wish to leave his litter. Women, children, and invalids of the poorer classes sat upon a "Haml Musattah," —rugs and cloths spread over the two large boxes which form the camel's load. Many occupied Shibriyahs; a few, Shugdufs, and only the wealthy and the noble rode in Takht-rawan (litters), carried by camels or mules. The morning beams fell brightly upon the glancing arms which surrounded the stripped Mahmil, and upon the scarlet and gilt conveyances of the grandees. Not the least beauty of the spectacle was its wondrous variety of detail: no man was dressed like his neighbor, no camel was caparisoned, no horse was clothed in uniform, as it were. And nothing stranger than the contrasts: a band of half-naked Takruri marching with the Pasha's equipage, and long-capped, bearded Persians conversing with Tarbush'd and shaven Turks.

—RICHARD BURTON,
Personal Narrative of a Pilgrimage to Al-Madinah & Meccah (1855)

THE NINETEENTH-CENTURY TRAVELER who left Europe or America for the Middle East, generally by steamship after 1840, usually landed at Alexandria, mistress of the world two thousand years before, at the mouth of the Nile, most mysterious of all rivers. From there upriver to Cairo by sail was a hundred miles. From Cairo, desert routes older than history led west to Morocco and Gibraltar, 2,500 miles; south to Khartum, 1,500 miles; north to Constantinople, 1,200 miles; east to Jerusalem, 300 miles, and to Beirut another 150; Beirut to Damascus 50 miles, Damascus to Mecca a long thousand; Damascus to Baghdad 500, from there to Basra 300; Baghdad to Tehran 600 miles. These are crow-flight distances, shorter than the actual routes that wound about from well to well, along impassable wadis, and zigzagged through mountains. By sea, from Suez to Aden was 1,400 miles, and a few hundred fewer to Hodeida, seaport of the Yemen; from Cairo to the borders of India was several thousand miles. Rail connected Alexandria, Cairo, and

The Nile flows northward, but the wind from the Mediterranean blows south up the Nile into Africa. With their towering sails, Nile boats overcame the current on their way up. Furling the sails, they floated back to the Mediterranean on the current. Passenger boats, called dahabiyas, could be any size (this one was 90 feet long) and were designed for luxurious sleeping and dining.

A. Beato, after 1868.

Suez by the 1850s, and by 1900 trains were running on several short lines in Anatolia and Syria and later from Constantinople to Medina. Until then, and on any other routes, the traveler journeyed with caravans exactly as he would have since the days of Sumer.

A caravan was an assemblage of camels whose bedouin owners rented them to the caravan organizer and to individual passengers and accompanied them as drivers, or of camels owned by entrepreneurs who leased them out and hired the drivers, always bedouin. Driving could be a lifetime profession, but many drivers were also renegades, smugglers, or murderers hiding from the law or from vengeful enemies. The captain, or *rais*, hired by the principal investors in the caravan, had to cope with this motley crew in his strategy and tactics against brigands,

marauding bedouin, tyrants of remote districts, all of whom lived off taxes and plunder. Government troops or mercenaries were often attached to the caravan, but they obeyed their own officers, who did not have to heed the rais, not even when the train was attacked.

The main goal of the rais was to shepherd sometimes a thousand or more loaded camels and hundreds of passengers across deserts and mountains from one watering place to another, through howling sandstorms that buried everything, and through flash floods started by cloud-

Although the photograph is titled "Soldat Abyssin à Dogal" ("Abyssinian Soldier at Dogal"), the soldier is probably from the southern Sudan, not Abyssinia. He rides behind the racing camel's hump, without the usual saddle.

Zangaki, after 1860.

The first automobile caravan in the Middle East consisted of a thousand Model T cars carrying a British expeditionary force through Persia, at the end of World War I, with orders to cross into Russia and help the White army fight the Red army. It never completed its mission. Cars and trucks appeared on city streets everywhere after the war, but even as late as the 1930s camels such as these in Persia were far more reliable transportation on unpaved caravan routes through the roadless mountains and deserts than were engines and tires.

Anonymous, ca. 1900.

bursts. His word was law, but he had to make it stick. Sometimes caravans broke up completely or groups detached themselves and followed their own leaders.

What made caravans run at all? Profit. And usually big profit on both merchandise and passengers.

Under decent conditions a freight camel carrying over five hundred pounds padded steadily at two or three miles an hour and might cover an average of thirty miles between rests, twenty in summer heat. A good riding dromedary clipped along twice as fast for a day and a night with short rests, and on racing camels a messenger could cover a hundred miles in ten hours. In the summer, caravans generally started before dawn and rested from midmorning to midafternoon, or they set off in the late afternoon and moved through the night till dawn, but in winter they plodded on all day. Bedding down the animals, feeding them daily, and watering them several times a week, depending on the season and the terrain, rearranging the loads, repairing harness, doctoring the lame and the sick, and so on, took hours at each rest. Long journeys took months. The huge pilgrim caravans from Damascus to Mecca and Medina made the round trip in four months. But this was a slow train, with many thousands of passengers, some of them walking all the way.

The routes were strewn with the bones of men and beasts that had run out of water, been choked or lost in a

The photographer who took this, J. Pascal Sébah, set up many scenes that he knew appealed to tourists who wanted to take home startling pictures. Probably he posed the five riders, as they have no baggage for any kind of journey. Such skeletons, however, lined all the caravan routes.

J. Pascal Sébah, after 1868.

Caravans from Jidda to Mecca, going through the barren mountains, usually took two days. Women rode in litters, often covered, of various designs. Before World War I pilgrims were preyed upon by customs and other officials, by bandits, bedouin, and townspeople. After Ibn Saud unified Arabia and eliminated the hazards of travel, pilgrimages flourished. (Detail.)

Dr. F. G. Clemow, 1906.

sandstorm, had sickened, or had been ambushed, or slaughtered in pitched battles. The vultures circled above, black spots in the radiant blue sky, waiting comfortably for the next feast of merchants, soldiers, thieves, or pilgrims.

A prospective traveler hunted in a city for someone connected with the passage he wanted to make — bazaar merchants, consular officials, bureaucrats, outfitters, wholesalers. It might take a week to find the right contact and strike a deal with some rais or agent. Ideally, the traveler and other passengers met and formed a group under an experienced old hand who knew how to bargain collectively with the rais, or for camels. Everyone carried his own leather bags, his own pots, camping gear, cot, tent, depending on his budget. Food was sometimes provided by the rais, but generally passengers hauled their own — rice, dates, coffee, flour, sugar, nuts. Someone was always generous enough to boil a poor companion's ration with his own. On some routes hunting for gazelles, birds, or lizards was possible, or sheep could be bought from bedouin. Most women and all the wealthy rented or bought a litter, usually covered, which was strapped on a camel's back. Any self-respecting Middle Easterner was accompanied by a household servant or slave, or two, and a general servant to handle the baggage, and even the poorer people had servant-cooks. At least one baggage camel was obligatory for supplies and a servant. Small parties sometimes rented or bought their own riding and baggage camels, hired their own servant-drivers and even armed guards, and negotiated with the rais as an independent unit attached to his train. Everyone carried daggers, swords, pistols, sometimes guns. Even women wore concealed knives.

If the lonely stranger was Western and knew no Arabic, he attracted predators and risked his life on a long journey. Consequently foreigners had to be rich, with bodyguards, loyal servants, and powerful letters from governors ordering officials to help them. If they were not rich, knowing Arabic was necessary and it was almost imperative to masquerade as a citizen of some distant part of the Ottoman Empire, and to rely on friends of friends along the way for help in dealing with rapacious officials. On the other hand, short journeys on well-traveled routes were safe for anyone.

And not all the tales about caravans were dire by any

The University of Chicago Expedition gets ready at Amara for a trip with, apparently, no confusion; or perhaps the hullabaloo has not yet started. Camels, the most patient beasts of burden, were also cantankerous and willful and only the bedouin knew how to get kneeling camels, facing every which way, into an orderly train in the right direction, instead of an explosion of camels in all directions.

Friedrich Koch, Breasted expedition, 1905–1906.

means. In fact, the friendliness of fellow passengers, the intelligence and valor of the rais, the community spirit of the drivers, the many, many Good Samaritans everywhere, were commonplace. One reason, of course, was that most people did not join a caravan to loot or murder. But there was also the fact that the code of the desert, tribal traditions, and Koranic law worked for mutual survival. Hostile or wolfish individuals were constrained by the culture into civilized behavior, at least for a while, or were often forced into it by other Muslims.

Also dangerous for Europeans was the fanatical hatred of "Franks" by provincial Muslims, although this was blunted by the tolerance of worldly Muslims and educated city dwellers. Less serious was Middle Easterners'

dislike of European contempt for all things not European and of their reluctance to accommodate to local custom; this irritation was again tempered by a tradition of laissez-faire toward all non-Muslims who were permanent citizens of the empire.

The big caravans arrived and left on schedule, give or take a few weeks when the route led through mountains that winter snows locked up or through dunes where the wells dried out in summer, or where sandstorms prevailed in season. The largest caravans were assembled in Cairo and Damascus for the annual pilgrimage to Mecca during the eleventh month of the Muslim year. By 1850, travel agents in Cairo were organizing special expeditions for tourists under government protection, with all the luxuries that camels could carry and with armies of cooks, servants, colorful guards, and sumptuously bedecked and armed dragomans.

Deir-es-Zor, in Syria, was built in the 1860s on the Euphrates near the ruins of ancient Azaura by the Ottoman government. Note the sidewalks, paved street, and gutters, and the geometric precision of the houses. It was the seat of a provincial governor and a bureaucracy that was to develop irrigation systems for raising cotton, grain, and cattle. As the site was an ancient caravan crossroad that had always attracted bedouin raids, the new town was also a military garrison. (Detail.)

D. D. Luckenbill or assistant, 1919–1920.

Obviously, shelter and food for travelers were necessary at staging points and were available at such places in caravansaries. Sometimes these shelters were enormous stone buildings, several stories high, covering many acres with a labyrinth of passageways, unfurnished rooms, and small apartments. Others were a few dirt-floored huts roofed with palm fronds. A caravansary pro-

vided nothing but water, often from its own cellar-well, and some kind of toilet facility — an outhouse or a hole in a corner room with a collecting cesspool below. There was not a stick of furniture and there were usually no glassed windows, just shutters. The owner was supposed to provide security but seldom did. Fires could be lit in hearths or braziers. People moved in bag and baggage, servants and friends, to wait for a caravan, and made themselves a little home away from home, with their own rugs and pillows and cookware.

Richard Burton wrote of the caravansary in Cairo:

It is . . . , as at Constantinople, a massive pile of buildings surrounding a quadrangular "Hosh" or

courtyard. On the ground-floor are rooms like caverns for merchandise, and shops of different kinds — tailors, cobblers, bakers, tobacconists, fruiterers, and others. A roofless gallery or a covered verandah, into which all the apartments open, runs around the first and sometimes the second story: the latter, however, is usually exposed to the sun and wind. The accommodations consist of sets of two or

Korosko.

Félix Teynard, ca. 1852.

three rooms, generally an inner one and an outer;
the latter contains a hearth for cooking, a bathing-
place, and similar necessities. The staircases are
high, narrow, and exceedingly dirty; dark at night,
and often in bad repair; a goat or donkey is tethered
upon the different landings; here and there a fresh
skin is stretched in process of tanning, and the
smell reminds the veteran traveller of those closets
in the old French inns where cat used to be prepared
for playing the part of jugged hare. The interior
is unfurnished; even the pegs upon which clothes
are hung have been pulled down for fire-wood: the
walls are bare but for stains, thick cobwebs depend
in festoons from the blackened rafters of the ceiling:
the windows are huge apertures carefully barred
with wood or iron, and in rare places show remains
of glass or paper pasted over the framework. In
the courtyard the poorer sort of travellers consort
with tethered beasts of burden, beggars howl, and
slaves lie basking and scratching themselves upon
mountainous heaps of cotton bales and other
merchandise.

A large part of Islamic literature and storytelling is
concerned with events in the caravansaries. Nowhere else
could such a continuous socializing of races and cultures
be found, or such tremendous variation in wealth and
goals, such a range of types from saints to devils. Lifetime friendships were welded between people who could
not speak the same language, and enmities suddenly separated brothers forever. Romance was harder to come
by, but it all depended. Guests were always cautioning
each other against con artists, thieves, muggers, for they
were a constant threat. Sometimes duels were fought to
the death. But a caravansary was a steady source of income for many local merchants, and peace could not be
violated for long before the authorities crashed in to
make order. Still, it was not unusual for guests to die not
only of old age, disease, or hunger, but by the assassin's
knife.

Steamships had been crossing the Atlantic since 1840,
and scheduled service between England and India
through Egypt had been inaugurated by then. The European sea leg ended at Alexandria; from there cargo and
passengers were hauled by camel — later by train — to
Suez, where ships of the East India Company took over.
After 1869 the Suez Canal opened the seaway to Asia.

Armed escorts at Korosko wait for the caravan.

J. Pascal Sébah, after 1868.

Passenger dahabiyas—with cabin windows—and a freighter (nearest the camera) tied up at Luxor. The relative size of the sailors climbing the yard of the mainsail indicates the astounding height reached by lateen rigs.

Francis Frith, 1856–1859.

But large steamers bypassed ports that did not offer enough business or had no proper anchorage or adequate facilities. For this reason, in the Middle East sail did not lose its importance until World War I, and even today it serves the Red Sea, the Indian Ocean, the Persian Gulf, and the Nile. In the Arab world nearly all boats were rigged with a towering fore-and-aft type of sail called the lateen, invented when Christianity was a few centuries old. It allows efficient tacking into the wind, whereas square-rigged ships can barely do so; they go only before and across the wind and are therefore slower. Thus a lateen rig sailed circles around any square-rigger. Yet European shipping generally neglected all types of fore-and-aft sails until the seventeenth century when modified

forms combined with square sails became popular. (The nineteenth-century clipper ships, designed to race against steam, used a combination.) The Arabs adapted the lateen rig to a variety of hull and deck designs, each having a distinctive name (but all called *dhows* by Europeans), for many kinds of work and for a wide range of waters. A big high-pooped seafaring ship—up to a thousand tons—made of hand-hewn timbers with treetrunk

masts and an enormous spread of lateen sails reaching many times higher than the masts, could foam through the translucent, phosphorescent seas at better than ten knots.

The desert people of the Arab world, within a few centuries after beginning their conquests, became the master mariners of the Mediterranean, the African and Indian oceans, and into the China seas. They were merchant sailors par excellence and the fiercest of all pirates. The Barbary pirates of North Africa terrorized European shipping and raided the coasts of Italy and France without opposition. (The Muslims of the Pacific also turned into unbeatable pirates.) The Arabs brought the lodestone from China long before Europe felt a need for it, and for many centuries Arabs wrote the best books on astronomy, geography, map making, and navigation. These works were translated reverently into Latin, and no European could dream of equaling their scholarship. Yet, because the Arabs were not forced into exploring the open Atlantic and Pacific, they never acquired the sophistication that Europeans had to after 1500, in their less maneuverable, smaller, and slower square-riggers. It was the Europeans who developed ship designs for worldwide voyages. Even in the nineteenth century,

The round kufa *of the Tigris and Euphrates, woven of rushes, appears in pictures from Babylonian times. It is a reliable water craft, though here overloaded.*

Underwood & Underwood, 1914.

A daguerreotype of dahabiyas with two Frenchmen aboard.

Jules Itier, 1845–1846.

Arab skippers carried few charts, no instruments, went by rule of thumb, memory, stars — seat-of-the-pants navigation — as they skirted the shores of Arabia, Africa, and India.

To go by sea, a traveler had to hunt for a ship's captain, also called a *rais*, in a seaport, although leads might begin in a city with agents, consuls, and so on. The risks were considerably higher than on a land journey — hair-raising, in fact. Shipwrecks along unmarked shores, piracy, and mutiny were not uncommon, but the dangers began in port. Unemployed sailors, smugglers, renegades, deserters, and corrupt officials preyed with impunity on all travelers. Still, shipping was big business, and pilgrim ships carried untold hundreds of thousands every year to Jidda, seaport of Mecca, from as far away as the Philippines.

The port of Alexandria, largest in the Middle East, was the site of the world's first lighthouse, on the island of Pharos. One of the Seven Wonders, built about 280 B.C., it functioned for over 1,500 years before falling into ruins. The lighthouse, center, and pylon, left, mark the entrance to the harbor, where a mixture of steam and sailing ships were celebrating something on the day this picture was taken.

Anonymous, ca. 1870.

The town of Kuwait at the head of the Persian Gulf had few wells. When they ran dry, sailing ships hauled water from Basra, about 150 miles away on the Shatt-al-Arab, a channel into which the Tigris and Euphrates flow. In this photograph the relief boat is anchored offshore and people are wading out to it with jugs on their heads. Today the largest desalinization plant in the world provides ten million gallons of water daily to Kuwait.

W. H. I. Shakespear, 1913.

Through Jidda, seaport of Mecca, have streamed untold millions of pilgrims from all over the world for a thousand years. They came by caravan and sailing ship and after the mid-nineteenth century by steamer. Until the gold tailings of King Solomon's mines were discovered a few miles northeast of Jidda in the 1930s and the oil fields were proved in 1938, pilgrims were Arabia's chief source of income, meagerly supplemented by the sale of camels and horses. In 1906 these small boats carried the pilgrims to and from steamships anchored in the harbor.

Dr. F. G. Clemow, 1906.

In Their Own Words

Photographers who worked in the Middle East, like most anywhere, rarely wrote about their experiences. Frédéric Goupil-Fesquet, Maxime Du Camp, Francis Frith, E. L. Wilson, and Adrien Bonfils were exceptions, and the following are statements about what they encountered or felt while photographing in these antique lands. Full sources appear on page 202.

It seemed to me most humiliating to go back to Cairo without bringing a single souvenir of the world's most famous monuments, in spite of the disparagements of my companions who threatened to throw the whole daguerreotype apparatus in the Nile as excess baggage. I alone had the patience to prepare another dozen plates, which I polished somehow or other and with all possible speed; I dared to do the opposite of M. Daguerre's directions and, thanks to that expedient, I got four or five plates of the Sphinx and the Pyramids, with exposures of fifteen minutes. These pictures, although not perfect, because of the haste with which the polishing was done, give nevertheless, a very good, truthful idea of the construction and the size of the monuments. The Sphinx, especially, at the foot of which a human figure serves as a scale of proportions, gives the lie to the tales of certain authors who have little conscience or are too rushed. But we had to leave for Cairo, and I didn't have time to pack up my apparatus, so I had to carry it piece by piece.

FRÉDÉRIC GOUPIL-FESQUET

Mehemet's [Mohammed Ali's] face is full of interest, his eyes, in spite of himself, betray an uneasiness which grows as the room is darkened so that the plate can be put over the mercury. An awed and anxious silence falls. No one dares to make a move. It is broken by the sudden scratching of a match, picturesquely lighting up the bronzed faces. Mehemet Ali, who is standing close to the apparatus, jumps, scowls and coughs — a habit, it is said, which he has when he is unexpectedly moved. His Majesty's impatience gives way to the liveliest expression of astonishment and admiration. "It is the work of the Devil!" he cried. Then

Although photography in the Middle East was extremely difficult, often the results had a tranquil, if idealized, beauty.

R. M. Junghaendel, ca. 1890.

he turned on his heels, still grasping the hilt of his sword, which he had not released for a single instant, as if he feared some secret conspiracy or some kind of mysterious influence, and went rapidly to his room.

FRÉDÉRIC GOUPIL-FESQUET

. . . Every time I visited a monument I had my photographic apparatus carried along and took with me one of my sailors, Hadji Ismael, an extremely handsome Nubian, whom I had climb up on to the ruins which I wanted to photograph. In this way I was always able to include a uniform scale of proportions. The great difficulty was to get Hadji Ismael to stand perfectly motionless while I performed my operations; and I finally succeeded by means of a trick whose success will convey the depth of naiveté of these poor Arabs. I told him that the brass tube of the lens jutting from the camera was a cannon, which would vomit a hail of shot if he had the misfortune to move — a story which immobilized him completely, as can be seen from my plates.

MAXIME DU CAMP

The difficulties which I had to overcome in working collodion, in those hot and dry climates, were also very serious. When (at the Second Cataract, one thousand miles from the mouth of the Nile, with the thermometer at 110° in my tent) the collodion actually boiled when poured upon the glass plate, I almost despaired of success.

FRANCIS FRITH

Know, then, that for the purpose of making large pictures (20 inches by 16), I had constructed in London a wicker-work carriage on wheels, which was, in fact, both camera and developing room, and occasionally *sleeping room*. . . . This carriage of mine, then, being entirely overspread with a loose cover of white sailcloth to protect it from the sun, was a most conspicuous and mysterious-looking vehicle, and excited amongst the Egyptian populace a vast amount of ingenious speculation as to its uses. The idea, however, which seemed the most reasonable, and therefore obtained the most, was that therein, with right laudable and jealous care, I transported from place to place — my — harem! It was full of moon-faced beauties, my wives all! — and great was the respect and

consideration which this view of the case procured for me!

FRANCIS FRITH

I may be allowed to state, as giving additional value to good Photographs of eastern antiquities, that a change is rapidly passing over many of the most interesting: in addition to the corroding tooth of Time and the ceaseless drifting of the remorseless sand, Temples and Tombs are exposed to continued plundering — Governors of districts take the huge blocks of stone, and the villagers walk off with the available bricks, whilst travellers of all nations break up and carry off, without scruple, the most interesting of the sculptured friezes and the most beautiful of the architectural ornaments.

FRANCIS FRITH

Attempt not, I beseech thee, to square those door-panels or window-frames with the straight-edge of thine eye (in the East there are no straight lines, no squares, no circles); the shade is welcome, the green of the orange and rose trees is refreshing; blue and gold are beautiful colors; believe, smoke, and be happy!

FRANCIS FRITH

The picturesque figures of these rascally Arabs, with their flowing robes and long lances, were of course very desirable ''accessories'' to the pictures of Petra; but they wanted heavier pay for ''sitting'' than any professional models. I had to pay thirty dollars for the privilege of making my picture of the six scoundrels on their horses.

E. L. WILSON

In this century of steam and electricity every thing is being transformed . . . even places. Already in the ancient Plain of Sharon one hears the whistle of the locomotive. . . . The immortal road to Damascus, witness to the apostle Paul's conversion, has become no more than a vulgar railway! . . . Before . . . progress has completely done its destructive job, before this present which is still the past has forever disappeared, we have tried, so to speak, to fix and immobilize it in a series of photographic views we are offering to our readers in this album.

ADRIEN BONFILS

6 THE VILLAGES

The villagers were of a kindly humour; and pleased themselves in conversing with the stranger, so far as their short notice might stretch, of foreign countries and religions. . . . I thought the taste of their bitter green tobacco, in this extremity of fatigue, of incomparable sweetness, and there was a comfortable repose in those civil voices after the wild malignity of the Bishr tongues. A young man asked me, "Could I read? — had I any books?" He was of Mogug, and their schoolmaster. I put in his hand a geography written in the Arabic tongue by a learned American missionary of Beyrut. — The young man perused and hung his head over it in the dull chamber, with such a thirsty affection to letters, as might in a happier land have ripened in the large field of learning: at last closing the book, when the sun was going down, he laid it on his head in token how highly he esteemed it, — an Oriental gesture which I have not seen again in Arabia, where is so little (or nothing) of "Orientalism." He asked me, "Might he buy the book? — (and because I said nay) might he take it home then to read in the night?" Which I granted.

—CHARLES M. DOUGHTY,
Travels in Arabia Deserta (1888)

TENS OF THOUSANDS OF VILLAGES and hamlets nestled in their fields along the irrigated banks of the Nile, Tigris, and Euphrates, the rain-visited Mediterranean and Black Sea shorelines of Anatolia, Lebanon, and Palestine, the cloud-catching mountain slopes of Anatolia, Iran, and Yemen, the small and large oases above underground lakes, like the Faiyum in Egypt and Taif in Arabia. Their inhabitants might be a few hundred souls, seldom more than a thousand.

Surprisingly few villages were photographed in the nineteenth century, probably because during daylight almost everyone was in the fields and village architecture was not traditionally picturesque.

Anonymous, before 1877.

Although the building style of each region depended on the environment, the basic material was sun-dried brick. Usually the houses were cube-shaped with flat roofs, sometimes with low parapets turning the roofs into rain-catchers. Sometimes the mud-colored walls were plastered or whitewashed. In eastern Arabia and the Yemen, blocks of coral cut from the floor of the Red Sea were used for building. Villages in Syria, with no timber for rafters, had conical roofs. Turkish mountain homes were of fieldstone, and grass was planted on their sloping roofs for insulation. Many had only one room, with tiny windows and low doors. Houses shared walls with stables and barnyards, pocket-sized to nestle into alleys meandering along ancient property lines. Or a village might be a single long row of huts side by side, each with its small yard. Above the twisting alleys, only as wide as the span of cattle horns, nodded olive trees, or-

(5)-11632-View from a "bee-hive" village of the Arabs, north-ward over Haran. © Underwood & Underwood, U-144161

This is a view overlooking Haran or Harran, a village in Syria. Because there was no wood in the region, the houses, built of sun-dried brick, could not have flat roofs. They were shaped instead as conical structures. Haran, on the road to Nineveh from Ur, was important in Biblical times, and when Abraham led the Hebrews away from Ur, their caravan settled here for a while.

Underwood & Underwood, 1915.

ange, lime, lemon, plum, apricot, peach, walnut, almond, fig, grapevines. Date palms ripened their orange clusters and dropped their fronds. Poplar, aspen, cedar, sycamore, acacia, mulberry, and various evergreens snuggled against the walls and marched along the ditched dirt roads. Every square foot of land was precious, so people and animals were crowded together by the plow. In every yard a manure and compost pile, a cooing dovecote, clucking chickens and bleating goats wandering in and out, a buffalo in her stall, occasionally a camel, and always a donkey. No public buildings except a mosque in the largest village of a group, no hotel or inn, no restaurant but always a corner house turned into a roadside coffeehouse and minimal store. Whoever visited a village came from the nearest town on foot, in a hired buggy, or on donkey-back, and stayed with relatives or friends.

Seldom was there a school but often a retired teacher—a mullah or a sheikh who had been to school himself—might chose to settle in a village and hold classes in the mosque, where he taught the Koran by rote. Occasionally he started the brightest and most eager child on his alphabet and prepared him for entrance in the nearest town school. If he was paid anything, it was in food and shelter.

Sometimes a landlord built a villa with high walls, planted an orchard, kept a clutch of rapacious servants, and spent weekends or even a whole summer there with his children. His presence never benefited the peasants, who had to tend his private garden in addition to laboring in his fields.

From one end of the Middle East to the other, villagers regarded outsiders with a mixture of contempt, ridicule, and fear, as creatures who knew only how to buy and sell and count money, who created nothing and yet strutted importantly, whose thin smiles and cunning eyes did not hide the fact that they were the villagers' mortal enemies. When village sons drifted into town to make a living, they remained tied to the village as if all their energy flowed from that insignificant mud nest, every bit of

Here is a view of the village of Luxor that tourists seldom looked for.

Anonymous, no date.

which usually belonged to absentee landlords. Westerners seldom paused as they rode past a village; they all looked alike to Western eyes and seemed to be islands whose inhabitants hid from the real world, performing monotonous tasks as if in a timeless dream. And truly the tools and techniques for watering, digging, plowing, planting, hoeing, defending against birds, insects, and robbers, the gathering, breeding, butchering, storing had all been depicted in fine detail on the temple and tomb walls of despots thousands of years before, as if there really were something mysterious in all that, something that no Westerner could grasp.

But in fact, the Middle Eastern peasants were no more interesting to Europeans than their own peasants, who may have seemed better off but were also caught in a mesh of tradition, economic exploitation, and laws maintained by cooperation between governments and landlords. (Slavery was not abolished in the British Empire until 1933, serfdom in Russia ended in 1860, and the Civil War freed slaves in America only in 1865. There were neither serfs nor slaves in the villages of the Middle East.)

A shaduf, the oldest mechanical aid throughout the world for lifting water from a well, uses the lever principle. A long tree trunk, stripped, is suspended on supports close to its thick end, which is weighted with stones and dried mud. Because this is so much heavier, it lifts the other end, to which is tied, with a long rope, a bucket made of skins, reeds, or baked clay. The empty bucket is lowered into the well by pulling on the rope hand over hand, thereby lifting the opposite, weighted, end of the lever. When the bucket fills it is just balanced by the weight, and thus the operator can easily raise it and then empty it into a flume or ditch running into the fields. Here a series of shadufs is worked to lift water through several levels; at each level there is a pit into which the bucket is emptied, until the last one pours the water over the ridge into the ditch beyond. (Detail.)

Probably J. Pascal Sébah, after 1868.

A more complicated water-lifting device than the shaduf is the sakiyeh, *partially visible here. A blindfolded animal plodding in circles turns a horizontal cogged wheel; a vertical cogged wheel meshes with the first. The axle of the vertical is fastened to a larger wheel, which has pots tied to its rim. As this wheel is turned, the pots dip into the water, rise, and at the top are automatically turned over, spilling into a flume. These wheels, which can be twelve feet or more in diameter, last hundreds of years with repairs that village carpenters can make. As the wooden cogs grind together they emit groans and squeals that can be heard for miles — music to the fellahin but maddening to the stray tourist.*

H. Béchard, 1870s–1880s.

Because they hardly knew their own peasants, Westerners found it impossible to imagine — if they ever tried — what Middle Eastern villagers talked about, felt about anything: did they rut like their animals or fall in love, marry, and raise children like fully developed human beings? Because their isolation from cities and their servitude to landowners was total, their lot seemed sealed forever. Nowhere was anyone interested in them, not since the time of the pharaohs, even though civilization itself depended on their knowledge, ability, and labor, and their willingness to rebuild their villages and rear

new generations into the same life. Yet it was popularly believed that the peasant was lazy, a liar, sly, untrustworthy; that he cheated the landlord as a matter of course, committed crimes without number, and escaped punishment by vanishing into the maze of village kinships linking whole regions; that he was diseased, slovenly, ignorant, and stubborn; that he believed in demons and witchcraft. He refused to be a good soldier when crammed into a uniform, and he ran from the battlefield. He knew too much about all kinds of things the rest of society ignored, yet he was as stupid as the beasts he tended. Like an animal, he had to be watched constantly and beaten regularly. Europeans agreed that their own peasants were the same sort of incorrigible, beastlike morons. Yet despite this universal prejudice, the peasants in the Middle East, as elsewhere, had outlasted all

A main ditch, filled by shaduf or sakiyeh *or other means like the Archimedes screw, often runs along property lines. Small breaks are hoed in the raised wall of the main ditch to trickle away the water into the fields. This method of irrigation was worked out thousands of years before the first pharaohs. (Detail.)*

H. Béchard, 1870s–1880s.

There are several ways to thresh grain: that is, to separate the husks from the kernels. The simplest is to beat the seeds with a flail. Greater efficiency is obtained if a wooden toboggan weighted with stones and people is pulled by bullocks around and around over a heap of grain. After the threshing, the mixture is tossed into the air; the light chaff floats away on the breeze, and the kernels fall to the ground.

J. Pascal Sébah, after 1868.

the empires. How did they do it?

They were up before dawn tending animals, cooking, preparing for the long day. Some had already left for the town marketplace with produce. Most of the men, the boys, the strong girls, and a few young women went into the fields or brought water in buckets from wells or the river to the ditches. In the village were playing children, women at house chores or carrying water in jugs on their heads to the house, the old and sick and pregnant, and perhaps a weaver or pot maker. At dusk, small fires glowed outside and inside the homes, and the smells of spicy food drifted under the trees. On dark nights the inhabitants slept like the dead cheek to cheek, but often in moonlight the field work continued.

The village had no ramparts, nobody was trained in soldiering, and weapons were the tools of farming—scythes, shovels, axes. Nobody could read, nobody knew the law. The villagers with their animals, families, and houses were sitting targets for armies, police, tax collectors, loan sharks, bedouin raiders, highway bandits, though they had paltry sums of money, no jewels, and only small hoards of food.

One force in the villagers' baffling survival was the blood and marriage ties that provided mutual support for everyone, a kind of cooperative that hid a little of what had been raised before the landlords seized the rest. A corollary was the primitive realization by rulers that if they wanted to feed their cities and armies they couldn't squeeze the peasants into extinction, either at sowing time or at harvests.

A psychological element of kinship was folk art. Every region fashioned its own utensils and tools, wove its own carpets and cloth, made its own clothes and footwear. Although artisans lived and worked in towns and passed on their skills to their own children, many villages also nourished a craftsman or two. Each piece of work—jug, rug, slipper, wheel, brazier, saddlebag, earring, basket, hoe—had traditional form and color that identified the place where it was made, but the craftsmen deviated from the models century after century for their own pleasure and according to their talents. The most famil-

Here camels walk away from a well, pulling up buckets; they are then led back to repeat the process endlessly. Such photographs showed Westerners the incredible drudgery of the preindustrial world, which the steam engine had eliminated in Europe.

Anonymous, no date.

iar object to Westerners was the hand-loomed and vegetable-dyed carpet, which took the place of furniture in bedouin tents, village huts, city mansions, and in the sultan's palace. In any great city hall or mosque carpeted with rugs from a score of villages, the different patterns and colors never clashed. After a few hours of sitting amid them one was calmed. No one would weave a pattern to live with if it did not produce a harmonious state of mind; every style of Oriental rug had been tested for compatibility for many, many generations. Thus a dirt-floored hut contained creations of the imagination to walk on, sleep in, eat from, live with, and leave to the children, thinner and frayed but glorious still, and still a panacea for body and mind.

All classes bought the same basic housewares, so that everything in the village hut appeared also in the villa and the palace, the only difference being the quality of workmanship. (In the nineteenth-century West the rich man, the middle class, the laborer, the peasant bought altogether different objects to live with, designed in terms of a machine's limitations at different cost levels; the designs changed as the machines changed, and the West was becoming used to seasonal fashions that did not try to please sensibilities generation after generation. The difference was profound.)

But an even greater cultural sharing by rich and poor in the Middle East, rulers and ruled, was the limit imposed by the desert on the exploitation of the environment. Without machines the environment had to be lived with, accommodated to. It could not be overcome. The whole Ottoman Empire lived at the pace of camel, donkey, and ox, no matter who one was, long after the West had shifted to the railroad, telegraph, and steamship.

Every village had a headman, generally granted the title of sheikh, who was picked by agreement as the most reliable spokesman for dealing with higher authorities. Never an inherited position, it carried vaguely defined powers and duties, such as adjudicating feuds, family disputes, and legal squabbles that otherwise would have to be taken to court in town. When cooperative effort was needed the sheikh made the decisions, as at planting and harvest times and during natural catastrophes. He counseled and persuaded on all sorts of things, including marketing and irrigation; probably he knew how to read a bit. But he was especially respected for his pacifying talents, sense of justice, wisdom, shrewdness, toughness — not always in that order. Above all the villagers trusted him to be absolutely loyal to them against the greedy world.

Thus, an important part of his job was to flatter and fawn on landowners and district governors in the ways they expected a village sheikh to fawn, while he pursued secret plots, aided by the whole village, to bamboozle, fool, cheat, and wrest whatever profit was possible from any confrontation whatever. Those bovine faces stared as if incomprehensibly at shouting officials, at the hate-filled gluttonous face of a landlord, at the cruel faces of soldiers, who were children of their own kind conscripted and trained to use a whip on them.

In the larger villages one other resident had formal authority, as a member of the rural police force. His duty was to protect property against thieves, bandits, or madmen, organize firefighting or flood rescues, stop fistfights: in other words to help the sheikh. But his real job

*Perhaps the most important task for Egyptian farmers'
daughters and wives, while the men toiled in the fields
and on the irrigation ditches, was to carry water from
the Nile to their homes. Washing clothes and scrubbing
the family donkey were less important chores. The pleasure
of it all in that climate was the daily dip. The usual
splash and shriek is missing from this photograph because
the photographer had to persuade the bathers to hold
still while he took their picture. As anywhere in the world
before plumbing brought water into the house, women
exchanged vital gossip at the well, fountain, river, or lake.*

Gaston Braun, 1869.

was to provide the tax collector with confidential information and carry out the wishes of the landowners. This policeman tended to be a busybody, a bully, or a lazy oaf, his hand perpetually held out for baksheesh, partly because his bosses stayed in town miles away and partly because only certain types of villagers would volunteer to be trained for the job. He carried an old gun of sorts, wore some kind of uniform or insignia, reported whatever was happening to headquarters, and occasionally bit his master's hand by informing the sheikh. He was always a figure of fun in folk stories, a buffoon, someone to torment.

It is hard to generalize, however, on the structure of village government because so much of it was influenced by the whim, greed, or indifference of governors and their appointees, and the landlords bribing them. The peasant had no recourse anywhere.

Nor did the desert relent, burning steadily at the end of all the little ditches. And above every village hung a cloud of dust in which circled the scavenger hawks and, higher, the mighty vultures planing in off the desert for a look.

Every villager knew when every baby was born. Weddings were big, several days of feasting and dancing. Funerals were quick: death, wake, procession, wailing, and burial all in twenty-four hours. Seasonal celebrations, holidays of forgotten origin, ceremonies left over from pagan times, interrupted the year liberally, and every village had its own remembrances that demanded exultation a few times a year. Under a full moon a parade might form and, ululating, chanting, clay drums throb-

Any view of a palm-shaded village on the Nile illustrates the simple fact that the river and the desert ignore one another and need the peasant's brain and hand for a fruitful marriage between them.

John B. Greene, 1854.

The photographer Bonfils titled this picture "Femmes de Siloé Palestine" (Women of Siloam, Palestine). On the back of the print, the tourist who purchased it wrote: "2 Moslem peasant women. Dark blue robes, bound round waist by girdle, white veils — Note coins on head-dress of woman on right — her dowry carried in this safe way. The round baskets contain farm produce of all kinds, carried thus long distances from the villages to the Jerusalem market, — often a great weight. Peasant women noted for upright & graceful bearing. Note: Moslem peasant women go unveiled: only Moslem townswomen veil —"

Bonfils, after 1867.

bing, wind out to the cemetery to chase away the evil spirits. Incantation linked the living with the dead in defiance of the Koran's admonition against pagan rituals.

As for the oasis village, the solitude of the desert wrapped it far, far, away from the friendly congregation of villages around a market town. But the oasis had its own enchantment, at the heart of which were pure air and silence, and the greater miracle of green crops and palm trees, as on an island in the yellow sands. The same tools were used as in the river- and rain-watered lands but the camel was far more important. The inhabitants, sometimes a single family, had to be expertly self-reliant, not only because of their isolation but because wells on occasion dried up and sometimes sandstorms covered the farm. Memories of such tragedies ennobled rather than brutalized the spirit of the oasis dweller, who, in a way, had to share the bedouin's love for the desert or else flee to the rivers to save his sanity.

Stereographs:
Mass Media Entertainment and Education

. . . Most of us have been enabled by the labours of [David] Roberts and other painters to realize with some approach to accuracy what the great Egyptian monuments are like; but the revelations of [Charles] Wheatstone's marvellous invention [the stereoscope], applied to this subject, carry us far beyond anything that it is in the power of the most accomplished artist to transfer to his canvas. You look through your stereoscope, and straightway you stand beside the fabled Nile, watching the crocodile asleep upon its sandy shore, with the superb ruins of Philae in the distance. The scene changes, and you are in the Desert. . . . In an hour the schoolboy will learn more from these views than it was possible, ten short years ago, for the most learned man to know who had not traversed the scenes depicted. It is the education of the eye in the most striking and effective sense which is thus practised, for nothing is omitted in these sun-painted revelations, and the simplest intellect is at once filled with a new light, whereby to measure the past with the present, to feel that if we are great in our works so have been the generations of men who lived, and the forms of civilization which flourished before authentic history began. How strange it is that . . . a boy in this 19th century, gazing at a small double picture of Egyptian ruins in a curiously constructed box, will know how to think with due humility of the works which the Pharaohs and Ptolemies left behind them!

—THE TIMES (*London*)
January 1, 1858

The set of one hundred stereoscopic views referred to above was made by Francis Frith on his travels to Egypt and Nubia in 1856 and 1857 and published upon his return to England by the firm of Negretti and Zambra. This group of views, because of its early date and subject matter, is probably the most renowned in the history of stereography.

Westerners in the late nineteenth and early twentieth centuries saw the Middle East through the stereoscope more often than in any other way. It was the "optical wonder of the age," as television is of ours. Stereo-cards of faraway places, news events, daredevil exploits, funny tales, famous buildings, exotic people, arts and crafts were all for sale and considered valuable educational entertainment. One of the most popular subjects of all was the Holy Land.

A stereoscopic camera made two separate pictures at the same instant through two lenses separated by the distance between human eyes. When the two images, mounted on stiff cardboard, were viewed through the optical arrangement of lenses called a stereoscope, the pair of two-dimensional pictures was transformed into a single three-dimensional illusion. With a stereoscope in the corner and a box of slides, the parlor became, for a while, the most exotic of places and the viewer a world traveler.

By the 1860s many photographers had taken their binocular cameras into the desert. Even the British War Department published 150 views of nomad life and topographical studies. More than seventy-five photographers issued stereoscopic views of the Holy Land before 1900. Most, however, traveled the same routes—the safe routes—and focused on similar subjects.

One William E. James, an entrepreneur, had the idea in 1866 that stereo-cards would make excellent teaching aids in Sunday schools. The cards themselves could be manufactured inexpensively and so could the viewers (modeled on Oliver Wendell Holmes's 1861 design). Each student in class could hold a stereoscope and gaze at Bethlehem while listening to the teacher talk about the infant Jesus.

The number of titles on the same theme that a photog-

Type.—Arab Dancing Girl, Upper Egypt.
Copyright 1896, by Underwood & Underwood.

A dancing girl of Upper Egypt.

Underwood & Underwood, 1896.

rapher issued with his name could range from 150 to 650. Of course, some photographers had never set foot in the Holy Land. They dressed up actors to portray characters in the Bible, copied passages from the Bible, and made reproductions of religious paintings.

Stereo-views were produced continuously from 1851 to 1940. Although the format remained the same, the method of marketing them changed, and subsequently the demand changed. In 1879 Ben Kilburn started selling door-to-door, and Underwood & Underwood soon followed. The latter firm by 1901 was printing 25,000 cards a day. And it was not alone in manufacturing cards in these numbers. Keystone View Company, H. C. White and Co., Kilburn Brothers, and the London Stereoscopic Company were all hugely successful. One marketing device was the issuance of "boxed sets," particularly appropriate to the Middle East. A boxed set of cards looked like a book from the outside, but inside was a pamphlet written by an authority, perhaps a clergyman, and enough stereoscopic views to tell a complete story or to satisfy the viewer that he had had a thorough tour of the country. Card collecting was a popular pastime, and even Sears, Roebuck and Company offered a 200-card series of the "Holy Land" (also called "Palestine").

Stereoscopic cameras had shorter exposure times than large-plate cameras, and the pictures made with them often seem more spontaneous. Bert Underwood's pictures of 1896, for example, show Middle Easterners eating, working, walking down the street. These and many done by others give a rare glimpse of life in the Ottoman Empire. They were documentary studies to show the folks back home: a sword maker in Damascus, a silk weaver in Beirut, a Maronite priest in Jerusalem, a bedouin family in Palestine, a marketplace in Jaffa, a dancing girl in Upper Egypt, or a carpet maker in Persia. The stereo-views of the early twentieth century are wonderfully direct, but the long captions on the backs of the cards were usually pretentious. Perhaps this was because stereoscopic photographers, working for the big publishing houses, were on a tight schedule. They had to do everything quickly. They had no time to stage events, pose people, hire models. Neither did they have time to evaluate the subject matter and develop a strong point of view. They had their instructions about which antiquities to shoot, tradesmen to find, and shrines to record. Captions were written, either by the photographer or someone else, in a more contemplative mood afterward.

7 THE TOWNS

In Persia the usual order of shopping is reversed: you buy not when you stand in need, but when the merchants choose to come to you. Moreover, the process is very deliberative, and a single bargain may stretch out over months. The counters are the backs of mules, which animals are driven into your garden whenever their owners happen to be passing by. As you sit under the shadow of your plane-trees you become conscious of bowing figures before you, leading laden mules by the bridle; you signify to them that they may spread out their goods, and presently your garden-paths are covered with crisp Persian silks and pieces of minute stitching, with Turkoman tent-hangings, embroideries from Bokhara, and carpets from Yezd and Kerman, and the sunlight flickers down through the plane-leaves into the extemporary shop. There is a personal note about these charming materials which lends them an interest other than that which could be claimed by bright colour and soft textures alone. They speak of individual labour and individual taste. Those tiny squares of Persian work have formed part of a woman's dress — in some andarun, years of a woman's life were spent stitching the close intricate pattern in blended colours from corner to corner; those strips of linen on which the design of red flowers and green leaves is not quite completed, come from the fingers of a girl of Bokhara, who, when she married, threw aside her embroidery-needle and left her fancy work thus unfinished.

—GERTRUDE BELL,
Persian Pictures (1894)

THE BASIC DIFFERENCE between the towns and the villages was that any village could be self-supporting in every way, whereas no town could survive without its cluster of villages and without its ties to the big cities, ties maintained by caravans. In the villages everyone could do everyone else's work and all the tools could be made for household, barn, and field. But the towns were

Lunch break for the donkey-taxi and its young Egyptian drivers. The donkey, more than any other animal, shared the everyday life of people in the Middle East.

Anonymous, before 1877.

inhabited by specialists, professionals, and bureaucrats. If war destroyed a region, the ruined town was abandoned, while the peasants all by themselves rebuilt their villages and irrigation systems and were harvesting crops again, perhaps only a few years later. The town came back to life totally dependent on the vigor and ingenuity of the villagers — who were then once again squeezed as hard as possible by the townspeople with rents and taxes, loans and control of wholesale prices. The town markets, the only place where the peasants could sell, were run by a network of landlords who chose to hoard or distribute the harvests as they saw fit.

Unlike the villages, every town was individual and had a history. It could be that of a seaport like Jaffa, Smyrna,

Before 2000 B.C. a Hittite town called Halap (present-day Aleppo) appeared on the hill rising above the Syrian plain about sixty miles inland from the Mediterranean. Egyptian, Persian, Roman, Byzantine, Arab, Mongol, Mameluke, Turkish, and French armies conquered Aleppo, at times destroying it, at other times turning it into the most important trading center in the Middle East, with miles of covered bazaar. The forbidding walls were built in the thirteenth century under the reign of es-Zahir Ghazi, the son of Saladin, who liberated Jerusalem from the Crusaders. The citadel and entrance are shown here.

D. D. Luckenbill or assistant, 1908-1909.

The bazaar of Riyadh, capital of Nejd (now of Saudi Arabia), received its vegetables and fruit from the oasis whose date palms are visible just beyond the walls. (Detail.)

W. H. I. Shakespear, 1914.

The ancient city of Emesa near the Orontes River in Syria had a temple to the sun-god Elagabal. The town was named Hims or Homs when it was seized by the Arabs. Crusaders built the fortress of Krak des Chevaliers nearby, visible here rising above the sun-dried brick houses. As in every town and village, the habitations are packed tightly together so that as little arable land as possible is used for building.

Bonfils, after 1867.

The town of Qum or Qom in Persia has been a place of pilgrimage for Shiite Muslims for hundreds of years, because of the shrine to Fatima, sister of the ninth-century imam Riza. This shows the shrine's dome and minarets. Ten kings and several hundred saints are buried around Qom.

Sevruguin, after 1880.

Basra, a caravan crossroads like Aleppo, a garrison town or seat of provincial government like Riyadh, a holy place like Medina or Qom, the heart of a large oasis like Mersa Matruh, or a manufacturing center, like Shiraz with its carpets. It could be famous for its melons, or flower gardens, or balmy winters, or the fighting spirit of its men, or the loose morals or the chastity of its women, or because it was the abode of an oracle, or supported an ancient university. It could have been built by Crusaders as a fort, like Krak des Chevaliers. Sometimes a town was a wasted capital of a former nation, like Baghdad for centuries after the Mongol invasion, or world-famous for long-vanished culture, like Alexandria, which had shriveled to a fishing village before Mohammed Ali began to

The farmers' market in Jaffa, as everywhere else, was in an open square, the draft animals being separated from the fruit and vegetable stalls. The number of hucksters varied with the day of the week. The covered permanent bazaar can also be seen here.

Bonfils, after 1867.

Jaffa, ancient seaport and fortress in Palestine, boasted this narrow-gauge track for a traveling crane to unload lighters from steamships and sailing ships. (Today Jaffa is part of Tel Aviv.) (Detail.)

C. [G.] Krikorian, 1892.

rebuild it, or Antioch, which had led the early Christian movement. But no Ottoman or Persian town in the early nineteenth century had fine shops, luxurious homes, good hotels, elegant cafés and restaurants, beautiful dancing girls, a lively nightlife. In no way were towns small cities. Whatever their history, they shared the sort of atmosphere that was familiar in the provincial towns of Europe as well—insular, lethargic, dreaming of cities, fawning on visitors who were contemptuous of the fawners, although cities could not have existed without them. Arabic literature is full of confrontations between city people, townfolk, and villagers, sometimes one winning, sometimes another, and the same joke fits any region.

The town bazaar supported not just the merchants and their servants, salesmen and clerks, but also officialdom, the military garrison, the gendarmes, a few lawyers, a judge or two, schoolteachers, perhaps even a poet, as well as all the artisans, porters, drovers, and laborers. There were a caravansary, a third-class hotel and its restaurant, and a few small coffeeshops and eating places that served the lower classes, as Europeans called them, some of whom slept in the streets or nooks of walls. From before dawn till deep into the night the farmers came and went with donkey carts, and caravans ambled in and out of the desert. Everything was priced on two levels of economy: one used currency related to the outside world; the other used fractions of the smallest coins but depended chiefly on bartering with eggs, chickens, melons,

Samarra was rebuilt on the Tigris in 836 by the Abbasid Caliph Al-Mutasim who fled from Baghdad and made Samarra the capital of Mesopotamia for about forty years. It stands on a prehistoric settlement where Chinese pottery has been found, proving that it was a trading center. An Arab legend tells of a Baghdad servant who said to his master, "I saw Death in the bazaar and he beckoned to me. You must help me escape." The master gave him money and a horse and the servant rode like the wind to Samarra, where he hoped to hide. In the bazaar he met Death, who said, "I have been waiting for you." The ruins in the foreground are those of Al Malwiyah (see page 26).

Gertrude Bell, ca. 1910.

goats, bales of hay, cucumbers, for footwear and clothing, pots, implements, harness, trinkets, pretty things for holidays, sweetmeats.

Any town was a maze of ancient and new stone walls woven together to create twisting alleys, dead ends, and courtyards with massive gates. Fruit trees nodded above them; palms and shade trees shadowed the main street. Small workshops were everywhere: a weaver at his loom, boys pounding out copper trays, a cabinetmaker cutting inlay, a potter and his wheel. Goats clattered on cobbles and on tops of walls and even roofs in search of food, bleating to each other. Donkeys tied everywhere munched meager rations and split the air with their brays. Most households kept a few hens, doves, dogs, and even a cow.

Tiberias on the Sea of Galilee, one of the four holy cities of Judaism, has been a center of Hebraic scholarship since it was built early in the first century A.D. by Herod Antipas. The most widely accepted Hebrew text of the Bible was worked out there. Like all the cities close to the Mediterranean, Tiberias became Byzantine after Rome declined, the Arabs captured it, it was occupied by Crusaders, and then the Arabs recaptured it. The great Jewish philosopher Maimonides is supposed to have been buried here.

Bonfils, after 1867.

One translation of Bethlehem, a farming center in Palestine reaching back into antiquity, is "House of Bread"; another is "House of Meat." The lives and deaths of Rachel, Ruth, David, and Benjamin were linked to Bethlehem; it was believed by some that the Messiah, a descendent of David, would some day reveal himself there. The Emperor Hadrian, in A.D. 135, planted trees over the supposed site of the manger where Jesus was born, and dedicated it to pagan Apollo, to combat the spread of Christianity. In 333 the Church of the Nativity was completed over the same site by Constantine the Great and his mother Helena. It is invisible here in the center of the town. St. Jerome finished writing the Vulgate translation of the Bible in Bethlehem.

Francis Frith, 1857–1858.

Tripoli, a seaport in modern Lebanon, was founded in the
seventh century B.C. Later it became the capital of a
Phoenician federation of three cities (hence the name),
and thereafter it was occupied by all the well-known
conquerors of the Mediterranean including the Crusaders,
who destroyed its great library. Today the pipeline from
Iraq ends here. In 1859–1860 Louis de Clercq took
two photographs and joined them into this panorama.
The narrow strip of beach shows how precious land was.

The nameless scrubwomen of the world have touched the
hearts of many artists. So have children running errands
for their masters. These two salted paper prints appeared
in Pierre Trémaux's book Voyage au Soudan oriental,
issued over a period of fifteen years from 1847 on.

A curious fact about bread is that it does not transmit disease. These enormous flatbreads in Persia will be handled by many unwashed hands before being eaten.

Anonymous, ca. 1890.

No one paid attention to their noise and smells, strong in the morning dew, faded under the broiling sun, and strong again at dusk, which mingled with the smoke of lime kilns at the edge of town, and the smoke of charcoal braziers, scorching meat and spices, and the fumes of pitch-soaked torches for light. All day the bazaar bustled under its variegated roof against the sun, and at night a few cooks continued to serve the restless, the celebrators, the gloomy, the travelers, the lucky and unlucky. Sometimes musicians tootled and thumped on a corner, a few modest whores idled past, or a pimp, and in a backroom a belly dancer tinkled. The Koran forbade alcohol, but in parts of the empire the law was broken openly or secretly, and hashish was always available.

Town life was a long, long step removed from the village's mingling of human, animal, and vegetable worlds, but earth gods still breathed in towns. Dancing in a square under moonlight to a clay drum was still worship of a kind, not just entertainment: the laborer's energy was as mysterious as the farmer's dancing in the fields where fertility rites roused the village instead of the baadia rhythms of the street.

The photographer titled this portrait "Femme de Cheik," that is, a sheikh's wife. Sheikh was a general title for any leader or distinguished person. She is expensively dressed and one can imagine her more the wife of a rich village sheikh — there were some — who had her own servants than of a poor bedouin one. But respectable wives would not sport such elegant décolletage, and so most likely she is a courtesan. Photographers frequently used whatever title they thought would sell their pictures best.

G. Lekegian, ca. 1880.

A falconer was often a professional who earned his keep. This Mesopotamian trainer is not dressed for bedouin tents and would have been employed by a wealthy merchant or a member of the ruling family in the town, or a prince. Falconry seems to be as old as history and, although a falcon — or any of several other trained predator birds — was just a hunting tool for killing game birds and small animals, the sport was always a privileged one.

E. J. Banks or assistant, 1903–1904.

These martial Kurds visiting Tehran from a mountain town were photographed before a makeshift backdrop.

Anonymous, 1867.

A street in Jidda. This walled city was one mile square, its four- and five-story houses built of coral blocks, with dark latticed windows overhanging the alleys. It was the the only place in Arabia where foreigners — with diplomatic missions and trading companies — were allowed to stay. The tomb of Eve was believed to be a mound a hundred meters long just outside Jidda's Medina gate. In 1927 the site was demolished by puritanical Wahabis who claimed that it generated pagan worship.

Dr. F. G. Clemow, 1906.

Kerman, in southern Persia, was built in the third century A.D. and eventually became one of the most important centers for hand-woven carpets. They have been world-famous for centuries. The dress and demeanor of this group of men in Kerman suggest that they are teachers, or members of a religious sect. (Detail.)

Major P. M. Sykes, 1901.

The people of Yezd, or Yazd, in Persia, founded in the fifth century A.D., produced a great deal of silk cloth and built many mosques, minarets, and mausoleums. This lineup of men represents the police of Yezd. (Detail.)

Anonymous, 1916.

A note on the back of this photograph, taken in 1905, reads: "There are no regular jails in Seistan [a former province of Persia]. Prisoners are chained in irons, one end of the chain which passes round their neck being fastened to a nail in the ground. They cannot move about but once only in the evening they are taken under proper custody to the town to beg their food & are brought & confined to their cellar. Their term of imprisonment is indefinite. Those who have no money to condone their offence are imprisoned for life."

N. Ganga Singh, 1905.

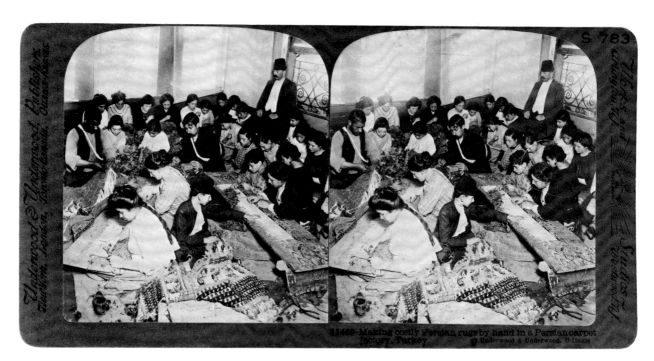

Rug weaving in Turkey, as everywhere, was done by
men, women, and children in workshops run by a master
craftsman. Stereographs showing Middle Eastern crafts
were popular in Europe and America.

Underwood & Underwood, 1914.

Although the nursing madonna was a well-known theme
in Renaissance art, Westerners generally were shocked
by breast-feeding in public. This photograph was probably
made in Egypt.

Auguste-Rosalie Bisson, 1869.

Dancers and musicians posed for this photograph in Persia.

Anonymous, ca. 1900.

Studio Photographers

The work of photographers who operated commercial studios in the Middle East during the nineteenth century was mostly of ancient Egyptian and Biblical architecture, romantic genre studies of so-called Oriental types (probably paid models), and posed street scenes. The prints were sold in the photographers' shops and in hotels. A town rarely had a studio, and a city might claim only two or three. Guidebooks listed them and noted which were best.

Photographers in the Ottoman Empire were almost exclusively non-Muslim. Most came from Europe; a few were Levantines. By background they were far better suited for the profession than any Sunni Muslim, whose religion forbade pictorial representation of God's creatures, including human beings. Levantines and foreigners were also financially better able to learn the trade, buy the equipment, and set up studios; their own

kind, as well as some rich Muslims, provided the market. But in Persia, where painting flourished because Shiites did not believe that images were sacrilegious, some native photographers seem to have made a living, though even there the market was restricted to the rich, a tiny minority.

Tourists did not start carrying cameras until the late 1880s, so for several decades they were the big market for photographs of professional quality. Painters at home in the West wanted them, too. Abdullah Frères, Arnoux, Béchard, Beato, Berggren, Bonfils, Dumas, Hammerschmidt, Lekegian, Sébah, and Zangaki were all known as reliable cameramen. Working in the second half of the

This montage, made from six negatives, purports to show an encampment of pilgrims on the shores of the Jordan River.

Bonfils, after 1867.

nineteenth century, they used either exclusively or at one time the wet-collodion process. Their equipment was a large plate camera, a tripod, a darkroom or dark tent in which they could sensitize glass plates before exposure and develop them immediately after, and many bottles and jars of chemicals and distilled water. Even under the blazing sun exposures took at least a minute and candid pictures could rarely be made.

Bonfils was best at creating a feeling of spontaneity in his views of marketplaces, Biblical subjects, cities and towns. La Maison Bonfils (Félix Bonfils, his wife, Marie Lydie Cabannis, and his son Adrien all photographed) also produced dramatic studio portraits, creating an extensive inventory of "native types." And at times they combined negatives to make a montage that purported to be a real scene but was actually a fantasy.

H. Béchard and Antonio Beato were fine architectural photographers who show columns soaring to the sky and make the viewer feel the power of the gods for whom the temples were dedicated. Beato lived in Luxor beside the ruins of Karnak and knew intimately every carving and massive statue. Béchard made sensitive, though posed, portraits of water-carriers, on whose labor everything in the Middle East depended.

The signature that appears at the bottom of commercial prints does not always identify the photographer. J. Pascal Sébah and Béchard apparently exchanged or sold each other negatives, scratched out the other's name, and wrote in their own. Both men staged scenes ostensibly portraying everyday life in Egypt in the 1870s and 1880s. Often their aim, however, was to please tourists by producing genre scenes fitting the Westerners' conception of the Orient. One finds in this work the same model dressed as a sheikh and a pilgrim, the same woman identified as a Lebanese Christian and a Turkish dancing girl. Generally the signature does identify the photographer and the caption is correct. But given that there is a problem of attribution and of correct captioning, a critical analysis of much of the work of these photographers is problematic.

Two commercial photographers working in partnership who did develop a personal style were the Armenian brothers Abdullah Biraderler. Converts to Islam, they were court photographers to Sultan Abdul Hamid II, who commissioned them to make a record of the social, educational, and military innovations he had launched at the end of the nineteenth century to modernize the Ottoman Empire. Anxious to arouse sympathy and support in the West for his plan, and as proof that the plan was working, he had the Abdullah Frères photograph school children, sometimes in Western suits, firemen in their Austro-Hungarian uniforms, officers and soldiers in their notion of up-to-date military trappings handling the latest hardware of war from swords to cannons, medical students with their cadavers, and nondescript new buildings. The stances and expressions that the brothers caught were striking proof of the revolution these people were going through; the lack of gesture and the disciplined bodies focus one's gaze upon the faces, which look back with calm, confident self-awareness of their role in the empire. Some of these portraits are the best of the period.

There are many questions concerning studio photographers in the Middle East in the nineteenth century. One of the most challenging is their relationship to local communities, given the religious strictures. We have portraits of distinguished Muslims, but because often they are not identified, we group them with genre studies. We know, too, that the Ottoman and Persian courts had official and semiofficial photographers with definite responsibilities. One of these was to photograph heads of state, high officials, visiting diplomats, court functions, palace ceremonies, and nationally important events. The court photographers were both native and foreign, Muslim and non-Muslim. One of the shahs, Nasr ud-Din, who ruled from 1848 to 1896, bought his own camera on a European trip, encouraged others to use cameras, and collected 20,000 pictures of all aspects of Persian life, his court, royal families, and European pornography.

Most of the people in the Middle East before World War I were peasants too poor to visit a studio, regardless of tradition. After the war, incomes rose, the tradition faded, Western influence became greater, and wedding, baby, engagement, and commemorative photographs started to become popular. The few Muslims who were now setting up shop had their own ideas about hand-coloring and composition and by the 1920s new images of the Middle East were evolving from an entirely different point of view and for very different purposes. Middle Easterners wanted records of their own lives made by individuals who valued and shared their customs. And they wanted the pictures to be dignified and beautiful according to their, not European, standards.

8 THE CITIES

Egypt has long been celebrated for its public dancing-girls; the most famous of whom are of a distinct tribe, called "Ghawazee". . . . [They] perform, unveiled, in the public streets, even to amuse the rabble. . . . They commence with a degree of decorum; but soon, by more animated looks, by a more rapid collision of their castanets of brass, and by increased energy in every motion, they exhibit a spectacle exactly agreeing with the descriptions . . . of the female dancers of Gades. The dress . . . is similar to that which is worn by women of the middle classes in Egypt in private; that is, in the hareem; consisting of . . . handsome materials. They also wear various ornaments: their eyes are bordered with the kohl; . . and the tips of their fingers, the palms of their hands, and their toes and other parts of their feet, are usually stained with the red dye of the henna. . . . In general, they are accompanied by musicians. . . . They are never admitted into a respectable hareem; but are not unfrequently hired to entertain a party of men in the house of some rake. In this case, as might be expected, their performances are yet more lascivious than those which I have already mentioned. . . . To extinguish the least spark of modesty which they may yet sometimes affect to retain, they are plentifully supplied with brandy or some other intoxicating liquor. The scenes which ensue cannot be described. . . . Many of them are extremely handsome; and most of them are richly dressed. Upon the whole, I think they are the finest women in Egypt. . . . In general they deck themselves with a profusion of ornaments, as necklaces, bracelets, anklets, a row of gold coins over the forehead, and sometimes a nose-ring.

—EDWARD WILLIAM LANE,
An Account of the Manners and Customs of the
Modern Egyptians (1842)

A courtyard in Cairo illustrates the general air of seediness for which Middle East cities were known in the West. Stone and wood deteriorated so slowly in the dry climate that there was no need to hurry repairs. But there was also the more important fact that Ottoman tax collectors were attracted by ostentation and extensive areas of fresh plaster and new brick.

H. Béchard, before 1878.

THE CARAVAN DISTANCES connecting Constantinople, Beirut, Cairo, Alexandria, Damascus, Baghdad, Mecca, and Jerusalem have been mentioned. Eight cities. In that enormous territory larger than the United States, three thousand miles from the tip of the Sudan to the tip of Persia and three thousand miles from the Bosporus to Aden, only eight cities. Few had a population much over half a million, and only Constantinople and Cairo were intimate with the West and its ways. These figures suggest how sparse was the urban population and

A fountain in a private courtyard somewhere in Turkey that was not built in Islamic style. Perhaps it was ordered by a Greek or Italian resident.

Anonymous, before 1877.

how tightly it was tied to the scattered islands of fertility in the sweep of deserts. A few more cities would have to be added to a contemporary list: Tehran, Riyadh, Ankara, Jidda, Al-Kuwait, Amman, each of which has become a center for a national bureaucracy, for education, and for electronic and air communication with the rest of the world.

A city in the Middle East was, like cities anywhere, rich with a variety of occupations and opportunities, social resources, religious, educational, financial, judiciary and artistic institutions, shopping, sports, amusements, theater, international nightlife, first-class hotels and restaurants, large congregations of foreigners, diplomatic representations, a flow of tourists, manufacturing, trade, communications; rich in the sophistication that allows private freedoms forbidden in the countryside.

And most of all, it had implacable power of all sorts over the towns and villages that supported it and were protected by it. Caravans were put together and were profitable because they served cities.

History is about the birth, growth, decay, and death of cities, not of towns and villages. And each city preserved relics of its long-ago glories and defeats so that streets, palaces, mosques, bazaars echoed that past within the ring of its own unchanging farmlands and the desert beyond. All the cities, unlike the towns, harbored a polyglot population segregated by religion, race, and traditions. An apprentice artisan memorized his craft and transmitted it to his apprentices when he became a master. Storytelling in coffee shops was a profession, too, highly prized, and storytellers trained fledglings to memorize the repertoire. Even servants learned their tasks from one another. There was no other school for the vast majority. Book learning belonged to those who in the West would have been part of the bourgeoisie but in the Ottoman Empire or Persia were simply rich, small in numbers. A few of their children studied to be doctors, lawyers, architects, engineers, or bankers, according to traditions centuries old.

The conqueror of a city in the past had a choice: accept the iron-clad traditions or destroy everything. Some chose the holocaust and on the ruins, or nearby, built a new city, bigger and better. But the ghosts insinuated themselves into the new culture. In Europe, the ghosts of pagan, feudal, medieval, Renaissance, and Age of Reason times were laid to rest by the scientific and technological revolution that began in the eighteenth century. In the Middle East the machines did not drive them out until after World War I. There were no factories spewing soot and waste, no related businesses, warehouses, transportation, communications, special housing, special schools for laborers and clerks. No traffic was geared to the clock. No segregated suburbs existed for the affluent.

The commonplace architectural sight everywhere was the random cementing together of ancient, medieval, and contemporary structures; ruins were picked apart and the bits reused century after century. Even as concrete and fired brick came into use, antique stone walls were not bulldozed until after World War II.

Western books were not translated into Arabic until well into the nineteenth century and then only in a trickle,

A Byzantine tower looks down on a Turkish cemetery near Constantinople.

Francis Bedford, 1862.

which says a great deal about how efficiently tradition preserved itself — without readers. It did not oppress the hearts and minds of those who believed in it and knew nothing else, and the exuberance of swiftly changing times, to which industrialization was adapting the West, was unimaginable in the Middle East.

There, the main sources of income were farming with near Stone Age techniques, hand craftsmanship with technologies as old as Egypt, commerce with primitive methods of finance and transportation, government bureaucracy, the military, and domestic servitude. Islamic universities taught law, philosophy, history, and diplo-

macy. That is why Europeans with professional competence were employed in the Ottoman Empire in key positions. It was also part of a tradition begun by the Arabs of hiring non-Muslims for certain kinds of office. Thus for most of the people the machine was merely an exotic and not very interesting object, a plaything for plutocrats and a gamble for governments. It could not be fitted to the

The contrast between the blaze of sunlight and the inky shadows on a street in the Cairo bazaar no doubt gave the photographer considerable trouble in judging his exposure time.

H. Béchard, ca. 1870–1880.

traditional technology based on muscle, for it did not aid human beings but replaced them without creating a modern community into which they could have moved. (Even in the 1930s, one spark plug cost many days' wages.)

And it was in this milieu, lingering until World War II in the countries carved out of the empire, that all the leaders who now confront the West were born.

Farmers prodding water buffaloes, herding goats and sheep, trundling pushcarts piled with apricots and trussed chickens, had the right of way in the city over carriages. Caravans filled the streets that led to the main gates of the city (even as late as the 1930s). The camels plodded under their swaying, creaking loads while their diminutive drivers, hawk-faced, famished-looking, dan-

gerous as drawn daggers, padded barefooted alongside, tapping the necks of their beasts with little sticks and talking to them. A rag for a turban, a smock their only covering. Men and camels seemed to carry in every movement a knowledge of the ends of earth. On the safe, tree-lined avenues all the deserts could be seen in the camel's large liquid brown and beautiful eyes fringed with double thick sweeping lashes, imperious, utterly indifferent to the inhabitants in their sumptuous homes and hovels. He had been stepping steadily from Isfahan to

Carpets have had far more significance and uses in the Middle East than in the West; they were handed down from generation to generation. These Cairo merchants are as serious as bankers.

Anonymous, no date.

Cairo, perhaps, balancing crates and sacks, pilgrims and nabobs, on his back, past temples buried in the sand, for a month or two since the last city where he was loaded. In the old city, always in the oldest quarter, the train snaked about to park in squares at the confluence of alleys and, suddenly groaning and burbling, the drivers shouting, the camels lunged to their knees on ground redolent of uncountable other caravans.

Every city's hub, its raison d'être, its heart, was the bazaar, sukh, or musky, which was far, far more than a shopping center. The first thing a traveler noticed in the bazaar was the smells: smoldering charcoal, spices, perfumes, leather, metal, sawdust, raw meat, fruits, incense, candy, vinegar, oils, coffee, tobacco. The shops were an integral part of a magnificent human endeavor from the

planting of seeds to holy wars, from citadels to the shape of a water jug, from caravans to thousand-year-old irrigation systems, from jewels to the muezzin's cry.

The guilds organized everything. Coppersmiths, slipper makers, potters, weavers, tailors, and so on, all had their own quarters. Shops were shallow caves in walls with doors folded back; stock was crammed on shelves, hung from above, piled on mats; an apprentice or two hammered or stitched while the owner met customers. Not all the shops were owned by craftsmen, but

Eight porters carry a drum of rope through the bazaar in Cairo, their dress and headpieces declaring their trade. The sign above them advertises English provisions.

G. Berggren, 1860s–1870s.

The workshop — this is a weaver's in Cairo — was often apart from the shop that sold the goods.

Anonymous, 1860s.

all had to obey guild regulations backed by laws and tradition. In this medieval system for marketing hand-produced goods, all the merchants had connections in cities other than their own. The sources of raw materials, the training for a master's ticket that kept journeymen moving about, and the urge to gamble developed an international outlook. Because rivals in each quarter watched each other, habitual dishonesty, steady smuggling, or profiteering was impossible; but clever manipulations or lucky deals were common, as were disasters and bankruptcy. It was possible for a merchant who cut corners and was not interested in having many friends to become wealthy, sometimes very wealthy, with a string of shops from Smyrna to Baghdad.

Peasants and pashas, their wives and servants, came to the bazaar to bargain for everything they needed, most importantly for food every day. Bargaining was necessary because the quality of goods varied with each slipper, and coffeepot, even when made by the same craftsman. But there were other reasons. Bookkeeping was minimal: cash flow, amortization, investment in stock, interest on debts, taxes, and all the other vital considerations of modern business methods were ignored. Each sale was pregnant with possibilities for a seller's or buyer's deal: yesterday's poor showing could be balanced out today with tougher haggling, yet a customer should be charged according to his or her means — why make a poor woman pay as much as the rich? After the price was agreed on, a tip had to be added for a number of subtle reasons: for example, as a token of esteem and a promise to return, as recognition that the bargain was fair, and so on. It could also be a slight, either way, by the buyer or the seller. In any case, bargaining was always interesting and often memorable.

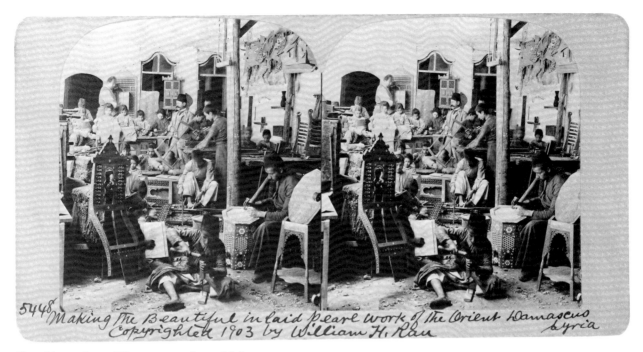

5448 *Making The Beautiful inlaid Pearl Work of the Orient Damascus Syria*
Copyrighted 1903 by William H. Rau

The cabinetmakers of Damascus made world-famous furniture inlaid with mother-of-pearl and metals. Girls as well as boys were apprenticed.

William H. Rau, 1903.

The picture of two swordmakers in Damascus was a popular stereograph for Underwood & Underwood, 1900.

A Sword-maker of Damascus, whose swords were once considered the finest in the world, Syria. Copyright 1900 by Underwood & Underwood.

Bazaar alleys could be roofed with fabric or palm fronds or they could be under a vaulted stone colonnade. Shafts of sunlight lit the displays and moved as the earth rolled under the sun. The trampled dirt or the cobbles were sprinkled several times a day to keep down dust. Coffee shops, seating half a dozen on stools, earned most of their livelihood with carry-outs: trays of little cups and little pots of coffee or tea, delivered by little boys when the merchant signaled. Bargaining for every serious purchase had to be concluded with coffee and sometimes a water pipe, called a narghile or (by Westerners) a hubble-bubble, and half a dozen other names. Pastry shops and bakeries were never far away. In general, a bazaar had more excitement for the senses and the mind than the shopping avenues of Paris or the streets of London.

Any agency that had anything to do with the life of the bazaar was there: the moneylenders and -changers, the

The interior of a house usually belied its street appearance; a courtyard like this one was not unusual in the city. It had several functions: it provided many windows away from the street's racket and dust, and cross-ventilation for all the rooms; it offered a pleasant view of trees, flowers, mosaics, and fountain; and it enabled the household to stroll in privacy and enjoy the open sky of evening. Gala affairs were held in courtyards. This one belonged to a Jewish house in Damascus. Such photographs were made to satisfy Western curiosity.

Anonymous, ca. 1870s.

government bank, bureaus that handled the movement of goods and people and money, collected taxes and rents; the police station, some of the consulates, foreign shippers, wholesalers, travel agents, messenger services, and the coffee shops patronized by porters, drovers, camel men, captains, smugglers, even hired killers.

Turkish ladies, lightly veiled, are taking the air in an ornate carriage drawn by bullocks. There is no road visible, not even tracks, the dog is either dead or fast asleep, and the attendants seem planted into the sod, as the party gazes down upon the unnamed body of water far below. The tufts swinging above the animals' necks are both decoration and fly chaser.

Anonymous, before 1877.

In lieu of newspapers, gossip was a vital part of business and daily life. Some member of every household went daily to buy food, deposit a bit of information and take away other bits that travelers of all kinds — caravan drivers, salesmen, scholars, pilgrims — carried with them not just within the empire but from as far away as China and deep Africa, although sparingly from Europe. Every shopkeeper had relatives and colleagues here and there in a dense network of communication that kept the public better informed than was the government through its official messengers, spies, and hierarchical exchange points wrapped in secrecy, lies, and red tape. The accuracy of bazaar gossip astonished Westerners even during World War II because although newspapers, radio, and telephone had become commonplace, they could be censored or tapped while the gossip never could be. (The bazaar in Alexandria had better information about the German army in the western desert than had British headquarters.)

In the second half of the nineteenth century, international trade revived and grew as the power of European representatives expanded, and secondary centers of business developed in the cities because the bazaars could not expand physically. They were patterned on the European custom of clustering offices, elegant shops, luxury hotels and restaurants, apartments, large cafés, and cab stands along the new wide avenues. The old bazaars did not suffer because the new districts catered only to the fashionable, rich, and mostly foreign trade and only in certain goods like clothing.

Just as in the towns, city life was on two mutually exclusive levels. At the top were the fabulously rich and powerful and the well-to-do, who thought in pounds, francs, dollars: in gold. The bottom class, the vast majority, thought in farthings and milliemes. An uneasy in-between class earned a respectable wage because its members knew how to read and write and speak several languages. They sent their male children to schools where they learned secretarial work and got them into clerical jobs in government and big trading firms as effendis (the Turkish word is the equivalent of *mister*; no women were employed anywhere). Mostly they were Levantines, non-Muslims who had been doing the bookkeeping, filing, and office management for the empire from its very inception. They thought in terms of gold during work, but much of their lives was spent haggling with the bottom class over pennies for food and housewares.

It was a mystery how the bottom managed, even considering the rabbit warrens where their rent was in farthings and the kind of food they bought cost fractions of farthings: a handful of fried beans, an onion, a few dates, and half of an unleavened bread was the principal meal on which a porter or pick-and-shovel laborer worked ten hours. The usual explanation by the wealthy—when a Westerner asked—was that they had been doing it for thousands of years and had discovered a magical technique for staying alive on almost nothing. They did not expect more from life than bare survival: that was all they wanted. Another explanation of why they didn't

The photographer's caption reads: "Imperial Gate of the Seraglio" in Constantinople. The seraglio was where the sultan's wives, children, divorced wives, concubines, slaves, and eunuchs lived. In that fiercely protected world, some children were raised with legitimate expectations of inheritance, others with only the ambitions of their mothers. An astonishing number of important political events, including succession to the caliphate, began with intrigue in the harem. The men in this picture seem to be merchants waiting for an invitation to show their wares to the harem women.

James Robertson, 1853.

deserve more was that they were lazy or diseased; five men were needed to accomplish what one European laborer could do alone; therefore it was all their fault. Semistarvation, schistosomiasis contracted in the irrigation ditches, malaria to which everyone in the villages was exposed, endemic trachoma from overcrowding, tuberculosis, venereal disease, cataracts, scrofula, and so on were all the result of their laziness and way of life. It was the way they wanted to live. So why pay them more?

A Turkish family photographed in the studio has the appearance of working-class people with a comfortable income.

Anonymous, before 1877.

Shoeshine boys in Cairo probably posed in exchange for the cigarettes they hold.

Edition, Photoglob.

At the same time, the quickness with which a ten-year-old apprentice learned a trade, or reading and writing if he had the chance, his industry and ambition, were recognized. The trouble was, it seemed, that in their teens something happened to these bright boys and they reverted into the general hopelessness of their class. The fact that even the most ambitious boy gradually realized that he had not a chance of getting anywhere unless he found a patron did not seem relevant to critics. They could always point to a wonderful exception: the Prophet himself had worked in caravans. In any case the idea of paying higher wages was ridiculous when so many were eager to do anything for a pittance. If they got more they would only squander it. (The same argument was used in Europe and America throughout the nineteenth century, not just by employers but by preachers in Sunday sermons, angrily denouncing the clamor of the factory workers for more than bare survival wages.)

But the true details of survival in the Middle East were the same as anywhere else. The man who was paid in pennies went home to starving children and the memory of several others he had already buried, an invalid wife, a demented relative no one else would look after, and perhaps an orphan or two willed to him by a dying cousin or brother. He moonlighted to keep his household alive until he dropped, when some relative or perhaps his young son stepped into his harness—he never owned shoes—not only in obedience to the Koran and tradition, but because there was simply nothing else to do.

Her simple dress, bare feet, and veil indicate a woman of lower class, meaning a wage-earner's wife or daughter. The metal piece on her forehead is an ornament attached to the cord that ties the veil to a headband. The naked toddler carried in this fashion was a common sight in the poor sections of the cities. The subject was a favorite of European painters who visited Egypt in the nineteenth century.

Anonymous, no date.

Mother, child, and servant or slave are posed in the photographer's studio in Constantinople for a carte-de-visite *portrait.*

B. Kargopulo, ca. 1870s.

Of all the livelihoods in the cities, that of servant supported more people than any other. It was impossible to imagine getting through a single day without servants to help. Servants themselves hired servants. The occupation was as old as the first village and as natural as father and mother. The cities drew adolescents from villages and towns to apprentice as houseboys, cooks, stable hands, gatemen, errand boys, porters, gardeners, and so on, and to learn the traditions and skills that city folk required in their servants. Men did all the housework including the laundry, ironing, polishing, dusting, marketing, cooking, rug beating and so on. Girls worked as ladies' maids and tended children, but after marriage they stayed home, usually in their village, to raise their own children, so males were often quasi-nursemaids and nannies. A servant in a good house, whether in Alexandria or Damascus, often came from a faraway district where he had a wife and children; in the city he kept another wife and batch of children, and he supported both families in equal poverty. He could manage this because

A street in Baghdad.

Underwood & Underwood, 1914.

tradition allowed him to filch 10 to 15 percent of the money he was given by his master to shop and maintain the house. The merchants all worked kickbacks with him. It was not such a bad thing to be a rich man's servant because although one could never rise above the penny-farthing system, one lived in relative comfort, wore decent clothes, was well fed, and got a few holidays.

Household slaves, not uncommon throughout the Ottoman Empire, were bought as children, raised with the owner's brood, and sometimes elevated to silent partnership in the family firm because their loyalty was absolute. Usually, however, when they came of age they claimed freedom, which the master had to grant according to Koranic law. Slave labor on farms or in construction had never been popular in the Middle East. But because of Koranic law that accepted slavery, and the tremendous importance of the Mameluke armies earlier, slavery had quite different connotations than in Christendom, where the practice was debated even when church and state made it legal. Visiting Europeans were not at all bothered by the house slavery they came in contact with.

Thus, because there was no industry, those who could not be farmers, soldiers, artisans, laborers, or clerks had of necessity to be servants. As population grew in the nineteenth century, the workshops did not increase fast enough to employ all the new applicants, and then around midcentury factory-made goods from Europe were dumped into the market, bankrupting many *ateliers*. Villages expanded irrigation systems to increase production, but the work was not enough to employ all the newborn peasants, and in Egypt the greed for cotton profits squeezed land for food to a minimum, making it harder still for the fellahin to stay alive. All over the empire agricultural workers drifted into the cities to swell unemployment. Those who found no work turned to begging. They joined gangs and became expert in extortion and protection rackets, as well as in organized begging. Professional cripple-makers broke legs and arms and set them to heal at ghastly angles, burned out eyes, disfigured faces, knocked out teeth, amputated anything.

The status of women during the early history of Islam was comparable to that in parallel cultures, and the laws continued in force in the nineteenth century. Society was patriarchal and marriages were arranged by fathers, usu-

The first impression is terrifying: the heavy silk cloth is pinned together, not held by hands, the head wears a flat crowned cap under the silk, and the flowered veil has no eyeholes. A bride sometimes danced for friends after the wedding night with her face completely veiled by a printed kerchief. The photographer seems to have assembled such a costume here.

Bonfils, after 1867.

way, including lodging, money, number of servants, clothing, and so on. Sometimes several wives chose to live in one house, sharing their days and bringing up the children together, but often the husband felt obligated to buy each wife a separate house, and sometimes he lived apart from all his wives, visiting them when he chose. Thus, polygamy was far too expensive for all but the very wealthy and the very poor. Given the perpetual threat of thieves, marauders, vendettas, feuds, raids, the constant rumors of war and riots, it was not surprising that most Muslim women could not imagine a better life than that of the harem, whether in desert tent or palace.

A husband could announce his desire for divorce without explaining why he wanted one, but he had to return the dowry. A wife could also sue for divorce but had to explain her reasons: for example, cruelty or neglect. Women could own and manage property, and they were frequently business partners of their husbands and relatives. Farmers' and artisans' wives worked side by side with their husbands, and the bedouin women shared the labor of nomadism. As anywhere in the nonindustrialized world, there were simply no jobs for women of the middle class, meaning respectable households in towns and cities. But everything Westerners learned about the harem told them that the institution ruled most mens' lives far more deeply, and often grimly, than single wives did in Europe.

On city streets everywhere women were prominent, often in small groups accompanied by servants, shopping, going to the baths, or visiting friends and relatives. (Visiting was the chief entertainment for all classes and for both men and women, but the men met in coffee shops.) Both sexes haggled passionately; bargaining was the second most common form of entertainment. Women even squabbled with cabbies, had a knack for caustic and ribald language, laughed a lot, lost their tempers, made big scenes, and in every way showed that they had strong minds and that they were used to getting their way. Women in veils — a custom that varied from quarter to quarter in every city, region to region, tribe to tribe, sect to sect — did not behave differently in public from their unveiled sisters. It was the Turks who had long ago introduced the veil, and it did not become popular everywhere in the Muslim world but depended on tribal or local tradition. Generally women who worked,

ally in agreement with their wives, for both sons and daughters. Women and children lived in the harem, a protected part of the house where only specified male relatives and friends could visit. Women were segregated in public, too, and at prayers in the mosque, which, for other purposes, was open to all.

Mohammed's original intention in the pagan world he fought against was to provide security for women and children. For example, Islamic law assures all the wives of a man (up to four, by law) equal treatment in every bedouin or peasant, tended not to be veiled. Among upper-class city women a transparent scarf drawn across half the face satisfied decorum, but in some rural parts of the empire even the rich were heavily veiled. In any case, the kohl-circled eyes, glistening and curious, coquettish or brazen, had none of the humility and fear that Europeans thought harem life instilled. A very large part of Islamic literature is concerned with errant wives who find ways to select and hold lovers, to make or break husbands, to become rich with secret schemes based on outwitting the greed and duplicity of men. One can say without equivocation that the men in the Muslim world were far more dependent on the women in their lives than were men in the Christian world, ironical as this may seem. At the same time prostitution, although forbidden by the Koran, was practiced freely in every part of the empire. Usually the women were forced to inhabit a specific quarter of the city, but sometimes streetwalkers were tolerated. Although they were considered to be a necessary part of the community, they were not accepted in society and so they lived as exiles of sorts, often embroiled with the law, and exploited by pimps and madams. Every town and city had its famous harlots who could pick and choose customers because they had become wealthy. Male prostitutes were usually employed at the baths.

In the cities, as on the caravan routes, it was simple to identify anyone's profession, economic and social standing, ethnic group, religion, and place of residence by accent and idiom, wit and banter, but primarily by dress. Perhaps the most important clue was the headpiece, whether skullcap, fez or tarbush, or turban that came in many shapes, sizes, and colors; the bedouin wore kaffiyahs, kerchiefs of various sizes and colors fastened to the head with different sorts of agal (cords). A teacher of the Koran from Isfahan wore a turban utterly unlike that of a teacher from Izmir. Someone who had completed a pilgrimage to Mecca wore a green turban and had the title *hajji*, but the rest of his clothing, which would include footwear, trousers, gown, cloak, belt, identified his origins. Women were no harder to identify, although they often wore sacklike outer cloaks that covered everything. The veil, trinkets, bangles, bracelets, anklets, earrings, cap decorations, slippers, tattoos, henna on hair, hands, and feet—all added up to background. Traditions were

The caption reads "Zofia femme du Caire" (Zofia, woman of Cairo). She is posed outdoors, and her cool attitude and her dress indicate that she was a prostitute. This is a print from a paper negative and, like all such prints, tends to be somewhat fuzzy.

E. Benecke, 1853.

rigid, fashions did not change for centuries, and some aspects of dress and manners were out of Byzantium, with roots in Roman fashion. Western clothing for men began to appear in offices toward the end of the nineteenth century.

Every city had holy places for Jews, Christians, Muslims, and accommodations for pilgrims were part of the pattern of life throughout the Middle East. Close around the ancient heart of any city were the remains of walls, buttresses, and citadels, and not far were the ruins of ancestor cities, which began to draw foreign tourists early in the nineteenth century and generated new accommodations for them.

In this view of the Hagia Sophia mosque, the perspective has been deliberately dramatized to give the impression of a series of cascading waterfalls transmuted into stone columns and arches above a reflecting pool.

James Robertson, 1855.

Everywhere in the cities grew palms, jacaranda, bougainvillea, oleander, acacia, rusty pines. Parks and gardens flowered mightily to water bucketed from barrels on carts drawn by donkeys and camels. Above spread a brownish cloud of dust. In its visible updrafts circled kites, heads tilting, fierce eyes hunting for garbage. Folding narrow wings, they dove into alley or boulevard, sailed inches above the ground, to seize the booty, and then beat up and away. No one harmed these hawks that cleaned the streets, competing with wild dogs and rats and, sometimes, hyenas and jackals that ventured into the outskirts or lived permanently in the cemeteries. Huge owls and bats patrolled the nights.

Everywhere the stones were relaxing from the tensions the builders had placed on them, flowing impercep-

A row of apartment houses in Cairo illustrates the crowding in Middle Eastern cities because of real estate values near water. The overhanging windows are box seats to the spectacle of street life, and they also catch the breezes. The ground floor with its barred windows was used only for storage. Entrances and exteriors were generally neglected, as the stones could weather for centuries without attention. But the air of shabbiness had a purpose: it was hard to tell a rich man's house from a poor man's, and this fact presumably discouraged thieves and tax assessors.

John B. Greene, 1853–1854.

tibly back into the sands. Elsewhere rain and snow and frost eroded cities, and they had to be constantly rebuilt. But in the Middle East the decay was a different sort.

Below — that is, north of — Cairo the Nile flows into the Mediterranean through many branches that create an enormous delta. Alexandria, built on a western branch by Alexander the Great in 332–331 B.C., became the cultural center of the Hellenistic world. A museum, a great university, and the renowned library all attracted scholars of the civilized world. It was here, about three centuries later, that Cleopatra seduced first Julius Caesar and then Mark Antony in a futile attempt to save Egypt from becoming a Roman province. About four hundred years after that, the Byzantine Empire absorbed Alexandria, where the strongest of the early Christian churches had become established. Another two centuries, and the Muslims conquered Egypt.

After the Ottoman Turks seized Egypt in 1517, Alexandria declined, and when Napoleon landed it was a fishing village. Mohammed Ali ordered a navigation canal to be dug between Alexandria and the Nile just below Cairo, encouraged world trade to use Alexandria for overland shipping to Suez, and expanded the city and its harbor; the burgeoning cotton industry completed the metamorphosis of Alexandria into a cosmopolitan city. This view of the main square shows how Western notions were imitated, with trees and street lamps and promenade, to eliminate the dark, narrow alleys of ancient cities. After it was destroyed by British bombardment in 1882, the rebuilding, under the British, continued to follow conventional European architecture and city planning. This, together with its huge Levantine and Coptic population, and the international commerce, made it the least Arabic city in the Middle East. It could not compete with the power and elegance of Cairo, but its thickly shaded villas surrounded by rioting gardens, palm trees rustling in the sea breezes, and miles of sandy beach made it a resort city as well as a shipping center.

F. Merimin, ca. 1860.

· 152 ·

Mecca's origin is unknown, but its location made it a caravan crossroads. It is about fifty miles from Jidda on the Red Sea, has few wells, little rain, and sparse vegetation, and is surrounded by the barren Sirat Mountains, seen here looming over the city. In Biblical times the city was a link on the route between Marib in the land of Saba (Sheba, now Yemen), and Petra of the Nabataeans in Syria. Under the Romans it became more important, and under Byzantium many of the inhabitants were converted to Christianity.

Jews also settled in Mecca, and since antiquity pagans had been making pilgrimages there to visit the Kaaba, a sanctuary for a Black Stone that had magical powers. The Kaaba is in the courtyard of the Great Mosque, whose colonnades and minarets are visible here. It is believed that early builders of the Kaaba, meaning House of God, or Holy House, were Abraham and Ishmael. Rebuilt several times since Mohammed, it is the small, cube-shaped edifice covered with black draperies. Embedded inside one wall is the Black Stone, worn by millions of hands touching it. Near the Kaaba among other small houses in the court is one that protects the holy well called Zam Zam, whose water is reputed to have healing powers.

Thus, when Mohammed was born in 570, many foreigners of a variety of faiths lived in Mecca. His family belonged to the Hashim clan of the Quraysh tribe, whose leading merchants controlled Mecca, but he grew up with a desert tribe. Occasionally he retired to a cave in the hills to meditate, and when he was about forty years old he had his first vision. Jerusalem appealed to him as a holy city but then he chose Mecca, elevating the Kaaba into the principal shrine of Islam, for the religious center for the annual pilgrimage of Muslims from all over the world, and the site in whose direction all prayers are said. Pilgrims were Mecca's only source of revenue in the nineteenth century. The rulers of Mecca have been descendants of Mohammed's clan, the Hashimites, with the title of sherif. The Wahabi sect, which most of the tribes in the interior joined in the eighteenth century, seized Mecca but was driven out by the Egyptian army of Mohammed Ali in 1818. Eventually the Turks regained control and in 1908 the sultan appointed Hussein ibn Ali as sherif; his sons became the kings of Jordan and Iraq after World War I. In 1924 Abdul Aziz ibn Saud, descendant of the Wahabi leader, captured Mecca.

Although non-Muslims (then or now) were not allowed to enter Mecca, a few claimed to have done so in the nineteenth century. (Detail.)

Anonymous, ca. 1900.

When King Menes united Upper and Lower Egypt,
after 3000 B.C., he built Memphis as the new capital on
the border between the two former countries. In the first
century A.D., the Romans occupied a town called Babylon
fourteen miles north of Memphis and enlarged it; and in
641 the Arab conquerors turned Babylon into a fortified
city they renamed al-Fustat. The Fatimid caliphs in 969
expanded Fustat and called the new section al-Mansuriyal,
soon renamed al-Qahirah, or Cairo. It was at Cairo that
Saladin, who had rescued the city from Crusaders, established the Ayyubid Dynasty of caliph-sultans.

In the fourteenth century Cairo was not only the
wealthiest, most powerful, most glorious city in all of the
Middle East, Europe, and Africa, it was also the cultural center of Islam. The Mamelukes were its rulers. But
plagues, ravages by the Mongols along Egypt's borders,
and conquest by the Ottoman Turks in 1517 steadily
reduced its importance, except as the center of Islamic

studies and Islamic law at Al-Azhar University.

After 1805 Mohammed Ali began to rejuvenate and
Westernize Egypt, and his successors pursued that elusive
goal, goaded by the British, who by midcentury had
established their authority. Because of the influential
legacy left by the scholars Napoleon had brought to
Cairo in 1789, French was the preferred international
language and French law was the basis of the international
courts that were established.

New sections of Cairo were built in imitation of
Baron Haussmann's Paris. Thus in and about the city
there was an amazing variety of architectural styles —
the remnants of Memphis and the pyramids, medieval
houses crammed around the old bazaar, villas and small
palaces with gardens, mosques from every age, turn-of-
the-century parks and boulevards. The Nile sweeps majes-
tically through the city, its banks lush with shade trees
and palms that spread into the streets, and flowers bloom

· 154 ·

year-round in watered plots everywhere. In this view, the citadel at the right with its delicate minarets guards the city, but the wall seems designed to hold back the desert.

In the nineteenth century, Westerners made their preparations in Cairo for travel deeper into the Middle East, and it was here that entrepreneurism most quickly developed the means to satisfy every kind of visitor, to outfit explorers, and to help archeologists and scholars. The profits from the fruits of the Nile, harvested with less effort than produce anywhere else in the Ottoman Empire, were transformed far more generously into schools, newspapers, theaters, nightclubs, even the first opera house in the Middle East, and into sumptuous pleasure barges, Shepheard's Hotel, and elegant sport clubs.

Cairo dominated the Middle East culturally, commercially, and as a handicraft manufacturing center in the nineteenth century. Day and night caravans wound through the streets. Ironically, it was not its strategic situation for international trade, or for colonial expansion into Africa, or as a military headquarters overlooking the Middle East and North Africa, that pulled Cairo into the nineteenth century long before any other Middle East city stirred. It was the lure of the nearby pyramids, the Sphinx, and the ancient monuments hundreds of miles up the Nile that more than anything else reestablished its cultural connections with the outside world.

H. Béchard, ca. 1875.

Baghdad in Mesopotamia was a small town on a bend in the Tigris River when the Abbasid Caliph al-Mansur chose it in 762 as the new capital of the Arab Empire, shifting eastward from the former seat of power, Damascus. This bend in the Tigris, close to the Euphrates, had attracted builders since prehistory, so that all around Baghdad were ruins of the ancient empires of Sumer, Akkad, Babylon, Assyria, Persia, and Rome. Now Baghdad became the glittering center of Muslim civilization and might, which reached from Spain to India.

In 1258 the Mongols destroyed Baghdad and the seat of the caliphate was moved to Cairo, and although Baghdad was rebuilt, it remained a provincial town under the Ottomans into the nineteenth century. It continued to be the center of administration for the complicated irrigation system, in which villages had to be relocated periodically as the soil became saline, and to be a major caravan crossroads linking the Persian Gulf, Persia, Syria, and Mecca. And, as always, Baghdad was the fortress from which every government of Mesopotamia tried unsuccessfully to govern the unruly bedouin tribes.

In this picture, looking across the river at the city, the water buffaloes, kufas, peasant women, and the ancient mud brick walls to the left, suggest how intimately the life of Baghdad was woven into the life of its villages.

E. J. Banks, or assistant, ca. 1903–1904.

Jerusalem began as a Bronze Age city almost 6,000 years ago. In about 1000 B.C., King David made it the capital of Israel and, later, Judah, and his son, King Solomon, built his Temple, which became a symbol for belief in one God. The list of conquerors thereafter is long: Egyptian, Philistine, Arabic, Assyrian, Babylonian, Persian, Greek, and Roman. Under King Herod the Great, who was a Jew appointed by the senate of Rome in 40 B.C. to rule Judea, the Temple and the city were rebuilt. The life of Jesus culminated in events in Jerusalem. In A.D. 70 the city and the Temple were again destroyed.

Christian pilgrimages to Jerusalem began early, and Constantine the Great erected the Church of the Holy Sepulchre and other shrines. But in 614, the Byzantine Empire's great rival Persia destroyed Jerusalem and its temples and churches. A few years later the Muslims arrived under Arab leaders and in 691 completed the Dome of the Rock, to mark the rock from which Mohammed was believed to have ascended to Heaven in 632. The Rock was already sacred to Jews as the place where Abraham was believed to have prepared to sacrifice his son Isaac.

In the eleventh century, Muslims destroyed the Christian shrines and closed the pilgrim and trade routes, giving the Christian world a reason for starting the Crusades. Knights of the Crusade ruled Jerusalem for ninety years

until Saladin drove them out in 1187. The Mongols looted Jerusalem next, and then the Egyptians moved in. The Ottoman Turks captured the city in 1517 and held it until 1917, when the British took over.

Fragments of architecture, like fossils of this turmoil, abound in Jerusalem and its environs, and are held sacred by the three religions. To maintain the holy places and to shelter pilgrims have been Jerusalem's primary functions as a world city, although under the Turks each faith looked after its own. Jerusalem was the largest city on the Mediterranean curve of the Fertile Crescent; rainfall and adequate wells grew a basic food supply and the city was cherished by those who had grown up with its quaint alleys, ancient walls, and pleasant vistas from the surrounding hills. For the nineteenth-century Western tourist it was the focal point of any journey to the Middle East. Its commercialism and the vicious rivalry among sects never diminished the beliefs of the faithful.

In this panorama of the Old City within its walls, the Jewish quarter is top left, the Christian quarter is top center, and the Muslim quarter is top right. In the left foreground is the Tomb of Absalom. The Dome of the Rock dominates the center. The slope of the Mount of Olives with the Garden of Gethsemane are bottom right, closest to the camera.

Possibly Félix Bonfils, 1867–1877.

The city of Rey, or Ray, in Persia, four thousand years old, was a religious center and a capital when Alexander the Great stopped there in 330 B.C. on his way to India. Adjoining Rey as a suburb was the town of Tehran. The Arabs kept Rey as the capital when they captured Persia in 641, but the Mongols in 1220 destroyed it and the populace fled to Tehran. In 1788 the founder of the Qajar (Kajar) dynasty of Saba selected Tehran as the capital. (This dynasty was deposed in 1925 by Reza Shah Pahlevi.)

The city is about 60 miles south of the Caspian Sea and almost 4,000 feet high on the slopes of the Elburz Mountains. It may have been in this region that the first village farming in the Middle East began. The mountains are semi-arid though the peaks bear eternal snow. Two rivers water the territory, giving the city many gardens and orchards and a view of fertile plains below. Mountain resorts provide relief from the summer heat and dust. Throughout the nineteenth-century tribal, religious, and political turmoil in Persia, aggravated by European rivalry for concessions, Tehran grew only slowly, more remote from the West than any other Middle Eastern city except perhaps Sanaa in Yemen. But it remained one of the important caravan centers linking Asia and the Middle East up to World War I. The building of paved roads and railways did not get very far until after World War I, and Westernization was superficial until after World War II. This is Arsenal Square, which resembles European models.

Anonymous.

Women and children picnic in a Persian park.

Anonymous, ca. 1900.

Drifting sand cut the stones. The dust accumulated in slopes that stretched inches, then feet, then yards.

After centuries a wall shortened by a finger's breadth, and larger pieces would be about to fall. Part of an arch took five centuries to collapse, but nothing could stop that collapse, the blocks suddenly falling and rolling about before they stopped. The desert nibbling for a thousand years brought down a turret. Another thousand, and mounds half buried roofless columns. And yet five thousand years did not destroy the palaces and temples that waited to be dug out again.

Constantinople, queen of the Orient, had four seasons, with winter snowfalls now and then, on the romantic bosky hills of the Bosporus. Alexandria was drenched by Mediterranean wind; a cloudburst could flood the streets, which had little paving so that the sand could drink up the rain. Astride the wide Nile, Cairo baked by day, but the nights were enchanting and the road to the pyramids drew visitors into the spell of pharaonic times. In Jerusalem the weather was sticky; the River Jordan and mild rains had made Palestine a land of milk and honey to desert wanderers so long ago, but that land seemed stony and thorny to Western eyes. Most famous for gardens and lovely courtyards was Damascus, cooled by breezes off the Lebanon mountains. On the sea side of the mountains, clouds broke and gave Beirut the finest climate of the Middle East—Riviera summers, rainy

The English photographer Francis Bedford, who traveled with the Prince of Wales on his Middle Eastern tour of 1862, identified the sitter as Abd-el-Kader (1808–1883) and the location and time as Damascus, 1862. The military and political hero of resistance to French occupation in Algeria, he created an independent state there before he was defeated, imprisoned in France, and exiled to Damascus. This is a much more sensitive portrait than those of many other dignitaries, made in abundance a few years later by commercial photographers.

The photographer captioned this picture "École Persane" (Persian school). The lesson being learned concerns a form of punishment called the bastinado—having the bottoms of the feet whipped. (Detail.)

Anonymous, ca. 1890.

winters, and, on the peaks, snow that melted into spring rivulets. Baghdad on the Tigris boiled year round, and the people seemed to have no yearning for greenery. Nestled in an extinct volcano, Aden roasted and stewed forever. Red Sea shores were steamy, except for a few months in the winter, but the Persian Gulf was the hottest of all the seas all the time. The climate of Sanaa in the mountains of the Yemen was blissfully moderate, and its farms were the most productive in Arabia. Tehran was so hot that most of the year its inhabitants spent all the months they could in the mountains. And Mecca—

Mecca was a true daughter of the desert, being the only city in the Middle East without a river, without rain, and without adequate wells.

Because of their isolation and powerful tribal traditions, village and oasis populations remained regionally rather pure; and the bedouin fiercely maintained patrilineal bloodlines. But in the cities, white, brown, olive, black skins, kinky and straight hair, Semitic noses, Egyptian eyes, Turkish jaws, Circassian mouths mingled with red hair, Berber beaks, Negro lips, Italian eyes, French foreheads, Teutonic chins. Yet a man from Baghdad was recognizable from a Yemeni or an Egyptian; a Turk couldn't be mistaken for a Syrian; a Palestinian did not look at all like a man from Mecca or Tehran. Even more surprising, though each city had its distinct culture, dialect, vanities, all had a common denominator of activities. They really did belong to one civilization, and in many ways it was more uniform than the European civilization was from Ireland to Siberia, or its extensions in the

The caption on the photograph reads: "Sheikh professors at the national schools." (Detail.)

G. Lekegian, ca. 1900.

Americas from Alaska to Tierra del Fuego. No doubt this was partly because of the dominant single language. Arabic created a bond that reached all Muslims. And for all its schisms, Islam is a more unifying faith than Christianity. Certainly the sea of sand that the cities shared was also important.

The common denominator in the way of life was visible in the streets. Backgammon, called trictrac and other names, was played everywhere with a mindless passion. Strings of amber beads were circled, clicking, in every hand at the coffeehouse tables. At any time of day or night literate patrons enjoyed reading newspapers to the uneducated who gathered around to listen. And there were always storytellers and poets wandering about who for a cup of coffee regaled a little audience. Musicians plucked and blew and scraped and banged as they strolled, ready to be hired for any jollity but relying on the street to put farthings in their palms. Sometimes a male dancer per-

formed; acrobats and magicians were standard entertainment at certain places, as were trainers with their animal acts: trick dogs, goats, birds. And there were snake charmers. Cobras lived in gardens, and a man with a magical flute could make a living enticing them into his basket. Hawkers of too many things to list, vendors of snacks and sweets and water — each howled his own cries endlessly. A restaurant might be a charcoal brazier in a gateway, grilling morsels of meat or frying bean patties. Dishes of yoghurt, flat bread, pastries stacked on boards went by on the heads of chanting boys. At night, pitch torches flared in sockets on the walls. The cloudy smell of spices and charcoal fumes mingled with that of soups, bitter coffee, ripe fruit, and the rancid exhalations of bubbling water pipes, with the smell of sweat, animal droppings, urine, the vapors of stones as the cooling night squeezed them. The unconcerned emptying of bladders and bowels, and the open-air fornicating of beggars and scavengers, made Westerners dizzy and fearful. Street life made poverty bearable, made the desert bearable, made the boredom of the rich bearable. The streets of the Middle East were more democratic than anything dreamed of in the Western world, and not just because beggars were tolerated. The segregation of women in the home forced male friendships and business socializing at all levels to develop and be nourished in the marketplace.

Something should be said about the poor, who disgusted Westerners with their bad manners in public. The poor in the West were locked into factories for twelve hours a day and corralled into their slums all night; they were kept out of sight. In the Orient they lived everywhere and made what they could on the streets. Curiously, the Westerner, intolerant and afraid that the political potential of his own lower classes might be liberated against him, was far more intolerant of what he took to be the impudence of half-naked, homeless throngs in the Middle East, pestering everyone for a pittance. He never understood that in Muslim countries poverty was not thought of as the wages of laziness or of sin. It was all Allah's will, just as the richest man had collected his wealth with Allah's will. Beggar and millionaire (of whom there were not many) could look into each other's eyes and together chant, "There but for the grace of God go I!" And neither could say that he was being punished

*These vendors in Cairo are setting up their trays for
customers who are hungry for pastries, sweets, and bread.*

Both anonymous, before 1877.

or rewarded because nobody could read the Almighty's
total plan: they were equally important in that plan. This
belief was reiterated in prayers five times a day. Thus,
poverty smelled considerably less awful than in the
Christian West with its tendency to think that God had
an affection for the rich, that He helped those who helped
themselves, and that the poor had only themselves to
blame. The cry of baksheesh, the hand held out in the best
of shops and hotels and even by the suffragi who guarded
the gates of mansions, meant more than just begging for
a handout. The starving had a spiritual right, granted
them by the Prophet, to ask for a share of the nation's
wealth. Furthermore, Muslim history was full of spectac-
ular careers from rags to riches and of ghastly plunges
from palaces to penury. Almost all Muslims, good or
bad, obeyed the dictum of giving a tenth of their income

to the poor, orphans and widows, the aged, the sick; the
wealthy often left large slices of their fortunes to chari-
table organizations.

In a teetotaling society something had to take the place
of alcohol as a social lubricant and nerve soother. In the
Arab lands the remedy for most ills was coffee. Selecting
the beans, roasting and blending them, had long ago become a technique practiced in each household, but making
the brew was an art and the sharing of it a ceremony that
in itself was a joy, even in the hurly-burly of the bazaar.
Caffeine was the drug of choice and men and women were
addicts, observing rules that varied little from land to
land. The coffee bean was powdered in a mortar, a fresh
batch for each brew, and the ringing of the brass as the
pestle worked never ended in the streets and came out
of windows many times a day. One had to tell the host
whether he wanted the tiny cup sweetened with lots of
sugar, or "just right," or without any sugar. Bitter car-
damom was one of several flavors that could be added.

The game of mankalah *that these men are playing was as popular as chess, backgammon, and checkers. Although illiteracy in the lower classes made games take the place of newspaper reading in the coffeehouses, the literate society played them just as passionately. This scene is in Egypt.*

Anonymous, before 1877.

Photographers were attracted to the coffeehouses because they were such lively places, serving in effect as the bar-rooms, saloons, and pubs of the nonalcoholic Muslim lands. But they had several other functions. First, they were meeting places for gossiping and socializing in a society where the home was barred to all but relatives and close friends. Second, in a largely illiterate society all news traveled by word of mouth, and the cafés were receiving and transmitting stations. Third, men of the same trade congregated in the same cafés, and one went there to do business or to hire them. Some cafés were elegant, with chairs and separate tables; others had no more than squatting rights in the street. The shouted greetings and conversations, the racket of backgammon players, the smells of coffee and tobacco, the coming and going, the excitement and vitality of this Egyptian coffeehouse could not be captured by the long-exposure nineteenth-century camera. (Detail.)

Anonymous, ca. 1860s–1870s.

In the city the prime reason for drinking was addiction and cordiality. Just as among the bedouin, the coffee hour was a complicated affair, for it involved the status of the host, his guests, political rivalries, and a formal opportunity — therefore not subject to moods — to exchange information, gossip, affirm friendships, and be entertained by discussions, arguments, stories.

Far less ceremonial was tea drinking. This beverage, too, was brewed so strong that the caffeine and tannin in a thimble-sized glass were enough to jolt one's system heartily. Boiled black tea, in fact, became the standard drug for heavy laborers, who stopped regularly to ease their exhaustion and hunger with gulps of syrupy, revitalizing black tea.

An ear-filling sound in the city was the call of the muezzin from all the minarets three times in the day and twice during the hours of darkness. There was always a

*These women were posed before a bathhouse in an uniden-
tified city about 1880 (the entrance to the baths was once
through a Roman arch). The photograph with the donkey
is signed Béchard, the other is signed Sébah. Both were
probably taken by H. Béchard, but somehow J. Pascal
Sébah acquired one of the negatives and sold prints under
his own name.*

first one, then others here and there, until from all sides
came the chanting, as though those men were truly in
love with Allah, truly saw the world's transience as they
looked down upon its rooftops, and truly believed that all
good Muslims prayed according to the Prophet's directions. In every city except Mecca there were also a few,
very few, Christian bells, but they were designed to be
barely audible.

As prominent as anything else in the daily life of the
city were the bathhouses. Though they were used primarily for cleansing the body and were indispensable in a
sweaty climate, since no city had running water piped into homes, they also had a social function. Friends met
there regularly. Women especially loved to spend hours
away from home in a public place where they were not
under scrutiny by every passerby. Gossip at the baths
was as wide-ranging and vital as gossip in the bazaar.
And an air of sexuality pervaded the cavernous, steamy
rooms, the masseuse tables, and the pools. Tales of per-
versions were picked up by foreigners, who were also
excited by the relaxed attitude toward prostitution of all

kinds. The baths play a prominent role in Arabic literature's stories of intrigue and lechery. But the vast majority went to the baths simply for the delights of hot water,
rubdowns, and information.

In fact, it is possible to argue that exchange of information is the key to any community, whether village or
empire. Even the basic need of food cannot be met without it. History shows that in times of glory, communication reaches wondrous efficiency and that dark ages are
associated with impoverished or destroyed communication systems. The Arab empires were possible only because of the speed with which orders crossed deserts, and
for the Ottoman Empire, too, this was of primary concern. After the seventeenth century the sultanate's long
preoccupation with European entanglements, the growth
of provincial power in the face of deepening corruption,
and the weakening of official military authority went
hand in hand with the slackening of the imperial news
service. In the latter half of the nineteenth century, railroads and telegraph lines began to crisscross the Middle
East, largely in the service of government. Most of the
people benefited hardly at all. The newspapers of the
West, which grew with the development of industry, literacy, and democracy, had no counterpart in the Middle
East, where only the cities nourished a literate class, and
that was small in numbers. All news had to continue being disseminated by the ancient system of caravan, bazaar, and bathhouse.

Tourists, Kodaks, and the Sphinx

By the beginning of the twentieth century, tourists to the Middle East were carrying cameras wherever they went. Gone were the sketch pads, chairs, and umbrellas that young men and women of the preceding decades used as they sat for hours in the sun, delineating Abu Simbel, Karnak, camels under palm trees, Gethsemane, and the River Jordan. In 1900 George Eastman's Brownies sold for a dollar, were guaranteed easy to use, and princesses and the bourgeoisie toted them around.

The early snapshot cameras introduced in the 1880s produced small pictures, frequently fuzzy from shaky handling and under- or overexposed. They were placed in albums, prized for one or two generations, and then relegated to the attic. Every ten years or so their life would be endangered as the family reevaluated the contents of Granny's trunk, which by now had to compete against a flood of illustrated books and stereo-cards of the Middle East.

The second-generation photographers who had studios in the Middle East in the first two decades of the twentieth century differed from their predecessors. They did not make pictures as energetically as had Bonfils, Sébah, Zangaki, and the others of the nineteenth century. Rather, they tended to inherit or to buy large stocks of excellent negatives that included views of all the major sites. They printed these as their own, or kept the original photographer's signature, profiting from his reputation. They also printed and sold postcards and kept stocks of photographic supplies to sell to tourists. Sometimes they waited at monuments for tourists who might want to be photographed there.

One exception was G. Eric Matson, who lived in Jerusalem from 1881 to 1946 and signed his photographs "The American Colony." He photographed all over the region, mostly with a stereo-camera, and recorded street life, antiquities, news events, flora of the desert, farming techniques, and so on in over 20,000 negatives. He also made series of captioned photographs illustrating stories in the Bible, thus offering something particularly attractive to pilgrims.

It is instructive to glance at a series of pictures of the Sphinx. The first photographers were fleeing the industrialization that they knew they must return to, and they saw the Sphinx as the symbol of a totally different kind of civilization, one characterized by the serenity of traditions and the mystery of the sublime rather than by revolutions. They were also somewhat uncertain, perhaps secretly, about the function and esthetic meaning of the chemical kit they were using as against the brush and palette that they had discarded. But then, as more and more people photographed the Sphinx, it acquired familiar proportions and became easier to use as a prop. British Tommies, baseball players, charter groups, dragomans, donkey boys all nestled against that enigmatic, stony face, climbed on its head and waved their hats, and in general asserted equality with the Great Mystery. In the end, socialites, grandmothers, millionaires, and nobodies patronized the Sphinx by sitting proudly atop rented horses or dromedaries, on whose backs they had been hoisted by guides, with the Sphinx's eternal visage obligingly peeking at them out of the general background. No one questioned the power of the machine that could join the symbol of immortality with their own triumphant presence. The lands of the Bible and the pharaohs could never again be the same.

OPPOSITE AND OVERLEAF
(A) *Maxime Du Camp, 1849;* (B) *Felix Beato and James Robertson, 1857;* (C) *W. Hammerschmidt, ca. 1858;* (D) *Francis Bedford, 1862;* (E) *A. Beato, ca. 1865;* (F) *Anonymous, ca. 1880;* (G) *R. M. Junghaendel, ca. 1890;* (H) *Helen Hamilton Gardener, ca. 1903;* (I) **D. D. Luckenbill**, *1908–1909.*

A

B

C

D

E

F

G

H

I

9 THE FOREIGN COLONY

Each step [of the pyramid] being full as high as a dinner table; there being very, very many of the steps; an Arab having hold of each of our arms and springing upward from step to step and snatching us with them, forcing us to lift our feet as high as our breasts every time, and do it rapidly and keep it up till we were ready to faint — who shall say it is not lively, exhilarating, lacerating, muscle-straining, bone-wrenching and perfectly excruciating and exhausting pastime climbing the pyramids? I beseeched the varlets not to twist all my joints asunder . . . and they only answered with some more frightful springs, and an unenlisted volunteer behind opened a bombardment of determined boosts with his head which threatened to batter my whole political economy to wreck and ruin.

Twice, for one minute, they let me rest while they extorted baksheesh, and then continued their maniac flight up the pyramid. They wished to beat the other parties.

—MARK TWAIN,
The Innocents Abroad (1869)

ONLY IN THE CITIES, in the ruins, and in the holy places had most Western visitors to the Middle East anything to do, and only there could they reside throughout the nineteenth century if they wanted government protection. They began to arrive after Napoleon in increasing numbers, sent by French, English, Dutch, German, and Italian governments and various organizations, always on hardship contracts with per diem and other emoluments, including long vacations at home. The Middle East was considered by these formal representatives of the West to be somewhere between the jungles of Africa and the opulence of India.

Tourists, shepherded by dragomans to the pyramids, were hauled up to the top by men whom Mark Twain called "draggers."

H. Béchard, before 1878.

(There were several differences between the Middle East and India. Because irrigated deserts could never yield the wealth that many regions of Asia could, any maharajah squandered more in a year, over and above his plush existence, than the wealthiest landlord in the Ottoman Empire could accumulate in half a lifetime of greed. On the other hand, the mass poverty, famines, and plagues of overcrowded Asia generally were far more devastating than in the Middle East, where populations were thinly spread, and degradation of the destitute in a caste system was also immeasurably worse than where the Koran preached spiritual equality and charity. Thus the rich and the poor were more intimate in the Middle East. Finally, colonialism in India had established all the comforts of the Anglo-Indian way of life, the way of the rulers jealously guarded and aloof from the ways of the governed. In the Ottoman Empire there was no such separation possible between the citizens and the Europeans, who were guests and not the lords and masters.)

A German expedition to Egypt, with its local assistants, was photographed by the archeologist Johannes Dümichen, or by a member of his team, ca. 1870.

Women tourists of every age felt perfectly safe visiting antiquities with their guides, who demonstrated their mastery over the "natives" at every opportunity. The natives, however, were often participants in a setup that netted them a few small coins.

Anonymous, ca. 1885.

The Breasted expedition traveled 2,000 miles up the Nile into Nubia, photographing ancient inscriptions. This picture shows Horst Schliephack photographing the great stele at Tumbos, which celebrates a victory over the Nubians by King Tuthmosis I (ruled 1525–ca. 1512 B.C.).

Probably James Henry Breasted, 1907.

Hardship contracts notwithstanding, Westerners often lived considerably better on the same scale as well-to-do natives than they could have back home. They justified doing so in terms of giving to the Middle East Christianity, materialism, imperialism, and the machine. Resident foreigners included many hardworking people: teams of archeologists (who sanctioned the looting of tombs); the staffs of missionary institutions who built schools, a university, hospitals, hostels in hopes of making converts; engineers and technicians hired by local governments and by the sultanate; bankers, businessmen, manufacturers' agents, and diplomatic and consular officials whom the others accepted as their leaders. There were also genuine scholars, the forerunners of anthropologists and sociologists, who studied the Islamic world with a desire to explain it to the West. After 1850 photographers began to take up residence for extended periods. And there were wealthy eccentrics and jaded expatriates who settled in, mostly in Constantinople and Cairo, for a variety of sybaritic and esthetic reasons. The tourists were quite apart from the foreign colony, whether they came with retinues of servants, on their own

Russian pilgrims—peasants, intellectuals, young, and old—have reached the River Jordan.

G. R. Lees, 1891.

An elegant group of tourists poses with servants at Karnak.
Anonymous, ca. 1870.

yachts, or alone on a romantic tour or pilgrimage. Many tourists were famous writers and artists, but even they were usually herded along in groups. The residents shied from their ignorant, exhausted, complaining, homesick compatriots.

The Ottoman Empire had always followed the Arab custom of segregating foreigners in designated quarters of a city, where they enjoyed immunity from Koranic law, taxes, and import duties, and the red tape that strangled business contracts and travel and forced citizens of the empire into corrupting the bureaucrats. Any foreigner who committed a crime was handed over to his consulate for trial according to the laws of his own country. This remarkable privilege was exploited in all sorts of ways for profitable transactions forbidden to natives, and it contributed to the extravagant way of life in villas with many servants and at sport clubs restricted to Europeans. At the same time foreigners had to ride a merry-go-round of social calls within the colony, fitting themselves

Pig-sticking along the Euphrates and Tigris rivers was one of the few entertainments for the English in Baghdad. The rulers of Babylon thousands of years before had also hunted these big boars. (Detail.)

Signature obscured, 1858.

Sand, pyramids, Sphinx, donkey, camels, horse, dragomans, photographer, onlooker, and ladies — under the setting sun.

C. Chusseau Flaviens, before 1914.

For the foreign colony in Aden, the broiling heat was not as terrible as the boredom. Here members of the Polo Club line up in the shade, dressed precisely as if they were in green and misty England. The large staff of servants who made the club possible are not included in the picture, nor would they have been in England.

Anonymous, 1908.

The terrace of Shepheard's Hotel in Cairo was where the monarchs, millionaires, diplomats, financiers, and the famous for any reason hobnobbed. Mark Twain said it was "the worst [hotel] on earth except the one I stopped at once in a small town in the United States," but by others it was equated with the Ritz and Claridge's.

J. Pascal Sébah, after 1868.

fearfully into a complicated protocol that gave each one a status, or handicap, according to profession, rank, pay, seniority, length of residence, private wealth, influence back home. To ignore the pecking order in this little ghetto led to recall and broken careers. Those who survived were not necessarily the most intelligent or talented, or the most useful to their country or to the Ottomans, since protocol ignores such attributes. But they had an inflated respect for themselves as Westerners, Christians, Old Hands, Friends of Persons in High Places. Unquestioned authority, not just over servants and citizens who worked for them in their offices but over anyone who got in their way, was to them a God-given right.

In no city did they mingle easily with indigenous people, whether Muslim, Jew, or Christian, seldom inviting them and seldom being invited. One or two local officials educated in England or France and certified acceptable by the embassies might turn up at formal dinners or to watch polo or a tennis match at the club; they were generally assumed to be spies with whom it was wise to be cordial. Basically anyone who wore a turban or fez was considered inferior by the majority of foreigners simply because he did so.

The colony turned up posturing, secretly agog, at affairs of state put on for them by the regional satraps, but they just did not know how to fit Muslim society into their own social classification which seemed to them so vital to preserve. They heard endless stories about how complicated Muslim protocol was, of how subtle and flowery were manners, and how deeply a host could be insulted by a trivial oversight. And how confusing the presence of the harem! The very idea of locked up veiled women roused the newcomers' imagination to dream of wild sexual abandon and sadistic repressions. But the more intelligent and curious wives found ways of becoming friendly with Muslim women, and the tales they brought back from harem visits were ordinary ones of love, jealousy, infidelity, frustration, or power plays inside the family, the raising of children, problems with grandparents and in-laws, and accounts of the household, servants, shopping, holidays, and banquets.

But few Westerners, then as now, could cope with Arabic, one of the most difficult of living languages for Latin, Germanic, or Slavic speakers to learn. The script (traced to Syriac origin) runs right to left, the spelling uses diacritical signs instead of vowels, and there are decorative flourishes. Learning to read demands diligent study for at least a year. Moreover, written Arabic is classical and remote from the vernacular. It has complicated grammar, intricate constructions, and is full of figures of speech, alliteration, and metaphors not relevant to modern life. Contemporary books and newspapers use modified classical Arabic, and ceremonial speeches and drama are also classical. Even legal papers retain classical language. Every literate and a surprising number of illiterate persons understand it because it is the language of the Koran. But it is never used in conversation. After learning to read in Arabic, the foreigner must learn the vernacular. Street argot is even farther removed from the written, not just structurally but in terms of local slang,

The Pyramids.

Patsy.

Capt. Pierre. Evie. Martino Pacha. Capt. Y.B.

Baron Rálamb.

on the way to the Barrage. Col.

Patsy.

Col. Watson. Sir John. Patsy. A.W. The Khedive. L.M. Daisy. Gustaf.

Arthur, Duke of Connaught and Strathearn, visited Egypt in 1905 with family and friends, and this is one page from the album of photographs and small water-colors that he put together after he returned home. In the front row from left to right are a Colonel Watson; Princess Patricia of Connaught; the Duke; the Khedive Abbas Hilmi II; Princess Louise Margaret, the wife of the Duke; Princess Margaret of Connaught; and her husband, Gustavus Adolfus, Crown Prince of Sweden. Assorted officers, a knight, and a baron are in the back row.

· 175 ·

Bonfils

98. Caire, Allée de Pyramides.

*A road from Cairo to the pyramids was built in 1868
in honor of the Prince of Wales's visit. It considerably
reduced travel time by buggy or donkey-back. Many
guides lived in the village at left.*

Bonfils, after 1868.

mordant wit, and explosive obscenity. Arab curses are
violent. They accuse an adversary of every imaginable
moral and sexual perversion and damn his family, home,
religion, health, and afterlife. Ordinary bazaar talk is
flowery beyond anything familiar to Western business,
and government pronouncements and regulations are far
worse than Western gobbledygook. Mastery of Arabic at
any level of education has always been highly appreciated
both in the palace and in the village — part of the Muslim

tradition that admires creativity extravagantly in every
field.

The pronunciation of Arabic is as difficult as the writing. It uses sounds that range from sibilant to harsh, and
guttural to sonorous, unknown in the West and hard to
imitate. Just as incomprehensible for Westerners are the
passion with which natives spill out the words and the
exuberance of body movement that accompanies the
flow. It seems to captivate both talker and listener. An
exchange of greetings seems to set up an intimacy with
hugs and pats that is puzzling: what does fervor imply?
It implies nothing more than respect for one another.
Like many aspects of Middle Eastern society, this formal
intimacy is a residue of desert life and medieval chivalry.

A Beau Brummel in velvet suit and gaiters poses with his guide, in white turban, and servants.

Anonymous, ca. 1885.

For all these reasons, Westerners seldom bothered to learn Arabic, relying on interpreters even after years of residence. Lingua Franca, a heavily corrupted Italian French, was the international language of commerce until the twentieth century, when pidgin English began to squeeze it out, and foreigners who had to, did pick up enough to get along in the bazaar. On the other hand, most Westerners soon developed a vocabulary of curses and commands such as *give me*, *come here*, *get out*, *you're no good*, *carry this*, and so on, which they felt established their importance. And many wives allowed their cooks to teach them kitchen Arabic, a few-score words that took care of household needs. The abominable accents caused mirth because of the unintentional puns they turned, sometimes obscene, but anyone who even tried to speak Arabic was forgiven mistakes.

Casual friendships always developed in every city, usually on a jovial level with the more cunning merchants and lawyers in the bazaars, who spoke half a dozen lan-

The dragoman was a multilingual, educated guide-interpreter-protector, licensed for hire by foreign tourists. Applicants were usually local boys related to other dragomans who helped them get their education and license, but sometimes they were European expatriates who went through the same training. Touring the Middle East was extremely difficult unless one hired these handsome, extravagantly dressed and armed shepherds, whose jobs were to organize transport, arrange for meals and permits, keep beggars and thieves at bay, narrate the history of the ruins, and help out with bargaining in the bazaars.

Bonfils, after 1867.

· 177 ·

In the village of Bethany (now Al-Azariyah) at the foot of the Mount of Olives near Jerusalem, the New Testament places the sisters Mary and Martha. Here Jesus resurrected their brother Lazarus and from here Jesus ascended to heaven after saying farewell to his disciples. The village is holy to Christians and to Muslims, who revere Lazarus.

The English photographer James Graham made this picture in 1855 while traveling with two Pre-Raphaelite painters, Thomas Seddon and William Holman Hunt. Here and there among the modest ruins the freshly plastered walls of new houses glisten, and olive trees grow wherever there is room in the stony soil. The scene is typical of most villages throughout history anywhere in the world: as the ancient roofs cave in and walls crumble, new dwellings emerge out of the rubble in organic continuity. The Pre-Raphaelites sought accuracy of detail in their paintings and used photographs extensively. This one contains the dramatic contrasts of light and shadow, startling clarity and dense mystery, that the painters sought. The retouched figure in the lower right-hand corner has the contemplative air of a storyteller.

guages and traded gossip and tips for inclusion in import-export schemes and currency shuffles that involved the Capitulations. In other words, mutual profit softened prejudice on both sides, although it did not quench the foreigner's secret dread that local demagogues, fighting one another, might goad a mob into looting, making the wealth of strangers a primary target. Though not commonplace, friendships could run deep, deeper than any in the West, because bridging the two worlds demanded it. The rewards were profound, almost Biblical.

There were foreigners who lived sometimes for years in the Middle East but never asked to join the club, and probably would have been refused for questionable loyalty. They were the wanderers: artists, poets, adventurers, dilettantes, explorers, scholars, photographers;

This mosque rises from the ruins of Luxor. It was photographed in 1855–1856 by Frédéric-Auguste Bartholdi, the sculptor who designed the Statue of Liberty.

There was a big market for photographs that painters could copy. On this one has been drawn a grid to help a painter transfer the image to canvas.

Charles Lallemand, 1860s.

Ashkenazi (eastern European) Jews in Jerusalem were photographed by the Palestine Exploration Fund.

H. Phillips, 1866.

sometimes all these labels could be pasted on a single man, and, infrequently, on a woman. They rented lodgings in the native quarters, in villages or oases, even in ruins. They joined bedouin tribes on their migrations. Fluent in dialects, at home in native dress and with native food, tremendously knowledgeable about history, they made true friendships with sheikhs, pashas, porters, dervishes, carpenters, rug merchants, ordinary citizens. They won the hearts of loyal servants, and they rode camels as if they had been born on them. They laughed at the fears and pretensions of the colony, squabbled with their embassies, pulled strings in Ottoman quarters, ignored red tape, wrote exuberant letters and books, and in general found the Middle East's deserts, ruins, and cities the most exciting, beautiful, romantic, funny,

dreadful, and wonderful in the world—and the most dangerous. The known and unknown risks of nature and human society were a lure for testing their talents and courage. Nothing in the West could match the challenges of the Orient, nor the sweetness of survival by being accepted into the Muslim world.

There was another, far more important, non-Islamic population in the Ottoman Empire and in Persia, which has already been mentioned: the Levantines. They were permanently domiciled in every city and town and were not considered Western because their ancestors had lived in the Middle East for countless generations. They in-

In front of the studio backdrop, a European landscape, are posed seven old Jewish men around a make-believe campfire. The photograph, made probably in Anatolia, implies they are pilgrims, but they could have been collected by the photographer from other walks of life. Four of them look startlingly alike.

Anonymous, before 1877.

cluded Christians and Jews, originally from any country in Europe, as well as indigenous Jews and Christians like the Copts and Maronites. They wore a mixture of European and Oriental dress, furnished their homes partly in European style, often sent their children to mission schools and, if rich enough, to European universities. Multilingual, frequently possessing dual citizenship through deals with consulates, the Levantines had been

an integral part of the population since before the first Arab Empire, but they had resisted becoming Muslim, preferring to cluster by themselves and claim the rights of minorities granted by the Arabs. The monasteries they built in those early centuries still stand in forbidding deserts, still attract converts. Some Levantines in the nineteenth century were doctors, lawers, rich businessmen, who held important jobs in the Turkish government just as their ancestors had under the Persian, Arab, and Byzantine dynasties. Most were modestly employed as bookkeepers, clerks, office managers, but many owned small businesses, stores, restaurants, and coffee shops, pharmacies, haberdasheries catering to everyone above the penny-farthing level and below it, too. If one thought of a middle class in the nineteenth century, one thought automatically of the Levantines, whose clever brains managed the commerce, banking, and bureaucracy of the empire.

Yet as a class they had no political power at all, which, of course, was precisely what the middle class in the West had begun to acquire in the eighteenth century. They had their hands on the flow of money and goods but were denied equality with Muslims, and were not granted the sanctions foreigners had under the Capitulations. Thus they sought individual influence with local pashas and khedives, and long before had acquired a reputation for industry mixed with intrigue and double-dealing. They were considered to be corrupt as a class, yet they all had warm friendships with their Muslim peers at every level of activity in the empire. At the same time, whenever a revolution or fanatical riot broke out, the first victims were the prosperous Levantines, even before the foreigners.

Westerners considered the Levantines a cut above the Muslims but quite unreliable. Also, Levantine society lived by Orthodox Jewish or early Christian rules and seemed far too Byzantine to the Westerner: that is, medieval, repressive, clannish, seething with jealousies and feuds. The status of women was exclusively that of dependents; they were bartered in marriage and sequestered as rigidly as Muslim women. (Of course, most households were run by ambitious and demanding women and clandestine love affairs were common.)

Among the non-Levantines, most snobbish and prejudiced, most feared because of their singleminded drive toward empire, were the British. Yet they made more friends among the top natives than did any other Europeans, perhaps because many were eccentric, adventurous, and self-possessed enough to set aside haughtiness. The French had love affairs with Arabs and Levantines and were less formal than the British in all their relationships, but for that very reason seemed less predictable and therefore less likeable. At the same time, France was far more popular than England as a place to visit. Germans were dedicated salesmen currying favor in high offices for contracts. Italians were lowest on the list, probably because they had always been familiar middlemen between the Orient and Europe. Nobody knew any Russians. Dutch firms represented East India trade rather than Holland, and the Dutch kept aloof. Americans

In the summer of 1918, a few months before the end of World War I, these recruits enlisted in the 40th Battalion, Royal Fusiliers, in Jerusalem to fight the Turks. Two British noncoms, on either end, pose with the diverse ethnic types.

Anonymous.

before World War I, mostly Protestant missionaries involved with the university in Beirut and schools everywhere in the empire, were disliked for their disapproving smiles and teacherish manners, which seemed to conceal prejudice; they also had the reputation of investing in land and doing very well. (Prejudice remained; American oil-field workers in the 1930s called anyone who spoke Arabic a "rag-head.")

The Middle Easterner's contact with foreigners took place therefore largely in Western ghettos or with groups carted about in extraordinary and ridiculous luxury, guarded by richly adorned, fawning guides and servants. Clearly they were fair game. The cry of "baksheesh" followed the heavily dressed aliens everywhere because their fear and horror of street people were expressed not just by facial grimaces but by eloquent body gestures as well. The street people found these irresistible. Resident foreigners kept to themselves and were known mostly as members of a tightly knit community closed to the Ottoman or Persian citizen.

*In 1915 the Allies launched an attack against the Turks
at several points on the Dardanelles, with the aim of
capturing Constantinople. The expedition, which ended
with retreat from Gallipoli, was a disaster for several
reasons and led to Winston Churchill's dismissal as First
Lord of the Admiralty. Over 200,000 casualties were
suffered by English, Australian, New Zealand, Indian,
and Egyptian units of the British army. These two
pictures of a much-photographed war show a British*
*plane's forced landing at Chocolate Hill, Suvla, and a
divisional transport crossing a pontoon bridge on the
River Auja, September 19, 1918. British, Australians,
Indians, and Egyptians, horses, mules, and a donkey
were components of the cavalry force that captured the
Turkish army at the battles of Mejiddo, six weeks before
the armistice between Britain and Turkey.*

Anonymous, 1915 and 1918.

POSTSCRIPT

As the Germans left Damascus they fired the dumps and ammunition stores, so that every few minutes we were jangled by explosions, whose first shock set the sky white with flame. . . .

When dawn came we drove to the head of the ridge, which stood over the oasis of the city, afraid to look north for the ruins we expected: but, instead of ruins, the silent gardens stood blurred green with river mist, in whose setting shimmered the city, beautiful as ever, like a pearl in the morning sun. . . .

At the Town Hall things were different. Its steps and stairs were packed with a swaying mob: yelling, embracing, dancing, singing. . . . Damascus went mad with joy. The men tossed up their tarbushes to cheer, the women tore off their veils. Householders threw flowers, hangings, carpets, into the road before us: their wives leaned, screaming with laughter, through the lattices and splashed us with bath-dippers of scent. . . .

Meanwhile I made myself responsible for public order. . . . The conduit was foul with dead men and animals. . . . The resumption of street lighting would be our most signal proof of peace. . . . The streets were full of the debris of the broken army, derelict carts and cars, baggage, material, corpses. . . . Then the prisons [burned]. Warders and inmates had vanished from them altogether. . . . The citizens must be disarmed. . . . The destitute had been half-starved for days. . . . The currency was horrible. . . . The clamour hushed, as everyone seemed to obey the call to prayer on this their first night of perfect freedom.

—T. E. Lawrence,
Seven Pillars of Wisdom (1926)

During world war i the Allies signed several secret documents in which they detailed what parts of the Ottoman Empire would go to which victor after the war was won. Even ancient Anatolia, homeland of the Turks, was to be carved up. In 1918 the defeated sultan and units of the army still loyal to him were allowed to reside in Constantinople, largely because the Allies were suspicious of one another's greed for more land than had been agreed on. A year later Mustafa Kemal, an officer and former member of the Young Turks, rounded up remnants of the Ottoman army hiding in the mountains, recruited peasants for training, gathered patriotic intellectuals and politicians, declared war on the sultan and the Allies, and in 1920 formed a government in Ankara. Fighting pitched battles, skirmishing, using guerrilla tactics, retreating, burning, living off the villages that supported him, for two years with courage and masterful tactics Kemal led his rebel government and raggle-taggle army toward freedom from foreign powers under the hitherto unknown banner of patriotism: Turkey for the Turks. One by one the European governments signed treaties with Kemal Atatürk—Atatürk was a name he chose, meaning Father of the Turks—until he was sole and absolute ruler of Anatolia, the Dardanelles, and the

Bosporus. In 1924 he abolished the caliphate, having in 1923 created the constitutional Republic of Turkey, dedicated to Westernization. This meant cutting all traditional ties with the new countries formed out of the empire and, later in 1925, separating Islam from the state in law and in the schools. In 1930 Constantinople was renamed Istanbul, the capital having been moved in 1923 to Ankara, a provincial town Kemal proceeded to build into a modern city. To create a new country out of the ruins of empire was a brilliant triumph for Kemal and for Turkish nationalism, the very first example of a true "nation" in the Middle East's long history of empires that had always assimilated ethnic and religious groups. The move was not at all appreciated by the European governments whose armies Kemal Atatürk had defeated and who were hard at work trying to attach the rest of the old empire to their own possessions. And in fact only two other regions achieved the same absolute freedom as did Turkey: Saudi Arabia and Yemen.

To go back to 1918 and the Armistice, the first step made by the Allies to lull the Arabs was to extend President Wilson's Fourteen Points concerning self-determination of peoples to the population of the Ottoman Empire. In Paris, directly after the Armistice, however, the great powers plunged into fresh negotiations that canceled the secret agreements made during the war: England intended to keep Egypt, Mesopotamia, Palestine, the island of Cyprus, all of Arabia, and Persia (which had never been part of the Ottoman domains); France was determined to keep all of Syria; the Greeks demanded new territory, which they named Byzantium (including Constantinople, the Straits, and half of Anatolia). Italy was set on seizing the Dodecanese Islands and a large slice of Anatolia; several Armenian factions vied bitterly for their former lands in order to establish their own independence; the Zionists argued that the Balfour Declaration, signed during the war, meant to give them the whole of Palestine. Only the Russians had renounced all claims, being involved with the Bolshevik Revolution, which made them enemies of the West.

Not a scrap was reserved as an independent territory for the Arabs, who had actually put an army in the field to fight the Turks. A small delegation under Prince Feisal, son of King Hussein (the sherif of Mecca who had taken the title King of the Hejaz, backed by T. E. Lawrence and

Gertrude Bell), waited in the wings. Finally an Arab National Congress that formed in Damascus elected Feisal King of Syria and his older brother Abdullah King of Mesopotamia. After a year of complicated turmoil that involved nationalist parties, tribal loyalties, commercial blocs, and perfidious European diplomacy, Feisal was deposed and the French assumed full control of Syria. In 1926 they carved out of Syria a small republic of Lebanon, with a large Christian population and Beirut as its capital, leaving Damascus the capital of the rest of Syria, almost wholly Sunni except for the Druze in the hills. France maintained her rule in both countries, which were recognized by the League of Nations as mandated territories, by army garrisons, commercial controls, and by constantly setting tribal and religious factions at each other's throats for promised crumbs of power. This situation changed little until France fell in 1940, when the British took over for the duration.

When Feisal abandoned his brief kingship in Syria the British engineered his transfer in 1921 to a newly created throne of Iraq (formerly Mesopotamia), to which his brother Abdullah resigned his claim. A government was formed and a treaty signed giving Britain all power. A series of elected assemblies and cabinets tried to oust the British without success and although in 1927 Iraq was recognized as an independent nation, British commercial and political domination was hardly reduced, while Kurds fought Arabs, Sunnis fought Shiites, and the bedouin fought each other and any central government. In 1932 Iraq was admitted to the League of Nations. The next year King Feisal died, his son Ghazi succeeded him, but corruption continued, worse than it had ever been under the Turks. A succession of army coups and assassinations destroyed all hope of unification.

Another troublemaker was oil. Before the war, the sultan had granted concessions to the same German interests that had built the Baghdad railroad, and after 1918 a consortium of Allied companies took over exploration and development. But production was meager until the 1930s, when a new field came in and pipelines were laid to the Mediterranean. By 1939 British, Dutch, and American oil interests were deeply involved with the political scene.

By 1919 Ibn Saud was king of Nejd, the interior, and of Al Hasa along the Persian Gulf, and he now moved

Emir Feisal in Damascus was told by General Allenby that the Allies would rule most of the Middle East. Here Feisal is leaving the conference bitterly disappointed but cheered by the crowd. "They were a strange contrast," wrote T. E. Lawrence: "Feisal, large-eyed, colourless and worn, like a fine dagger; Allenby, gigantic and red and merry, fit representative of the Power which had thrown a girdle of humour and strong dealing round the world."

Anonymous, October 3, 1918.

against the Hejaz along the Red Sea, taking first Mecca and Medina and driving out the Hashimite family, and then capturing Jidda, the chief seaport. By 1922 he had unified Arabia for the first time since ancient days, except for the brief spell under his Wahabi ancestor. And although his own army consisted largely of tribes belonging to the Wahabi sect, and although he ruled without an elected government, he was not a tyrant or fanatic but a desert chief who lived up to the tenets of bedouin leadership. Through victory in battles, diplomatic marriages, and statesmanship, he had won the loyalty of the tribes. He maintained that peace, with the pilgrimage to Mecca his country's only source of income. When oil was discovered on the island of Bahrein in the Persian Gulf, he was besieged by foreign interests for concessions, but he resisted until in the 1930s he granted Standard Oil of California a limited area to search, and another American consortium the concession to process gold ores from an ancient mine. In 1938 the first major field was proved.

Just as everywhere else in the former Ottoman Empire, totally unexpected events took place in Palestine.

The population in 1920 was around 700,000, of which 50,000 were Jews, some indigenous for millennia as merchants and craftsmen, others newcomers working on agricultural communes, and all helped by international Jewish charity. The Palestinian Arabs expected to be incorporated with Syria into the new independent Arab state promised by the British, while the Zionists expected that Palestine would become a new Jewish state, also promised by the British. The British wanted to keep Palestine their mandate because of its key position on the

An Arab commission went to the Peace Conference at Versailles in 1919 to argue independence for the new territories carved out of the Ottoman Empire by the victorious Allies. Emir Feisal stands in the center. Colonel T. E. Lawrence, behind and second from right, was still hoping that Arab aspirations would be honored. Although eventually Feisal was made king of Iraq and his brother Abdullah king of Transjordan, all the territories, including these two, of the Ottoman Empire became mandates of Britain and France.

Signal Corps, U. S. A., January 22, 1919.

Mediterranean touching Suez and Egypt, Arabia, and Iraq. A British executive government, a Palestinian Jewish government, an international Zionist government, and an Arab government were created. At the top, Sir Herbert Samuel, the British high commissioner from 1920 to 1925, was the chief of chiefs, but he was subservient to the British colonial office in London, which was concerned with the British Empire and only minimally with Palestine. The expansion of farms by Jewish settlers on newly irrigated lands, and the influx of Jewish capital for increasing industrialization and urban growth, introduced problems where life had always been frugal and dominated by the desert. Administration of the Holy

Places, sometimes holy to two or three religions, was cause for fanaticism. Clashes, killings, riots, strikes increased. Both Jews and Arabs rose against the 1939 proposals for the partition of Palestine, and undeclared civil war broke out with sabotage, underground terrorist tactics, and cruel reprisals. Hitler, World War II, the end of the British Empire, and the withdrawal of all European governments from the Middle East were the deciding factors that enabled the State of Israel to be born in 1948.

The territory that became Transjordan—cut from Palestine—was mandated to Britain in 1920; Abdullah, brother of King Feisal in Baghdad, was made its king in 1921. But Britain remained in control of its foreign affairs, finance, and the armed forces which they built up until they were the best in the Middle East. The original function of the British presence in Palestine was shifted to Transjordan, now Jordan: to hold a key position relative to the Suez, to independent and not very friendly Saudi Arabia, and to the oil pipeline from Iraq.

In Egypt, headquarters in the Middle East for the war against the Turks (as it was headquarters in World War II for the war against Germany), the British created a throne and in 1922 crowned King Fouad, descendant of Mohammed Ali, to rule over both Egypt and the Sudan, but retained key power in finance, the military, foreign affairs, internal security, communications, and industrial development. In Egypt more than anywhere else after 1918 nationalist feelings were channeled into a single political party, which therefore had real power and could organize riots and street clashes at will either against the British or against political rivals who accepted British presence for their own purposes. The king also intrigued for as much power as he could seize, in effect forming a palace government through various constitutional revisions. In a crisis the British simply called out the army to set things the way they wanted. One great source of Egyptian anger was the Capitulations, left over from the Ottoman Empire, which the British would not give up until 1936. In every other new nation as well, Britain and France clung to the Capitulations. But Egypt prospered more than the other countries because the population was homogeneously Egyptian on the land, and in the cities the Levantines (including the Copts) had been residents from time immemorial. Also, the British had been running things since the mid-1800s and the hated, compli-

cated colonial system nevertheless benefited anyone who went along with it. Industrialization grew slowly but was on a better footing than anywhere else. Cairo and Alexandria were the most worldly cities in all the Mideast.

The sequence of events in Persia before World War I reads like a script for total chaos created by conflicts for power: the court, the British, Russian, and German commercial and diplomatic forces, tribal warlords, religious leaders, Persian merchants, political groups, and landlords all fought one another ferociously. None alone had any margin of authority against the rest, which created a permanent state of corruption through bribery, assassination, and reprisal. But the landlords formed the most coherent coalition, perhaps because control of food and of property taxes was the primary source of power in a non-industrialized society. They always collaborated with whoever strengthened their position, which included maintaining their status quo against modernization. Landlords filled the parliament, held offices high and low, controlled banking and the courts through judges, and had close relationships with the religious leaders, who, on the whole, had aims similar to the landlords'.

Just before the war the teenage Sultan Ahmad Shah turned toward Germany to escape from British and Russian pressures. After 1918 a standoff between now Bolshevik Russia and still imperialist Britain resulted in a withdrawal of both. In 1921 an unknown Cossack officer, Reza Khan, entered the leaderless confusion, seized Tehran with his troops, and soon made himself prime minister. He was inclined toward Westernization and a republican form of government along the lines drawn by Kemal Atatürk, but massive opposition from religious teachers and the powerful landlords and nobility turned him toward the traditional throne. In 1925 he deposed Ahmad Shah and proclaimed himself Shah Reza Khan Pahlevi. But his hero remained Atatürk and he tried to limit the cultural influence and political strength of the Shiite mullahs and ayatollahs. He planned state modernization of irrigation systems and state-owned industrialization, but most of these aims faltered because of the landlord system.

Oil dominated the Persian economy and was controlled by the Anglo-Persian Oil Company, formed in 1909. The company ran its business and its books as it saw fit, and

In 1908 an oil field was discovered near Abadan, Persia, and in 1913 the largest refinery in the world was completed there by the Anglo-Persian Oil Company. The picture indicates the technical ingenuity and the energy with which Europe colonized the Middle East, when it was profitable to do so, for every tool and bolt had to be shipped in thousands of miles and every drop of refined product had to be shipped out thousands of miles.

W. H. I. Shakespear, 1913.

the shah, though a total dictator, had to accept whatever royalties the company felt like giving him based on whatever production figures they cared to report. As part of modernization the name of the country was changed from Persia to Iran in 1935. In 1938 the shah wrangled much better concessions from the firm, newly named the Anglo Iranian Petroleum Company, but he remained subservient to British might. Furthermore, Russian interests squeezed him in the north, partly by controlling trade between the two countries. Just as his predecessor had done before the war, Reza Shah turned to the Germans for relief. German goods, technicians, tourists, and businessmen appeared in huge numbers in Iran and were clearly squeezing out those of Russia and Britain. Then World War II broke out. Two years later British and Russian armies forced the shah's abdication and shepherded his teenage son, Mohammed Reza Shah, to the throne.

Yemen's history is peculiar in that it was always more intimately related to Africa than to the Arab or Ottoman empires. It was closed to foreigners under a holy imam during the nineteenth century, and even after World War I permission to visit was difficult to obtain. Aden, to the south, was a British protectorate until after World War II, as was the Hadramaut, where, however, the tribes refused to recognize the British Crown. Muscat, Oman,

and Qatar were sheikhdoms more or less independent internally but recognizing British India as a watchful giant neighbor; after World War I the new kingdom of Saudi Arabia became their protector. Kuwait's sheikh allowed a British agent to counsel him, and Bahrein was a British Crown Colony. After 1945 all those faraway regions were pulled into the twentieth century because of their oil deposits.

This portrait of the Middle East has touched only the major events in its ten-thousand-year history, and only the largest details of life from the nineteenth century to World War I. The generation born during World War II is now in its late thirties and early forties, the prime age for achievement and for establishing power under the ruling sixty-year-olds, who were born during World War I. Far deeper conflicts than those of their counterparts in the West concerning the immediate goals of their nations separate these two generations.

They are divided by a modern turmoil, really a revolution in terms of nationalism, education, politics, economics, and industry, financed largely by oil royalties that the producing countries share with nonproducing neighbors. At the same time, they understand one another because they are all faithful to the concept that everything worthwhile can be attained within the teachings and laws of Islam. They quarrel over the means. Camels and shadoufs are being replaced by trucks and diesel pumps, but the primary task of the future will continue to be, as it always has been, the uninterrupted domestication of the desert in every part of the Middle East. Every sown acre must have a keeper who, with family and children and friends, can make a community prosper at the edge of the wasteland.

Bibliography

Articles, books, and exhibition catalogues with references to photographers who worked in the Middle East in the nineteenth and early twentieth centuries.

Borcoman, James. *The Painter as Photographer: David Octavius Hill, Auguste Salzmann, Charles Nègre*. Vancouver: Vancouver Art Gallery, 1978–1979.

Buckland, Gail. *Reality Recorded: Early Documentary Photography*. Greenwich, Conn.: New York Graphic Society, 1974.

Bull, Deborah, and Donald Lorimer. *Up the Nile. A Photographic Excursion: Egypt 1839–1898*. New York: Potter, 1979.

Carella, Elizabeth. "Bonfils and His Curious Composite." *Exposure* 17 (Spring 1979): 26–33.

Chappell, W. "Robertson, Beato & Co." *Image* 7 (Feb. 1958): 36–40.

"Comparative Photography: A Century of Change in Egypt and Israel. Photographs by Francis Frith & Jane Reese Williams." Introduction by Brian M. Fagan. *Untitled*, no. 17 (1979).

Darrah, William Culp. *The World of Stereographs*. Gettysburg, Pa.: W. C. Darrah, Publisher, 1977.

Dimock, George. "The Sunset of the Old World: A Portfolio from the Work of C. Chusseau Flaviens." *Image* 21 (March 1978)

"Early Photography in Egypt." Introduction by Gerry Badger. *Creative Camera*, no. 186 (December 1979).

Flaubert, Gustave. *Flaubert in Egypt: A Sensibility on Tour*. Translated and edited by Francis Steegmuller. Boston: Atlantic–Little, Brown, 1972.

Galassi, Peter. *Before Photography: Painting and the Invention of Photography*. New York: The Museum of Modern Art, 1981.

Gavin, Carney E. S. "Bonfils and the Early Photography of the Near East." *Harvard Library Bulletin* 26 (Oct. 1978): 442–470.

Gavin, Carney E. S., Elizabeth Carella, and Ingeborg O'Reilly. "The Photographers Bonfils of Beirut and Alès 1867–1916." *Camera* (March 1981).

Gill, Arthur T. "One Hundred Years Ago [Frith's Bible]." *The Photographic Journal* 102 (Jan. 1962): 39.

———. "Photography at the Great Pyramid in 1865." *The Photographic Journal* (April 1965): 109–118.

Gimon, Gilbert. "Les Daguerréotypes d'Égypte." *Prestige de la Photographie*, no. 9, pp. 13–30. Undated clipping.

Henisch, B. A. and H. K. "Robertson of Constantinople." *Image* 17 (Sept. 1974): 1–9.

Hershkowitz, Robert. *The British Photographer Abroad: The First Thirty Years*. London: Robert Hershkowitz, 1980.

Jammes, André. *French Primitive Photography*. Introduction by Minor White; commentary by Robert Sobieszek. New York: Aperture, 1970.

Jammes, André and Marie-Thérèse. *The First Century of Photography, Niepce to Atget, from the Collection of André Jammes*. Introduction by David Travis. Chicago: Art Institute 1977.

———. "Egypt in Flaubert's Time: An Exhibition of the First Photographers, 1839–1860." *Aperture*, no. 78 (1977): 62–77.

Jay, Bill. *Victorian Cameraman: Francis Frith's View of Rural England 1850–1898*. Newton Abbot, David & Charles, 1973.

———. "Francis Bedford 1816–1894." *Bulletin of the University of New Mexico*, no. 7 (1973).

Matson, G. Eric. *The Middle East in Pictures: A Photographic History, 1898–1934*. Introduction by George S. Hobart. 4 vols. New York: Arno Press, 1980.

Naef, Weston. *Early Photographers in Egypt and the Holy Land 1849–1870*. New York: The Metropolitan Museum of Art, Sept. 1973. Exhibition publication.

Newhall, Beaumont. "The Daguerreotype and the Traveler." *Magazine of Art* 44 (May 1951): 175–178.

Onne, Eyal. *Photographic Heritage of the Holy Land 1839–1914*. Manchester, England: Institute of Advanced Studies, Manchester Polytechnic, 1980.

Scarce, Jennifer. *Isfahan in Camera: 19th Century Persia through the Photographs of Ernst Hoeltzer*. London: Art and Archeology Research Paper, April 1976.

Schaaf, Larry. "Charles Piazzi Smyth's 1865 Conquest of the Great Pyramid." *History of Photography* 3 (Oct. 1979): 331–354.

Sobieszek, Robert. "La Maison Bonfils." *American Photographer* 4 (Nov. 1980): 48–57.

Sobieszek, Robert, and Carney E. S. Gavin. *Remembrances of the Near East: The Photographs of Bonfils, 1867–1907*. Exhibition catalogue. International Museum of Photography at George Eastman House and the Harvard Semitic Museum, 1980.

Thomas, Ritchie. "Bonfils & Son: Egypt, Greece and the Levant, 1867–1894." *History of Photography* 3 (Jan. 1979): 33–46.

———. "Egypt on Glass." *History of Photography* 4 (Oct. 1980): 329–335.

———. "Some 19th Century Photographers in Syria, Palestine and Egypt." *History of Photography* 3 (April 1979): 157–166.

———. "The Tin Box Photos." *Aramco World Magazine*, Sept.–Oct. 1975.

Two Victorian Photographers: Francis Frith . . . Francis Bedford . . . from the Collection of Dan Berley. Introduction by Dan Berley. Brockport, N.Y.: New York State University College, 1976.

Van Haaften, Julia. *Egypt and the Holy Land in Historic Photographs: 77 Views by Francis Frith*. Selection and commentary by Jon E. Manchip White. New York: Dover Publications, 1980.

———. "Francis Frith and Negretti & Zambra." *History of Photography* 4 (Jan. 1980): 35–37.

Wallach, Amei. "When Iran's Name Was Persia." *Newsday*, June 29, 1980, pp. 15–16. Interview with art historian Donna Stein.

Watson, Charles M. *The Life of Major-General Sir Charles William Wilson*. London: John Murray, 1909.

Biographies of Photographers

The following men and women photographed in the Middle East between 1839 and 1919. The list is not definitive. Sometimes there is a brief biography of someone whose work is not in the book. The omission of his or her photographs does not mean that the pictures are without merit or importance in the history of photography. Rather, they did not fit into the context of the book or were too subtle or delicate to reproduce properly (for example, some of the earliest calotypes), or showed subject matter that was already adequately covered (for example, antiquities). For some photographers in the book no biographical information is available.

Unless otherwise noted, photographers working in the 1850s used paper negative processes; those working in the 1860s, 1870s, and early 1880s used the wet collodion process; and those photographing from the mid-1880s on used dry (commercially prepared) plates or film.

ABDULLAH BIRADERLER (FRÈRES)

Armenian. Court photographers from 1862 to the sultans Abdul Aziz and Abdul Hamid II, Kevork and Wichen Biraderler began in photography as assistants to a German chemist, Rabach, who came to Constantinople during the Crimean War and established the first photographic studio in Anatolia. When Rabach left in 1858, the brothers took over the business. Because of privileges given them by the sultans, they became Muslim, were circumcised, and changed their name to Abdullah Biraderler. They photographed foreign rulers and Turkish dignitaries and made general studio portraits and stereo views. Abdul Hamid II commissioned them to photograph schools and military, public safety, and other facilities and institutions that showed the modernization of Turkey at the end of the nineteenth century. Hundreds of these pictures were mounted in fifty-one albums presented by the sultan to the Library of Congress in 1893. Their business was eventually hurt by competition, first by Febus Effendi, who was given the title "Sultan's Photographer," and later by the Apollo Photo Shop.

H. ARNOUX

Probably French. He worked in Egypt from the 1860s, sometimes with Zangaki. His photographs were often signed "Arnoux Photographie Port-Saïd." His *Album du Canal* contains 24 albumen prints of the Suez Canal and includes a portrait of Ferdinand de Lesseps.

EDGAR JAMES BANKS (1866–1945)

American. He served as field director for the University of Chicago Oriental Exploration Fund at Bismaya (in present-day Iraq) until 1904. In 1912 he published his book *Bismya* [sic].

HENRI DE BANVILLE (1837–1917)

French, of an ancient Norman family. Vicomte de Banville, an archeologist, traveled to Egypt in 1863–1864 with Vicomte Olivier Charles de Rougé, the curator of the Egyptian wing at the Louvre. He made the 158 photographs in the *Album photographique de la mission en Égypte* (1865), without payment, and was awarded the Croix de la Légion d'Honneur for his contribution.

FRÉDÉRIC-AUGUSTE BARTHOLDI (1834–1904)

French. The sculptor of the Statue of Liberty and the Lion of Belfort, he photographed in Egypt in 1855–1856.

ANTONIO BEATO (? –1903)

There is considerable confusion concerning the relationship of Antonio and Felix Beato and their nationality. They may have been brothers and they were probably Italian. Both were photographers. Antonio followed Felix to India and is listed in the *New Calcutta Directory* for 1859. He stayed only fifteen months and then left for Egypt, where he established a studio in Luxor in 1862. In 1907 his negatives were acquired by Gaston Maspero for the Cairo Museum. On many of the pictures taken by James Robertson and Felix Beato the signature reads "Robertson Beato & Co."; the "Co." could refer to Antonio.

FELIX [FELICE] BEATO

Reportedly born in Venice and a naturalized British citizen. He worked with James Robertson during the Crimean War (there is a reference in the *Illustrated London News* for July 21, 1860, to "Signor Beato, who has taken so many scenes in the Crimea") and in Constantinople, India, Athens, Egypt, and Palestine. Their photographs of the Holy Land were taken in 1857 and signed "Robertson and Beato" or "Robertson Beato & Co." Beato photographed the Indian Mutiny (1857–1859) and arrived in China in 1860 as the semi-official photographer of the Anglo-French North China Expeditionary Force. He then moved to Japan, where he lived and photographed for many years.

H. BÉCHARD

Probably French. He worked in Egypt in the 1870s and 1880s. He and Sébah exchanged or purchased negatives from each other. He won a gold medal at the Universal Exposition of 1878. His photographs were published as photogravures in *L'Égypte et la Nubie* (Paris: André Palmieri & Émile Béchard, 1887).

FRANCIS BEDFORD (1816–1894)

English, from an old, prestigious Cornish family. Bedford's father was an accomplished ecclesiastical architect and a painter. Of independent means, Francis, also a painter, turned avid photographer in the early 1850s and became known for his photographs of church architecture. He was commanded by Queen Victoria to accompany the Prince of Wales (Edward VII) on his Middle Eastern tour of 1862 and to document it. This was the first visit by the British Royal Family to the area since the Crusades. Prince Alfred, who was also on the trip, helped Bedford prepare the wet collodion negatives and expose the plates. Bedford made a total of 210

10×12-inch pictures, and in July 1852 he exhibited 172 of them at a Bond Street gallery. They were published the following year in 21 parts by Day & Son at 43 guineas under the title *Photographic Pictures of Egypt, the Holy Land and Syria, Constantinople, the Mediterranean, Athens, etc.* They were also offered in smaller units: "Egypt" (48 photographs, £12.12s), "The Holy Land and Syria" (76 photographs, £19.19s), "Constantinople, the Mediterranean, Athens &c." (48 photographs, £12.12s), "A selection of any twenty photographs from the entire series" (£7.7s), and "A selection of any photographs from the entire series, not less than three in number" (7s each). Except for the last category, the photographs came in a gilt-lettered half morocco leather portfolio. A book with 48 of the photographs, reduced in size, was published by Day & Son as *The Holy Land, Egypt, Constantinople, Athens, etc.*, with descriptive text and introduction by W. M. Thompson (1867).

GERTRUDE BELL (1868–1926)

English, born in Durham. Her grandfather was a founder of the iron industry in Yorkshire. After graduating from Oxford University, in 1892 Bell traveled to Persia, where her uncle was British Minister to the shah's court. She published her impressions of the country, *Persian Pictures*, anonymously in 1894, and in 1897 translations of Persian poetry, *Poems from the Divan of Hafiz*. Studies of Christian and early Islamic architecture led her to visit northern Arabia in 1913. Carrying a panoramic camera and a hand-camera that took glass plates $6\frac{1}{2} \times 4\frac{1}{4}$ inches, she was the first Western woman to penetrate the Great Arabian Desert. In 1915 British Intelligence recruited her to map Mesopotamia. As Assistant Political Agent there she was an important influence in the formation of the independent state of Iraq and became King Feisal's advisor and Director of Antiquities in Baghdad. Two of her best-known books are *The Desert and the Sown* (1907) and *The Thousand and One Churches* with Sir William Mitchell Ramsey (1909).

E. BENECKE

Probably French. A banker, he photographed in Lebanon, Egypt, and Syria in 1852 and 1853. Four of his photographs were included by the photographic publisher and printer Louis Désiré Blanquart-Évrard in his album titled *Imprimerie Photographique de Lille*.

G. BERGGREN

Worked in Egypt in the 1860s and 1870s. Among his photographs are two large panoramas of Constantinople, one of fourteen panels and one of eight panels.

PETER E. BERGHEIM

English, resident in Jerusalem 1850s to 1870s. A Jew converted to Christianity, he photographed in Palestine, Anatolia, and Greece. Twenty-six of his photographs are included in an album, *Palestine and Syria*, and his photographs also appear in Charles Warren's *Underground Jerusalem* (1876) and the *Ordnance Survey of Jerusalem* (London, 1865). The 1876 edition of Baedeker's *Palestine and Syria: Handbook for Travellers* mentions Bergheim's shop as being in the Christian Quarter of Jerusalem.

AUGUSTE-ROSALIE BISSON (1826– ?)

French. With his brother Louis-Auguste, he set up a daguerreotype studio in Paris in 1841. Ten years later they continued their careers as two of the finest practitioners of the wet collodion process. Famous for their architectural views of the 1850s and of the summit of Mont Blanc in 1861, they did not choose to compete for the carte-de-visite market in the 1860s and declared bankruptcy. Auguste-Rosalie entered the firm of M. Léon et L. Levy, Paris, photographic publishers, and was sent by them to Egypt for the opening of the Suez Canal in 1869. He also photographed in Syria.

FÉLIX BONFILS (1831–1885)

French, born in St.-Hippolyte-du-Fort near Alais (now Alès). Bonfils first arrived in Lebanon in 1860 with the French expeditionary corps sent to protect the Christian minority during the troubles with the Druze. Returning to France, he worked as a photographer. After his wife, Marie Lydie Cabannis, and his son, Paul-Félix-Adrien, had visited Beirut, Bonfils decided to move his family there in 1867. Between then and 1877 he became known as one of the finest and most prolific photographers of the Middle East. He also had a studio in Alais. In 1871 he stated he had made 15,000 prints and 9,000 stereoscopic views. He published the album *Architecture antique: Égypte, Grèce, Asie Mineure* (Paris, 1872). *Souvenirs d'Orient: Album pittoresque des sites, villes et ruines les plus remarquables de la Terre Sainte* was published in four volumes in Alais in 1877 and 1878. A small-format issue of *Souvenirs d'Orient*, containing 100 reduced-size photographs, was published in Alais in 1878, with captions in French, English, and German.

MARIE LYDIE CABANNIS BONFILS (1837–1919)

French, married Félix Bonfils in 1857. She worked with her husband in his Beirut studio and probably made most of the female portraits. Her pictures were used for the engravings in *Those Holy Fields: Palestine Illustrated by Pen and Pencil* by the Reverend Samuel Manning (London, 1874). In her *Catalogue général des vues photographiques de l'Orient* (Beirut, 1907) it is mentioned that the firm of Bonfils has studios in Jerusalem and Baalbek. She continued to photograph until she was evacuated from Beirut to Cairo in 1916. She was succeeded by Abraham Guiragossian, who kept the studio name of Bonfils.

PAUL-FÉLIX-ADRIEN BONFILS (1861–1929)

French, born in St.-Hippolyte-du-Fort. Educated in an Arab school in Beirut and in France, he joined the family business about 1877. His work, like that of his mother, father, and Guiragossian, is signed simply "Bonfils." About 1895 he gave up photography to run a hotel in Broummana, near Beirut. He left Lebanon for France after World War I.

GASTON BRAUN

French. The son of the well-known photographer Adolphe Braun (1812–1877) and his second wife, Pauline Baumann, he was sent by his father to Egypt in 1869 to photograph the opening of the Suez Canal and to record other aspects of Egyptian life. He returned to France with 80 wet collodion negatives. After 1870 he was briefly employed by Louis Pierson, whose daughter he married. The pictures from this period are signed "Braun and Pierson."

JAMES HENRY BREASTED (1865–1935)

American, born in Rockford, Illinois. A noted archeologist and historian of ancient Egypt, Breasted compiled a record of every known Egyptian hieroglyphic inscription and published a translation of them. He was Professor of Egyptology and Oriental History at the University of Chicago (1905–1933). From 1919 to 1924 he had a grant from John D. Rockefeller, Jr., to found and run the Oriental Institute there, which became one of the leading institutions of Egyptology in the Western Hemisphere.

Breasted's first trip to Nubia was from November 1905 to April 1906. Friedrich Koch, a German, helped him with the photographing of inscriptions at Abu Simbel, Wadi Halfa, and all the other pre-Ptolemaic temples of Lower Nubia, in the region between the First and Second Cataracts. On his second trip to Nubia, beginning in October 1906, he was assisted by the photographer Horst Schliephack. Together they photographed every inscription relating to the history of Nubia as an independent nation.

GEORGE W. BRIDGES

English. An acquaintance of William Henry Fox Talbot, the Reverend Mr. Bridges learned the calotype process from Talbot's assistant, Nicholaas Henneman. He left England in 1845 on a seven-year trip that took him to Malta, Italy, Greece, and the Holy Land. In each place he photographed, using chemically treated paper sent to him from Talbot's Reading establishment in England. When he returned to Britain in 1852, he reputedly had 1,700 pictures. The whereabouts of most of them are not known; a very small number taken in 1849 and 1850 were published in 1858–1859 in Bridges's album *Palestine as It Is: In a Series of Photographic Views . . . Illustrating the Bible* (London: J. W. Hogarth). From 1855 to 1862 Bridges was the curate of a parish in England.

HENRY CAMMAS

French. He worked in Egypt in the early 1860s, using paper negatives, and exhibited his large prints at the Société Française de Photographie in 1863. Smaller prints were published in his book *La Vallée du Nil: Impressions et photographies* by Cammas and André Lefèvre (Paris: L. Hachette, 1862).

ERNEST DE CARANZA

French. A manufacturing engineer and an amateur photographer, he traveled and photographed in Anatolia in 1852. He exhibited his prints from paper negatives in Brussels in 1856 and in Paris in 1857. He was a member of the Société Française de Photographie.

CHARLIER-BÉZIES

Probably French. An amateur photographer, he owned a bookshop in Beirut in the late nineteenth century. He later became a publisher of postcards until the beginning of World War I.

JOHN CRAMB

Scottish. He photographed in Palestine in 1860, making 8 × 10-inch and stereoscopic pictures by the albumen-on-glass process. His pictures appeared in *Palestine in 1860* by Robert Buchanan, *Jerusalem in 1860*, and in a version of the Bible published in Glasgow in 1861. He held the title "Photographer to the Queen."

LOUIS DE CLERCQ (1836–1901)

French. A traveler and archeologist, in 1859–1860 he photographed in Syria, Palestine, Egypt, and Spain using Gustave LeGray's waxed-paper process. He published 222 of his photographs at his own expense in a five-volume work titled *Voyage en Orient* (1859–1860), which was given to friends and some public collections. Many of the pictures were large panoramas, difficult to make. He was an avid collector; in 1968 the Louvre exhibited 600 items that he had gathered together during his lifetime and that his family had bequeathed to the museum.

THÉODULE DEVÉRIA (1831–1871)

French. The son of a painter, he studied Coptic and Arabic and in 1851 began working at the Bibliothèque Nationale. On the recommendation of the Egyptologist Vicomte Olivier Charles de Rougé, he was appointed to the Egyptology Department of the Louvre to help catalogue items sent back from Egypt by the archeologist Auguste Mariette, later director of the Egyptian Museum in Cairo. In 1858 he accompanied Mariette to Egypt and made paper negatives and sketches. He made four later trips.

MAXIME DU CAMP (1822–1894)

French. A photographer and writer, Du Camp traveled to Asia Minor, Greece, Italy, and Algeria in the year 1844–1845; *Souvenirs et paysages d'Orient* (1848) is an account of his journey. In the Revolution of 1848 he fought with the National Guard, was wounded and received the Croix de la Légion d'Honneur. From 1849 to 1851 he traveled with his friend the novelist Gustave Flaubert to Egypt, Nubia, Palestine, Syria, Anatolia, and Greece, with a commission from the French Ministry of Education to photograph the monuments and sites of the Middle East. He made more than 200 paper negatives, of which 125 photographs, printed by Blanquart-Évrard, were published in 1852 in *Égypte, Nubie, Palestine et Syrie* (Paris: Gide et Baudry). This was the first travel book with photographs. In 1851 he cofounded the *Revue de Paris*, which published much controversial writing, including Flaubert's *Madame Bovary*. He was made an officer of the Légion d'Honneur in 1853. Among his books are *Expédition des Deux-Siciles* (1861), about his experience as a volunteer with the Italian revolutionary Garibaldi, and *Souvenirs littéraires* (1882–1883), two volumes.

TANCRÈDE R. DUMAS (? –1905)

French. He had a studio in Beirut from 1860 and photographed the Holy Land through the 1870s. In January 1877 the American Palestine Exploration Society published 99 of his photographs taken in the fall of 1875.

JOHANNES DÜMICHEN (1833–1894)

German. An archeologist, he studied Egyptology under Karl Richard Lepsius and Heinrich Karl Brugsch, and was professor of Egyptology at the University of Strassburg from 1872 to 1894. He frequently visited Egypt, copying inscriptions and texts both by hand and with the camera. Seventy-three of his photographs appear in *Photographische Resultate einer . . . nach Aegypten entsendeten archäologischen Expedition* (Berlin: S. P. Christmann, 1871).

George Eastman (1854–1932)

American, born in Waterville, New York, and educated in Rochester, New York. Eastman made amateur photography a popular reality with the introduction of the Kodak camera. In 1880 he perfected a process for making dry plate negatives and started manufacturing them. Four years later he set up the Eastman Dry Plate and Film Company, and in 1888 placed the first Kodak on the market. One of the first hand-held cameras, it took small circular pictures on a 100-exposure roll of stripping film. When the roll was finished, the whole camera was sent back to the manufacturer for developing, printing, and reloading. When George Eastman traveled to Egypt in 1890, he photographed with the Kodak No. 1. He founded the Eastman Kodak Company in 1892.

L. Fiorillo

He had a studio in Aswan and photographed throughout the Middle East in the 1880s and early 1900s. He issued an album showing the aftermath of the British bombing of Alexandria on July 11, 1882.

C. Chusseau Flaviens

French. He photographed in Europe, the Far East, the Middle East, and North Africa prior to World War I. He had access to royalty, leading politicians, and celebrities, often at fashionable holiday resorts. Over 10,000 of his glass negatives are housed at the International Museum of Photography at the George Eastman House, Rochester, New York.

Francis Frith (1822–1898)

English. Raised as a Quaker by parents who were great students of the Bible, Frith attended Quaker schools until the age of sixteen, when he was apprenticed to a cutlery firm in Sheffield for five years. At twenty-one he had a mental and physical breakdown and spent the next two years traveling in Great Britain with his parents. He became a devout Christian. He moved to Liverpool and started a grocery business with another young man, cornering the Greek raisin market and becoming rich while still in his early thirties. In 1850 he started a printing company and began taking photographs. He sold the business in 1856 and three years later founded the photographic printing and publishing firm of F. Frith & Co., Reigate, Surrey, one of the largest photographic publishers in the world.

Frith made three photographic trips to the Middle East: from September 1856 to July 1857 he traveled to Egypt and up the Nile to the Second Cataract above Abu Simbel; from November 1857 to May 1858 he journeyed to Palestine, Syria, Jerusalem, Damascus, Mt. Sinai, and Baalbek; and in the summer of 1859 he became a true explorer, traveling over 1,500 miles up the Nile, past the Second Cataract. He had three wet plate cameras: a studio camera using 8×10-inch glass plates, a stereo camera, and a mahogany camera that took glass plates 16×20 inches. From his Middle East photographs three sets of stereos and eleven books were published: *Egypt and Palestine Photographed and Described by Francis Frith* (London: J. S. Virtue [1858–1860]), two volumes; *Cairo, Sinai, Jerusalem, and the Pyramids of Egypt: A Series of Sixty Photographic Views by Francis Frith. With Descriptions by Mrs. Poole and Reginald Stuart Poole* (London: J. S. Virtue [1860, 1861?]); *Egypt, Sinai, and Jerusalem: A Series of Twenty Photo-*graphic Views by Francis Frith. With Descriptions by Mrs. Poole and Reginald Stuart Poole* (London: W. Mackenzie [1860?]), republished by J. S. Virtue, London, 1862; *The Holy Bible . . . : Illustrated with Photographic Views of Biblical Scenery from Nature by Frith* (London: J. E. Eyre & W. Spottiswoode, 1862); *Egypt, Nubia, and Ethiopia: Illustrated by One Hundred Stereoscopic Photographs, Taken by Francis Frith for Messrs. Negretti and Zambra. With Descriptions and Numerous Wood Engravings, by Joseph Bonomi . . . and Notes by Samuel Sharpe* (London: Smith, Elder & Co., 1862); *The Holy Bible; Containing the Old and New Testaments . . . Illustrated with Photographs by Frith* (Glasgow: W. Mackenzie, 1862–1863; second title page reads *The Queen's Bible*); *Sinai and Palestine; Lower Egypt, Thebes, and the Pyramids; Upper Egypt and Ethiopia; Egypt, Sinai, and Palestine, Supplementary Volume* (London: W. Mackenzie [1862?]), four volumes; and *Photo-Pictures from the Land of the Bible* [1860s] with illustrations by Frith and Frank M. Good.

In 1860 Frith married. In addition to producing his books, he began making a photographic record of every city, town, and village in England, Scotland, Wales, and Ireland. Later, he employed others to photograph in the British Isles, Europe, and elsewhere, the pictures being printed and distributed as postcards and prints.

Helen Hamilton Gardener (1853–1925)

American, born Alice Chenoweth in Winchester, Virginia; married Charles Seldon Smart in 1875. She studied biology at Columbia University and lectured in sociology at the Brooklyn Institute of Arts and Sciences. She wrote newspaper articles under male pseudonyms and when she began lecturing in freethinking (agnosticism) changed her name to Helen Hamilton Gardener. A staunch feminist and suffragette, she wrote novels describing the plight of women. After her husband died in 1901, she remarried and traveled around the world with her second husband, Colonel Selden Allen Day, until 1907, taking snapshots of the places they visited. She was vice-president of the National American Woman Suffrage Association, and as its chief liaison with the Wilson administration she drafted several of the President's statements concerning women's suffrage. At the age of sixty-seven she was appointed by Wilson to the U.S. Civil Service Commission, the first woman to hold such a high federal position.

Joseph Philibert Girault de Prangey (1804–1892)

French. An expert on Muslim architecture, he traveled for two years in Italy, Greece, Egypt, Syria, and Palestine, making approximately 1,000 daguerreotypes. Some of these were copied as engravings for his book *Monuments arabes d'Égypte, de Syrie et d'Asie Mineure* (Paris, 1846).

Frank Mason Good

English. Possibly an assistant of Francis Frith, Good worked in the Sinai and the Near East in the 1860s. Some of his photographs appear in Frith's *Photo-Pictures from the Land of the Bible*. In the mid-1860s he published stereoscopic views of the Holy Land and *Photo-Pictures of the Holy Land*.

James Graham

English. One of the first resident photographers in Jerusalem, he was the Honorary Secretary to the London Jews Society. He photographed in Palestine and Syria in the 1850s, sometimes accompanying painters such as Thomas Seddon and the Pre-Raphaelite William Holman Hunt. Seddon's painting *Jerusalem* in the National Gallery, London, is probably based on one of Graham's photographs. Graham's work is usually dated in the negative 1854 or 1855 and signed and dated on the mount 1856 or 1857. Excerpts from the Bible sometimes appear under the photos. He made two magnificent panoramas of Jerusalem, one of six parts and one of ten parts. He exhibited his photographs in 1859 at the Exhibition of Fine Arts at the Palais de l'Industrie, Paris.

CARLETON H. GRAVES
American. A photographer specializing in stereoscopic views. He was associated with his father, Jesse A. Graves, from the 1870s, and active in the years 1880–1910 under the imprint of the Universal Photo Art Company.

JOHN BULKLEY GREENE (ca. 1832–1856)
American. An archeologist, the son of a banker in the Paris-based firm of Greene and Greene, he excavated the temple of Medinet Habu at Thebes in Egypt. He began photographing in 1852 and two years later Blanquart-Évrard published his book *Le Nil, Monuments, paysages, explorations photographiques*, with 94 salt prints. The following year *Fouilles exécutées à Thebes dans l'année 1855: Textes hiéroglyphiques et documents inédits* by J. B. Greene appeared in Paris. In 1855–1856 he photographed in Algeria. He was a member of the Asiatic Society and a founding member of the Société Française de Photographie. In the January 1857 bulletin of the latter, it was announced that Greene had died in November 1856 at the age of 24.

Although the above biography is given by photo-historians to identify the J. B. Greene who photographed in Egypt in the 1850s, confusion has arisen because Warren R. Dawson and Eric P. Uphill in *Who Was Who in Egyptology* (London: The Egypt Exploration Society, 1972) say that the man who wrote *Fouilles exécutées . . .* was an Englishman, John Baker Greene. According to Dawson and Uphill this J. B. Greene (ca. 1830–ca. 1886) was a surgeon and barrister who had studied Egyptology in France under Vicomte Olivier Charles de Rougé and went on an archeological expedition to Thebes in 1854–1855. He served as a surgeon in the Crimean War and then practiced law in London. He was a member of the Council of the Royal Historical Society (1880–1886), published *The Hebrew Migration from Egypt* (1882), and contributed to the Palestine Exploration Fund *Quarterly* in 1884 and 1885.

ABRAHAM GUIRAGOSSIAN
Palestinian. He was the successor to Marie Lydie Cabannis Bonfils, taking over the negatives and keeping the name of the Bonfils studio from between 1907 and 1916 until 1932. He published *Catalogue général des vues photographiques de l'Orient* (Beirut, n.d.) and sold platinum prints from Bonfils negatives.

SULEIMAN HAKIM
A photographer apparently working in Damascus at the turn of the century, he signed his pictures "S. Hakim." He is best known for his photographs of Mecca.

W. HAMMERSCHMIDT
German. He photographed in Egypt in the late 1850s through probably the 1870s. He donated some of his prints to the Société Française de Photographie, exhibited in their salon in 1861, and appears in their list of members in 1863.

ERNST HOELTZER (1835–1911)
German. An engineer, he lived in the Isfahan area of Persia and made 3,000 glass negatives between 1871 and 1898 of every aspect of life in that part of the country.

JULES ITIER (1802–1877)
French. The nephew of the Egyptologist Joseph-Marie Dubois-Aymé, he was the General Inspector of Customs in Senegal, Guiana, and the West Indies. In November 1845 he sailed for Cairo from Java, arriving in December. For two months he traveled in Egypt making daguerreotypes. Remarkably, his plates are still in existence in a private collection in Paris. He later settled in Montpellier, where he experimented with scientific photography.

JOAILLIER
He shared a studio with Sébah at 439 Grande Rue de Pera, Constantinople.

R. M. JUNGHAENDEL
Probably German. He worked in Egypt in 1890s. His book *Egypt: Heliogravures after Original Views* (1893), with a preface by C. G. Rawlinson, contained 22 of his photographs and 3 by L. C. Müller.

GEORGE SKENE KEITH
Scottish. A doctor and the brother of the calotypist Thomas Keith, he traveled to Palestine and Syria with their father, Alexander, in 1844. He made 30 daguerreotypes, over half of which were used as the basis for engravings in *Evidence of the Truth of the Christian Religion* by Alexander Keith (Edinburgh: W. Whyte, 1844). He was the first to photograph Petra.

BENJAMIN W. KILBURN (1827–1909)
American. One of the largest manufacturers of stereoscopic views, Kilburn Brothers and their successor B. W. Kilburn (later The Kilburn Company) were in operation from 1865 to 1909. Ben Kilburn took thousands of views in the United States, Europe, and in the Middle East (1870s). He initiated door-to-door salesmanship of photographs, based strictly on commission, with delivery of the stereo-cards within one week. The trade list exceeded 16,000 titles.

C. [G.] KRIKORIAN
Armenian. A deacon in Jerusalem, he gave up the diaconate to become a photographer in the 1860s. He continued photographing in Palestine, often for book illustration, until the 1890s. He made a series of pictures in September 1892 of the railway from Jaffa to Jerusalem. His son, J. Krikorian, was a photographer active from the 1910s to 1948.

CHARLES LALLEMAND
French. He produced a series of photographs in the 1860s to illustrate the native costumes and peoples of the world, titled *Galerie*

universelle des peuples; volume 1 was *La Syrie: Costumes, voyages, paysages* (Paris: Petit Journal, 1866). He also published *Voyage in the Orient: Maronite Syria*. He photographed over 600 subjects, primarily for the use of artists.

THOMAS EDWARD LAWRENCE (1888–1935)

English, known as Lawrence of Arabia. While a student at Oxford University, he toured Syria, and then in 1911 went on an archeological expedition to Mesopotamia. Until 1914 he lived in the Middle East, working on digs, learning Arabic, and traveling. He was attached to the Intelligence Section of the British Army in Egypt (1914–1919) and roused the Arabs under King Feisal to wage war against the Turks. He learned to use a camera while working as an archeologist and carried one with him during the Arab revolt. After the war he fought for Arab independence and twice joined the military under assumed names, eventually changing his name legally to Shaw. His book *Seven Pillars of Wisdom* (1926) is an account of the Arab uprising.

GUSTAVE LE GRAY (1820–1882)

French. A painter, photographer, teacher, and innovator of photographic techniques, he exhibited his photographs as early as 1848. He was a member of the Société Héliographique and a founding member of the Société Française de Photographie. In 1851 he invented the waxed paper process, an adaption of the calotype process. He taught photography to many people, including Maxime Du Camp. He is perhaps best known for his seascapes made on collodion negatives. Around 1859 he gave up his photographic studio in Paris and moved to Egypt, where he became a drawing instructor, having as one of his pupils the future khedive, Ismail. He continued to take photographs and teach photography. He died in Egypt after a fall from a horse.

G. LEKEGIAN

Probably Armenian. Holder of the official title of "Photographer to the British Army of Occupation" (in Egypt), he apparently worked from the 1860s to the early twentieth century. His prints are signed "G. Lekegian & Co."

DANIEL DAVID LUCKENBILL (1881–1927)

American, born near Hamburg, Pennsylvania. An Assyriologist, Luckenbill studied at the universities of Pennsylvania, Berlin, and Chicago and taught at the latter. He was curator of the Assyrian collections in the Haskell Oriental Museum (now Oriental Institute), was on the editorial board of the *Journal of Religion*, and co-editor of the *American Journal of Semitic Languages and Literature*. He excavated in Palestine in 1908–1909 and was a member of the University of Chicago Oriental Expedition 1919–1920. He published more than 34 monographs; his major works include *Annals of Sennacherib* and *Ancient Records of Assyria and Babylonia*. He died before completing his *magnum opus*, to be titled *Cuneiform Dictionary*.

G. ERIC MATSON (1888–1977)

Swedish-American, born in Nas, Dalarna, Sweden. As a boy he emigrated in 1896 with his parents and other farmers to Jerusalem, where they joined a group of Americans who had started a small Christian colony in 1881. The community prospered as it acquired property, livestock, olive and fig groves, and started taking photographs and selling them to tourists. The earliest ones were made in 1896 and signed "The American Colony." Matson taught himself photography, soon took over the studio, and in 1934 changed its name to "The Matson Photo Service." He photographed extensively all over the Middle East until 1946. Then he moved to the United States and eventually donated 20,000 negatives to the Library of Congress.

V. G. MAUNIER

French. He lived in Egypt for many years, working as a photographer, pawnbroker, and dealer in antiquities. In April 1854 the French periodical *La Lumière* described his discoveries at the Temple of Amenhotep at Luxor. Since several of his photographs, printed by Blanquart-Évrard in 1854 or 1855, are in the collection of the Société Française de Photographie, it is possible that an album was issued.

JAMES MCDONALD

British. Color sergeant, Royal Engineers, and one of two managers of the Photographic Office of the Royal Engineers' Establishment in 1869, he was part of Charles W. Wilson's survey team sent to Jerusalem in 1864–1865. Seventy-three of his photographs were published in the *Ordnance Survey of Jerusalem* (London, 1865). He participated in a second survey, also under Charles Wilson, which resulted in the much larger *Ordnance Survey of the Peninsula of Sinai* (Southampton, 1869). The photographs appeared in three volumes: 1. *Suez to Mount Sinai* (60 photographs), 2. *Wady Feiran and Mount Serbal* (60 photographs), and 3. *Sinaitic and Egyptian Inscriptions* (33 photographs).

A. DE MOUSTIER

French. A count, he was related to the French Ambassador to Turkey, the Marquis de Moustier, who obtained for him a firman so that he could travel and photograph safely within Asia Minor. His glass negatives, which were specially prepared in Paris in August 1862 with a solution of tannin for preservation, were exposed in Turkey in October and developed in Paris in December. This was an extremely uncommon procedure at a time when photographic plates were sensitized, exposed, and developed within minutes. His article "Voyage de Constantinople à Ephèse par l'intérieur de l'Asie Mineure, Bithynie, Phrygie, Lydie, Ionie" appeared in *Le Tour du monde* (second quarter, 1864), illustrated with wood engravings from his photographs.

H. PHILLIPS

English. A sergeant in the Royal Engineers, he was the photographer for the first surveys sponsored by the Palestine Exploration Fund. He took 164 photographs of Palestine from November 1865 to May 1866, and 179 photographs in 1867.

JAMES ROBERTSON (ca. 1813– ?)

Scottish. The photographer was probably the same James Robertson described as a "gem engraver," who exhibited between 1833 and 1840 four medallic portraits at the Royal Academy in London. Sometime between 1840 and 1850 he arrived in Constantinople, where he became Superintendent and Chief Engraver of the Mint and lived until 1881. On one of his trips back to England, he married Marie Matilda Beato, presumably Felix Beato's sister.

Robertson started photographing while on a trip to Malta in 1850, making calotypes with the help of Felix Beato. They photographed together in Constantinople, the Crimea, Egypt, Athens, Palestine, and India, changing their process to albumen-on-glass. *Photographic Views of Constantinople* was published in London by Joseph Cundall in 1853. *Description of a Series of Views of Jerusalem and Its Environs Executed by Robertson and Beato of Constantinople* (London and Paris: E. Gambart, n.d.) contains 21 photographs out of a set of 32 that are dated 1857. The pictures of Jerusalem are signed "Robertson Beato et Cie"; those of Egypt "Robertson & Beato"; and the one of Cairo "A. Beato." The Jerusalem pictures are titled on the negatives and are sometimes numbered.

Although Robertson is well known for his pictures of the Crimean War, mostly after the fall of Sebastopol on September 5, 1855, he may not have taken all or most of these. The *Journal of the Photographic Society* (vol. 3, June 21, 1856) reported under "Photographic Gossip" an article that appeared in *The Times* (London), June 18, 1856: "Mr. Robertson, Superintendent of the Imperial Mint at Constantinople, has sent up an intelligent photographer to the Crimea, and he is now engaged in fixing, as far as possible, every remarkable spot on paper." And the *Illustrated London News* for July 21, 1860, referred to "Signor Beato, who has taken so many scenes in the Crimea." Many of Robertson's photographs were copied as engravings and reproduced in books.

AUGUSTE SALZMANN (1824–27)
French. A painter of religious and allegorical subjects, Salzmann was also interested in archeology and photography. In December 1853 he left for Jerusalem, where he spent four months photographing to confirm Louis-Félicien Caignart de Saulcy's theories on the dating of Jewish, Christian, and Islamic architecture. He had an assistant named Durheim, who may have photographed under his supervision. Durheim did make pictures for two months after Salzmann left the city, and the work of both appears in Salzmann's two-volume book *Jérusalem: Étude et reproduction photographique des monuments de la Ville Sainte* (Paris: Gide et J. Baudry, 1856). It has 174 salted paper prints made at Blanquart-Évrard's establishment. In 1858 Salzmann went to Rhodes to study the excavations of Camirros and remained there until 1865.

J. PASCAL SÉBAH
Possibly Turkish. A commercial photographer who opened a studio in Constantinople in 1868, he worked with Joaillier; their photographs are sometimes signed jointly. He also had a studio in Cairo. He sometimes bought or exchanged negatives with Béchard, obliterated Béchard's name, and signed his own to them.

ANTOINE SEVRUGUIN
Probably Russian-Armenian. He had a commercial studio in Tehran from ca. 1880s to 1920s. He photographed the shah and his court, newsworthy events, and various aspects of Persian life. His name appeared in different spellings when his work was reproduced in books and articles at the turn of the century.

WILLIAM HENRY IRVINE SHAKESPEAR (1878–1915)
British, born in the Punjab; attended English schools and Sand-hurst. In 1898 he was posted to India, and in 1904 to Bushire, where he became assistant to Major Percy Cox, a diplomat in Persia. In 1907 he drove his automobile from Bushire to England via Persia, Anatolia, and Europe. Appointed Political Agent in Kuwait with instructions to meet Ibn Saud and draft agreement between British and Wahabis, he provided the British with almost all the information they had about Arabia; he made many excursions to map the interior and in 1914 crossed from the Persian Gulf to Egypt. To record the remote areas he visited and the leadership and activities of the Wahabis, he used a panoramic camera that had a clockwork mechanism and a hand camera that took glass plates. Remarkably, he developed his negatives even while traveling in the desert. Advisor and friend to Ibn Saud, he was killed during a skirmish between the forces of Ibn Saud and Ibn Rashid, emir of Hail.

B. LLOYD SINGLEY (1864– ?)
American. An amateur photographer, he founded one of the most important stereo publishing companies: the Keystone View Company. From 1892 to 1897 he took all the negatives for the company and composed the captions that appeared on the cards.

JOHN SHAW SMITH (1811–1873)
Irish. An affluent landowner who toured southern Europe and the Middle East in 1850–1852, he made about 300 photographs by the calotype process, adapting it, however, for hot climates. He used the paper moist and gave it an exposure of seven minutes in bright sunlight.

CHARLES PIAZZI SMYTH (1819–1900)
English. The Astronomer Royal for Scotland and the Director of the Edinburgh Observatory, he made photographs of the exterior and interior of the Great Pyramid, using wet collodion plates and burning magnesium. Among his published works are *A Poor Man's Photography at the Great Pyramid in the Year 1865, Compared with That of the Ordnance Survey Establishment, Subsidized by London Wealth, and under the Orders of Col. Sir Henry James . . . at the Same Place Four Years Afterwards: A Discourse Delivered before the Edinburgh Photographic Society on December 1st, 1869* (London: Henry Greenwood, 1870) and *Our Inheritance in the Great Pyramid* (London: A. Straham and Co., 1864), which went into many editions. Fifty of his photographs were published in the portfolio *Descriptive Album of Photographs of the Great Pyramid* (Manchester: J. S. Pollitt, 1879).

FÉLIX TEYNARD (1817–1892)
French. An engineer, he traveled and photographed in Egypt in 1851–1852 and again in 1869. His photographs were published between 1853 and 1858 by Goupil (prints made by Fonteny) under the title *Égypte et Nubie: Sites et monuments les plus intéressants pour l'étude de l'art et de l'histoire*. The book, with 160 plates, sold for nearly 1,000 francs.

PIERRE TRÉMAUX
French. He made calotypes in the Sudan from about 1847 to 1854. Beginning in January 1852, his book *Voyage au Soudan oriental* was issued in parts by Borani et Droz, Paris. Over the approximately 15 years during which it was published, the method of re-

production of the illustrations changed from traditional lithography from drawings, to salted paper prints from calotype negatives, to lithographs traced from original photographs, to photolithography.

BERT ELIAS UNDERWOOD (1862–1943)
American. With his brother Elmer, he began merchandising stereo views in 1882. In 1891 he learned photography from M. Abel in Menton, France, and thereafter traveled to Italy, Greece, the Holy Land, and Egypt making stereoscopic views. Originally Underwood & Underwood distributed Charles Bierstadt's views of Palestine made in 1872. In 1897 Underwood & Underwood purchased the photo-printing facilities of J. F. Jarvis and Bierstadt and, shortly thereafter, William H. Rau.

L. VIGNES
French. He and the photographer Jardin provided the photographs that were made into heliographs by Charles Nègre for an atlas of the Holy Land by Honoré T. P. J. d'Albert, duc de Luynes. He worked in the Middle East in 1864.

C. G. WHEELHOUSE
English. He photographed in the Middle East in 1849–1850 while serving as the medical officer of a yachting party consisting of Lord Lincoln, later the Duke of Newcastle, War Minister during the Crimean War, and other gentlemen. He made photographs of Baalbek, Petra, Karnak, Lebanon, Jerusalem, Damascus, Cairo, Thebes, Aswan, Edfu, Memnon, Philae, the Tombs of the Caliphs, the Convent of Mt. Sinai, and the Range of Horeb. All the calotype negatives were given to Lord Lincoln and subsequently destroyed in a fire. Wheelhouse put his prints in an album, which he titled "Photographic Sketches from the Shores of the Mediterranean," and wrote anecdotes and descriptions for each picture.

EDWARD LIVINGSTON WILSON (1838–1903)
American. A Philadelphia photographer, he published an "Eastern Series" of 650 stereo cards of Palestine, Syria, and Anatolia in 1883.

ZANGAKI
Possibly Turkish. He worked in Egypt from the 1860s, sometimes with Arnoux, from a studio in Port Said.

Index

Photograph Credits

The word detail has been used in the captions to denote photographs that have not been reproduced in their entirety. In almost all instances, however, only the slightest fraction of the picture has been eliminated. Photographs that bleed have approximately one-eighth inch taken off the edges.

The Art Institute of Chicago (photos Doug Munson): 4 top, 8 right, 104, 109, 167 top; BBC Hulton Picture Library, London: 2 left, 51, 60, 64, 122 bottom, 142, 145 right, 162 right; Bibliothèque Nationale, Paris: iv-v, vi, 11 bottom, 77, 126 bottom (both), 154, 166 top right, 178 bottom; The Brooklyn Museum, Courtesy Department of Egyptian and Classical Art (photos Scott Hyde): 3, 5 top, 23, 62 bottom, 134, 139, 168; Peter Coffeen (photos Scott Hyde): 98 top, 176; Arnold H. Crane Collection 11 top, 14 top left and xvii (both), 6 (both), 7 bottom, 8 left, (photos Doug Munson): bottom, 32–33, 40 right, 62 top, 68, 74–75 top, 81 top, 94 top, 98 bottom, 110 (both), 111 (both), 125, 132, 144, 149, 150, 163 (both), 165 top and bottom, 170 top right, 172 top, 174, 177 left, 197 center; John Fordham: 24; Freer Gallery of Art, Smithsonian Institution: viii, 52, 53 top, 54 top, 121; Collection of G. Gimon Photographique, Paris: 10, 29, 34, 43, 101 bottom; Harrison D. Horblit: 58–59 bottom; Imperial War Museum, London: 56 top, 58 top, 89, 181, 182 (both), 185, 186; India Office Library and Records, London (reproduced by permission of the Director): 54 bottom, 55, 152, 172 bottom, 173 bottom; International Museum of Photography at George Eastman House: i, 173 top; Janet Lehr Inc., New York (photo Scott Hyde): 151; Collection Gérard Lévy, Paris: 22, 115, 178 top, 179 left; Library of Congress: x-xi, 20, 36, 41 left, 65, 66, 67, 85, 101 top, 108, 112, 117, 130, 141 (both), 147; Middle East Centre, St. Anthony's College, Oxford University (photos David Buckland): 16, 17 (both), 26, 42 left, 48 bottom, 50 top, 80, 83, 114, 123, 128 bottom left, 131, 158; The New York Public Library, Astor, Lenox and Tilden Foundations. Art, Prints, and Photographs Division: 5 bottom, 7 top, 9, 14 top right, 18, 19, 100 bottom, 102, 140 (both), 170 top left, 197 right. From the Collection of the Jewish Division: 45, 50 bottom; The Oriental Institute, University of Chicago: ii, iii, xxii, 2 right, 46, 47, 48 top, 49 (both), 72 (both), 92, 95, 96, 97, 120 top left and bottom, 128 top, 155, 160, 167 bottom, 170 bottom; Peter B. Rathbone (photos courtesy Sotheby Parke Bernet): xii, 166 bottom; Royal Commonwealth Society, London (photos David Buckland): 61, 63; Royal Geographical Society, London: 56 bottom, 57, 74 bottom, 81 bottom, 82, 86, 94 bottom, 103 (both), 120 top right, 122 top, 127 bottom, 128 bottom right, 129 (all), 153, 171, 188; Royal Library, Windsor (reproduced by Gracious Permission of Her Majesty Queen Elizabeth II) (photos Elizabeth Johnston): 4 bottom, 99, 175; Royal Photographic Society Collection, Bath: 39; School of Oriental and African Studies, London University: 28, 40 left, 93 left; Science Museum, London (Crown copyright): 100 top, 165 middle; Semitic Museum, Harvard University: xvi, 13 bottom, 27, 42 right, 78, 84, 148, 177 right; Smithsonian Institution: 41 right (photo no. 79-4824), 53 bottom (79-4816), 93 right (79-4815), 127 top (79-4818), 146 right and left (79-4827, 79-4821), 157 right (79-4812), 159 right (79-4814), 167 middle (79-4837), 179 right (79-4828); Collection TEXBRAUN,

Paris: 70, 113, 126 top, 130 bottom, 197 left; Victoria and Albert Museum, London (photos David Buckland): 90, 137, 159 left, 166 top left; Stephen White's Gallery of Photography Inc., Los Angeles: 12, 25, 138; Daniel Wolf Inc., New York (photos Scott Hyde): vii, ix, 13 top left and right, 15, 21, 44, 106, 118, 124, 136, 143, 145 left, 156–157, 161 (both), 162 left, 180

Map (page xviii): Ann Lampton Curtis

Countless unsung water carriers kept everyone alive, as they still do where diesel pumps and iron pipes do not exist. Though they were paid almost nothing, their toil was honored and blessed by everyone. We give them their due by showing some portraits to remind us. *Page xvi: A. Beato, after 1862; xvii (both): H. Béchard, 1870s–1880s; 197 left: Auguste-Rosalie Bisson, 1869; 197 center: J. Pascal Sébah, 1870s–1880s; 197 right: Anonymous, ca. 1875.*

SOURCES FOR PAGES 104–105

Goupil-Fesquet: quoted in Beaumont Newhall, "The Daguerreotype and the Traveler," *Magazine of Art* (May 1951), pp. 176, 177.

Du Camp: quoted in Francis Steegmuller, ed., *Flaubert in Egypt* (Boston: Atlantic-Little, Brown, 1972), pp. 101–102.

Frith: "The difficulties" and "I may be": Introduction, *Egypt and Palestine* (1858–1860); "Know then": Doum Palm, and Ruined Mosque, *ibid.*, vol. 2; "Attempt not": Damascus, *Egypt, Sinai, and Palestine* (1862?).

Wilson: *The Photographic News* (Nov. 27, 1885), p. 754. Excerpt from *Century* (Nov. 1885).

Bonfils: quoted in Carney E. S. Gavin et al., "The Photographers Bonfils," *Camera* (March 1981), p. 14.

Library of Congress Cataloging in Publication Data

Vaczek, Louis Charles.
  Travelers in ancient lands.

  Includes index.
  1. Near East—Description and travel—Views.
I. Buckland, Gail. II. Title.
DS44.5.V32   915.6'041   81–9585
ISBN 0-8212-1130-7   AACR2

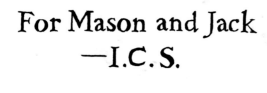

For Mason and Jack
—I.C.S.

For Henry Schwartz,
late of the SMFA
—B.L.

Houghton Mifflin Books for Children is an imprint of Houghton Mifflin Harcourt Publishing Company.

www.hmhbooks.com

The text of this book is hand-lettered.
The illustrations were created with acrylic paint and colored pencil on handmade paper.

Library of Congress Cataloging-in-Publication Data
Springman, I. C.
More / written by I. C. Springman ; illustrated by Brian Lies.
p. cm.
Summary: A team of well-intentioned mice saves a friend from hoarding too much stuff.
ISBN 978-0-547-61083-2
[1. Mice—Fiction. 2. Magpies—Fiction. 3. Conduct of life—Fiction.] I. Lies, Brian, ill. II. Title.
PZ7.S768468Mo 2012
[E]—dc23
2011025131

Manufactured in the U.S.A.
WOZ 10 9 8 7 6 5 4 3 2
4500345897

MORE

I. C. Springman   Illustrated by Brian Lies

HOUGHTON MIFFLIN BOOKS FOR CHILDREN

Houghton Mifflin Harcourt

Boston New York 2012

Nothing.

Something.

A few,

several,

more

and more

and more.

Lots.

and more

and more.

Lots.

Plenty.

A bit
much.

Much too much.

Way too much.

More than enough.

Less

and less.

A lot less.

Not so much.

Not much at all.   Enough?

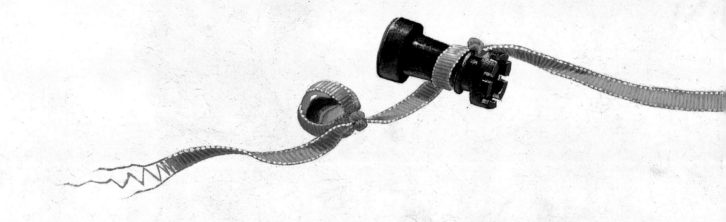

Yes,
enough.